Praise

"If there is any person I associate with HR and Agile, it is Pia-Maria Thoren. I don't know anyone in Europe who is so dedicated to bringing those critical areas together. I have worked with Pia-Maria on many occasions and know her to be very knowledgeable and a great pleasure to hang out with. A book by her hands will certainly end up high on my backlog."

—Jurgen Appelo, author of Managing for Happiness

"Pia-Maria is a pioneer in the area of Agile HR. We solicited her advice in the very early days of preparing for our transformation in way-of-work at ING's Dutch HR department. Pia-Maria helped us to get good at oversight in the complex matter of what it takes to become truly 'agile' as an HR department. Anyone interested in agile transformation should be interested in Agile HR (more appropriately phrased 'Agile people/ employee services') and I recommend all of them to pay close attention to what Pia-Maria has to say."

—Eric Abelen, Lean Coach, ING

Agile People

Agile People

A RADICAL APPROACH
FOR HR & MANAGERS

PIA-MARIA THOREN

Agile People

© 2025 Pia-Maria Thoren

All rights reserved.

Agile People

A Radical Approach for HR & Managers

ISBN 978-91-531-5484-6 Paperback (black-and-white edition)
978-91-531-7241-3 Paperback (color edition)
978-91-531-5485-3 Ebook

FOREWORD

When Agile People was first published in 2017, it set out to challenge traditional views on leadership and HR, offering a people-centered and agile perspective for the future of work. Since then, the world of work has changed dramatically, and so has our collective learning. The feedback and inspiration I have received from readers, course participants, and fellow practitioners over the years have been invaluable and are the reason this new edition exists.

While the contents of the first book remain highly relevant and are fully preserved in this edition, the second edition significantly expands on them with new perspectives, practices, and examples.

This edition includes several important additions and updates:

- A chapter on **Agility in Finance**, written by myself.
- A new chapter on **AI for Leaders and HR**, contributed by Thiago Brant.

- A chapter on Adaptable Organizational Design, written by Christophe Schnoebelen.
- An extended section on **Agile and the Brain**, now complemented with insights on *Neuroleadership* by Alexander Zaforek.
- A chapter introducing the **Agile People Coach**.
- An updated introduction with the **Agile People Manifesto** and the **Agile People Principles**.
- Many new illustrations and visual updates throughout the book

Since the first edition, two additional books have also been released:
- *Agile People Picturebook*, now translated into several languages.
- *Agile People Principles – Your Call to Action for the Future of Work*, currently available as an e-book and soon to be published in print.

I am deeply grateful to all course participants whose curiosity, challenges, and real-world experiences have inspired me to refine and expand these ideas. I also wish to thank the contributing authors – Thiago, Christophe, and Alexander – for enriching this edition with their perspectives and expertise.

Looking ahead, this book will soon be available in several translated editions, making it possible for even more people to explore, experiment with, and bring to life the ideas of Agile People in their own contexts.

My hope is that this edition, just like the first, will serve as both a guide and a call to action – encouraging leaders, HR professionals, and employees everywhere to co-create organizations where people can truly thrive.

Stockholm, January 2026
Pia-Maria Thoren

DEDICATION AND KUDOS

To you, Agile People, for supporting me in my mission to develop a network dedicated to creating better organizations. Thank you for putting all the hard work into making it possible to run our meet-ups and conferences. I hope this book will support our mission and that one day we will be able to look back and see Agile People as the beginning of a new world of work.

Also, thank you, Brooke, for your valuable support. Without you, this book would never have been written.

Thank you to all the contributors who have made this book come alive by participating in interviews and providing quotes and blurbs. The book was a team effort—in the true Agile spirit—more than an individual accomplishment, thanks to all your valuable contributions.

Thank you, Jennie and Alexandra, for helping me carry out all the interviews—it was hard work, but I'm very proud of the result.

Contents

FOREWORD 7
DEDICATION AND KUDOS 11
CONTRIBUTORS 15
INTRODUCTION 21
THE AGILE PEOPLE PRINCIPLES 29
1. THE BIRTH OF AGILE 49
2. AGILE ORGANIZATIONS 69
3. MODERN AGILE 97
4. PERFORMANCE MANAGEMENT 111
5. GOAL SETTING AND OKRS 137
6. AGILE REWARDS 149
7. AGILE RECRUITMENT 165
8. LEARNING AND DEVELOPMENT 183
9. THE REISS MOTIVATION PROFILE 211
10. AGILE LEADERSHIP 239
11. AGILE MANAGEMENT 263
12. AGILE TOOLS 283
13. EMPLOYEE ENGAGEMENT 303
14. AGILE AND THE BRAIN 331
15. AGILITY IN FINANCE 399
16. AI IN LEADERSHIP AND HR 407
17. THE AGILE PEOPLE COACH 419
18. ADAPTIVE ORGANIZATIONAL DESIGN 451
19. CONCLUSION 469
    AGILE GLOSSARY 479
    PRINCIPLES AND PRACTICES 483
    FURTHER READING 487
    APPENDIX 489
    ABOUT THE AUTHOR 525

Contributors

Leila Ljungberg

When Leila started to work with HR in the IT community, she soon realized there was a lot to learn from IT. She infiltrated the competence network that focused on Agile practices and then started to build an HR function from the base principles of Agile. They called it Agile HR back then. Nowadays, she keeps finding ways of using Agile values to evolve people and cultures to be the best they can be. She strongly believes we all have the leadership within us to grow and work hard to create an inclusive atmosphere with an impact on results.

Matti Klasson

Matti thinks motivated and happy people make really innovative and amazing products that delight their customers! He gives organizations, groups, and individuals tools and guidance. He helps them remove obstacles and waste to make it easier for them to grow and develop to be competitive and adapted to change. With twenty years of experience in systems and software engineering, Matti is a true believer in DevOps and Agile movements.

Bonnitta Roy

Bonnitta works with a network of leaders who are bringing participatory practices into the workplace. She is founder of APP Associates International and a member of the European Center for Leadership Practice. She designs transformative practices for individuals and hosts collective insight retreats for groups at Alderlore Insight Center.

Björn Sandberg

Björn has worked in various positions within HR and has been deeply involved in major transformations and changes, inspired by Lean | Agile. By getting into what it really was about, he realized it was possible to start developing next generation HR. It's a necessary step to be able to sustainably support businesses facing a fast-changing and complex world.

Fabiola Eyholzer

Fabiola is the CEO of Just Leading Solutions, a New York-based consultancy for Lean | Agile People Operations—the 21st century HR approach. She helps enterprises to accelerate their Agile transformation by focusing on their crucial asset: their people.

Riina Hellström

Riina has been recommended internationally by peers and strangers as a brilliant Agile and people professional. In 2010, she followed her passion and founded her own consultancy to drive the Agile organization development and Agile HR scene forward. Her company, Peoplegeeks Ltd Oy, is a modern people and business consultancy helping clients succeed in business through modern HR, Agile transformations, Agile management, people analytics, and by digitizing people services and developing and building modern leadership and collaboration across the organization.

Cecilia Westerholm Beer

Cecilia is a business-driven, curious, passionate leader focused on engagement and change management. She possesses extensive experience in most areas of strategic organizational development, performance, productivity, change management, employee and client engagement, workplace strategy, workforce planning, organizational design, and strategic implementation. Over the last fifteen years, she's worked in human resources, with jobs in management and at the director and VP level.

Thiago Brant

Thiago Brant is a purpose-driven, people-centered leader passionate about helping organizations become more human, agile, and innovative. With over 15 years of experience in organizational transformation, leadership development, and business agility, he combines deep expertise in Agile frameworks, change management, and people development to create thriving workplaces. As a trainer, consultant, and speaker, Thiago has guided leaders and teams across Latin America in building adaptive cultures and sustainable performance. He is also the founder of Agile People Brasil, representing the global Agile People movement in Brazil and promoting a more human future of work.

Alexander Zaforek

Alex is a change catalyst passionate about the human side of transformations. Blending systemic and solution-focused coaching with a deep expertise of agile frameworks and IT disciplines, his unique approach resonates strongly with teams and change leaders.

Known for fostering intrinsic motivation, boundary spanning collaboration, and mindset shifts, Alex is dedicated to enabling his clients to ensure lasting, sustainable change. His rich international background allows him to quickly connect and open doors at any level. He has successfully supported numerous agile transformations as agile people coach.

Christophe Schnoebelen

By day, Chris is a learning and development professional, executive coach and enterprise coaching expert. All these trendy titles simply mean that he is driven by two main concepts in his work: Firstly, he is convinced that the key to organizational performance lies in the link between empowering people and developing collective intelligence. Secondly, he believes that to achieve this, we need to invest in Secure Base Leadership, so that leaders create the best environment to perform and have a positive impact on people and the world around them. By night, apart from being a dad, he's a European debating champion and has won an innovation award. He's convinced that all great ideas start with a simple blank sheet of paper, choosing the right words and connecting with the right people. He's always on the lookout for new experiences, challenges and alternatives, while keeping his motto in mind: Work hard, laugh loud and shape the future!

Introduction

CHOOSING TO ADAPT

"In the struggle for survival, the fittest win out at the expense of their rivals because they succeed in adapting themselves best to their environment."
—Charles Darwin

Darwin was an early proponent of adaptability. He believed that plants and animals adapted to new circumstances and changes in their environment in order to survive. His famous phrase, "survival of the fittest," refers to a species' ability to adapt, not to its physical strength. The ability to adapt to a changing world is what allows some species to survive even the most dreadful environmental changes. The same is applicable for our organizations. The difference is that in the business environment, we don't have to wait two million years for the adaption; we will survive by actively *choosing* to adapt.

Choosing to adapt is the heart of the Agile philosophy. In the past, Agile was primarily associated with software development and the IT sector. Today, it's increasingly used by human resources teams and applied to entire organizations. Agile is a way of moving forward and creating value. It's a mentality that allows people and groups to meet challenges, learn quickly, and respond to change. It's a different and new way of managing teams, individuals, projects, and development.

> Agile is an operational strategy to meet a rapidly changing and complex world.
>
> —BJÖRN

My colleague, Tomas, introduced me to Agile in 2009, when I was working as a project manager in HR and IT transformations. We were implementing a talent management solution for a large international manufacturing organization. I was struggling with project management because I am not a structured person, although the job required structure. I did what I had to do, but I wasn't happy following time schedules, making detailed project plans, or mapping out exactly what everyone was supposed to do each day, and when. I learned to *behave* in a structured manner, though it's against my personality. And I did it well, but I did not feel good about my work.

The project management role didn't feel right to me. I couldn't understand why, until I attended a four-day course that transformed my life. My colleague had read a book about Agile and suggested we attend a workshop to learn how it could be applied to what we were trying to accomplish. During those four days, I learned there was a better way to run projects, businesses, and even my own life than the approach I'd been using.

In the 1990s, many IT companies embraced the Waterfall approach to management, which is a linear and sequential design process. We were using a variation of it for our big project. Agile, on the other hand, is an incremental approach. Work is completed in small batches or sprints, and then evaluated and tested. The method is collaborative and allows errors to be fixed or feedback to be taken into consideration as you move forward.

Later experiences and studies of frameworks for personality traits also taught me that people are very different on a foundational level. Some are flexible and spontaneous by nature and others crave order. How we operate and what motivates us is built into the fabric of our DNA. It's also taught during our early upbringing. The Reiss Motivation

Profile, which identifies an individual's sixteen primary needs, has been an invaluable tool in my life and in working with others. It will help you to better understand how you and your coworkers are wired so you know which roles and positions you will find most fulfilling. We'll cover it in depth in Chapter 9.

> I'm not prone to discussing the generational thing, like millennials, because to be honest, I think individual changes in people are a lot bigger than a group born in the '90s. Still, I think it's a shift; a shift in expectations. I don't think it's only the millennials. I think it's bigger than that.
>
> —LEILA

This book is about how to use Agile principles and practices in HR departments and throughout entire organizations. It is intended to inspire people to experiment with different tools and explore new avenues. Through experimentation and trust-based management, organizations can expect to increase employee engagement and ensure longevity in the marketplace. Although Agile originated in the tech sector, the philosophy applies to companies large and small in any rapidly changing industry and an ever-changing world.

> You can do a lot of different things and be a part of different communities. Your workday could consist of five or six different elements. I work part-time as an Uber driver, and I can work part-time as an online teacher. The possibilities to work are huge for people who see those kinds of opportunities. You don't really have to have a 9-5 workday anymore.
>
> —LEILA

My goal is to demonstrate, both through my own experiences and through the experiences of the companies I've consulted with, that when people feel better, they perform better. I'll show you how to adopt new leadership and management styles that promote the formation of self-directing teams. Together, we can help people feel safe and inspired so they will share their unique skills and ideas for the mutual benefit of individuals, teams, and entire organizations.

This book is for anyone interested in fostering more creative and productive work environments: consultants, customers, executives, employees, and educators. Those environments attract and retain top-level employees who are empowered to bring their A-game to the table every day. My intention is to share Agile principles and practices so that we can create better organizations together, without hierarchy or restriction. Above all, this book is for professionals within HR—a department that needs to find a new purpose.

Managers are taking over more and more HR-related tasks as a consequence of cost reductions and the old, controlling HR role is not valid anymore.

The mission for Agile People is both bold and broad, and I believe it has the power to make a huge difference in the world of work. I hope you find inspiration in it and allow yourself to explore its vast potential. Creating a better tomorrow starts today.

THE AGILE PEOPLE MISSION

There is a shift happening in the world of work. Organizations are becoming more inspiring, human, purposeful, and future-driven. Businesses are becoming a force for good. People's potential is freed up to have a positive impact on the lives of others, communities, and the world. Our purpose is to accelerate this transformation by spreading the Agile values of customer collaboration, energizing people, inspiring leadership, and rapid change to all areas of business and to organizations.

We take pride in being on the front lines of organizational change. We attract people from all types of industries that fulfill a diverse set of roles. Meeting across functions enables cross-learning, collaboration, and new solutions for the future of work.

The Agile People Principles

*"Leaders are like Gardeners, and Agile
People Principles fertilize the soil"*
– Agile People guiding metaphor

THE GARDENER METAPHOR

Think of an organization as a garden; the future manager/HR person is the gardener. Every garden has a purpose: for beauty, for producing fruits and vegetables, for respite and calm, to attract birds and bees. Regardless, a garden has a purpose. If the garden had no purpose, nobody would have bothered to create it in the first place.

Each garden contains different varieties and species of plants, flowers, fruit trees, bushes, shrubs, vegetables, ground cover, climbers, and/ or grasses. Each plant plays a different role, but together, they fulfill the purpose of the garden.

Yet, each plant needs different things. Some need sunshine, some prefer shade, and some need plenty of water. Some plants do well in clusters, others need space to grow. Some need support, while some manage well on their own. So who makes sure that every plant gets what it needs so it can grow and become big and beautiful?

The gardener's role is to care for and understand each plant's unique needs. It's his or her job to create the proper prerequisites for development, without forgetting about the whole garden's purpose. The most critical skill a gardener needs is to manage the conditions and the environment so the plants can grow.

The soil is like a company's culture —if it's not right for the plants, they won't thrive. The gardener cannot command and control the plants to grow faster or better. If the environment is not right, the plants will not grow well, regardless of how much they are commanded.

Let's say we plant a seed in our garden and it does not grow, or it grows very poorly/slowly. We can only give it the right conditions and environment, but if it doesn't grow, we need to deal with it. Personality change is rare, and it's a lot easier to change company environments—digital structures like systems, processes, policies, tools, methods, and the physical work environment—than it is to change a person.

It could be that the seed doesn't grow in our environment. It could be the wrong climate, soil, or something else. For example, wine does not grow well in Sweden. If that's the case, we need to try to change the conditions, perhaps plant the seed in another part of the garden where the conditions fit its needs better.

Or something is wrong within the seed. The seed could be sick or have other problems. If we translate the analogy to a human being, the person could be going through a divorce, be depressed, or have some other kind of issue. If this is the case, we can help in different ways. We can give the person some time off to deal with the issues, or have the company provide a therapist to help with the problems. Sometimes, the problem could stem from the gardener's insufficient skills, so we need to replace or develop the gardener.

Some seeds will never grow, regardless of what we do with our environment. If no attempts are made to fix the problem, we must help the plant grow into another garden.

The Gardener metaphor helps describe Agile leadership and the changing role of HR and management in complex environments. It amplifies the need to remove impediments to growth and create a system where people can develop, solve problems, and take ownership. The future lies in creating conditions for people to perform and be happy. By removing impediments, we can maximize engagement and employee satisfaction that will fuel speed and adaptability in a common, strategic direction. If we create this environment, it becomes easy to achieve the organization's purpose.

AGILE PEOPLE PRINCIPLES FERTILIZE THE SOIL

If leaders are like gardeners, then the Agile People Principles are the fertilizer. As we nurture and tend to the Principles, an organization and its culture can blossom into its unique environment.

The Agile People Principles were born from the Agile People Manifesto (as portrayed in the Introduction), the original Agile Manifesto, Modern Agile, and the Agile HR Manifesto (as portrayed in Chapter 3). These principles are governing ideals that support agile values.

Utilizing and increasing the Agile People Principles will be monumental for management and HR, especially in recruitment, training, motivation, engagement, compensation, development, and performance. The more the principles are practiced and absorbed, the better a company will function, like a well-tended garden.

The world is only getting more complex, and few competitive advantages remain for companies that want to survive and flourish. One such advantage is to learn faster than your competitors, to be innovative and creative, and to invent and produce products and services that your customers want and need.

Those activities require a different leadership style than what we have seen in the past. A style that provides room for people to make mistakes and learn from them. It also requires different principles for HR, which need to abandon policy making and process mapping to support speed, adaptability, and customer focus. It takes cross-functional business teams on all levels to create a learning organization, which has become a prerequisite for success, where everybody takes shared ownership of the company vision. The old structures with Top-down hierarchies and annual budgets linked to fixed performance targets and rewards will not support the speed and motivation needed to permeate future workplaces.

There will always be obstacles, but when given the choice, it's preferable to speak face-to-face rather than communicate another way. It's preferable to trust coworkers and managers rather than live in fear of them. Likewise, it is better to try new things and see what works than to remain unchanged. That said, companies that use Agile People Principles don't follow a fixed recipe or prescription. There are no clear, best solutions. The principles can be used to the degree they are applicable in a given scenario.

Ultimately, a company should be a network of self-steering nodes, instead of a top-down controlled organization. People must be free to act locally, make decisions quickly, and communicate freely with other departments and customers in real-time. When employees need to run every question or idea past a manager, the response time slows down. This will look different depending on the company and the industry. Still, essentially, companies should function as a network, instead of a machine— always moving, changing, and adapting to the external world, customers, and the environment.

Modern HR departments and leaders must embrace a bottom-up approach to foster efficient communication and empower staff members to make decisions faster. Moving away from a bureaucratic structure simplifies operations. There are fewer processes, systems, reports, and checklists to gobble up management's time and energy, which means that time can be better spent on facilitating work within the team. Do they have everything they need in place to be able to perform optimally? Time can also be better spent aligning and communicating with other departments within the company to ensure smooth cooperation. The intention is to create a great work environment for employees and value for customers.

When happy people serve customers, they will be more satisfied and loyal to the company. We also know that a satisfied and loyal customer is a profitable customer who can contribute to a profitable company. A profitable company can reinvest in employees and is more likely to reach its long-term goals and realize its vision. If management is wise, a substantial part of the profit should be reinvested in ensuring that all employees have the prerequisites for engagement and great performance.

Today's organizations place too much emphasis on specific projects. Instead, organizations must avoid project-based methods, where teams are put together to accomplish a particular task or goal. The people on the team are usually strangers. You can't expect a new team to perform well when it comes together. It takes time, sometimes years, for them to get to know each other and find an efficient way of working together. If you break up the team at the end of the project, just when team members started to work well together, you will never reap the benefits from high-performing teamwork.

Organizations should move toward creating stable, high-performing teams, and this takes time. When teams form organically in the workplace, they typically function at an elevated level. Those teams should be encouraged and rewarded for their output. They should be kept busy. Suppose a team requires increased competency in a specific area. In that case, that competency can be developed within the team or added to the team through a temporary or permanent person, so the team becomes cross-functional and more varied in its capabilities.

One-dimensional teams usually represent departments such as HR or IT. They serve a single function within the organization. Instead, the tasks within those departments should be broken up and dispersed to people with different competencies throughout the organization. This strategy allows for greater depth and fresh perspectives. This can be done in many different ways, and the result is usually a matrix-type organization.

A task like talent acquisition can, for example, be carried out by a team consisting of multiple members from different departments and functions, each with a unique competency to bring to the table. Marketing will add their competency when attracting employees, the recruiting manager knows best what skills are needed, and HR will contribute with their people skills to make sure the candidate is a good match for the organization as a whole. Also, the team onboarding the new team member needs to be involved in the selection process. They should all work together to make the best decisions regarding new hires. Instead of only managers, only HR, or only the team making all the key decisions, everyone participates. The more people involved in the selection process, the better the quality of the new hire.

In the book "Agile People Principles, Your Call to Action for the Future of Work", 35 Agile People Coaches from across the globe explore the practical application of the Agile People Principles. Through their combined experience, readers will gain a solid grasp on how those principles can strengthen individuals, teams, departments, and organizations. All principles are explored, explained, and put into the context of their value to a modern organization.

If you follow the Agile People Principles and constantly apply and improve them, you have a good chance of succeeding with your enterprise. The strength is not using one or two but all of them, and in combination.

AGILE PEOPLE PRINCIPLES

Here are all the Agile People Principles, a short description, and an illustrative example for each principle - follow them and change your organization for good ☺

AGILE PEOPLE PRINCIPLES

PRINCIPLE	EXPANDED DESCRIPTION	EXAMPLE
Accountability & Commitment	We hold one another accountable in respectful, adult-to-adult ways. Clear agreements, transparent follow-up, and peer feedback create ownership without blame.	Team members review progress together every Friday and adjust commitments openly.
Adaptability	We continuously sense changes in customer and employee needs and adapt accordingly. Adaptability is a daily habit—not just crisis response.	HR adapts policies quickly to remote work demands instead of waiting months.
Authenticity	People are encouraged to show up as themselves—values, voice, and all—while respecting others. Authenticity builds trust and reduces wasted energy.	A manager admits they don't have all answers and invites team ideas.

PRINCIPLE	EXPANDED DESCRIPTION	EXAMPLE
Boundary Spanning	We cross functions, disciplines, and groups to connect ideas. This dissolves silos and enables better solutions.	A finance expert joins a product sprint to give input early.
Clear Goal & Simple Rules	Leaders set the purpose and a few non-negotiables, then step back.	"We aim to improve onboarding in 90 days; keep costs under €5k."
Common Direction	We cultivate a shared vision and common metrics to orient work.	All teams track customer NPS as a shared success measure.
Continuous Learning & Improvement	We experiment deliberately and integrate insights daily.	Teams run retrospectives after each sprint to refine practices.
Collective Intelligence	We leverage diverse perspectives to make better decisions.	A workshop with people from HR, IT, and Sales generates more options.

PRINCIPLE	EXPANDED DESCRIPTION	EXAMPLE
Cross-Functional Teams	Stable teams with all skills deliver end-to-end value.	A product team includes design, coding, testing, and marketing.
Customer Value	Success is defined by value for external and internal customers.	HR redesigns performance reviews to save managers 10 hours yearly.
Diversity & Inclusion	We seek diversity and inclusive norms so all voices are heard.	Rotating facilitators ensure everyone contributes in meetings.
Emergent Strategy	We combine top-down intent with bottom-up insights.	Employee ideas feed into quarterly strategy reviews.
Empowerment	Decision rights sit where information is, paired with boundaries.	Customer support agents refund up to €100 without manager approval.
Focus	We limit work-in-progress and protect deep work.	A team works on two initiatives at a time, not ten.

PRINCIPLE	EXPANDED DESCRIPTION	EXAMPLE
Positive Feedback (Give & Receive)	We practice frequent, specific appreciation alongside candor.	Daily standups start with one "thank you" per person.
Grow People	Leaders and HR grow capability instead of commanding.	Offering coaching hours to help employees explore career goals.
Increase Happiness	We design for meaning, autonomy, mastery, and connection.	Regular check-ins on team mood with action on low scores.
Individuals & Interactions over Processes & Tools	We prefer conversation and collaboration to rigid procedures.	A conflict is solved through dialogue instead of a lengthy form.
Know People Deeply	We understand strengths, motivations, and constraints.	Managers use motivational maps to tailor development.

PRINCIPLE	EXPANDED DESCRIPTION	EXAMPLE
Make Mistakes & Learn	Errors are treated as data and curiosity is the response.	Sharing a failed prototype openly in a demo session.
Optimize for the Whole	We optimize end-to-end value, not local metrics.	Sales avoids overselling features that support cannot deliver.
Positive Peer Pressure	Norms and visible progress encourage responsibility.	A public team board shows progress, motivating timely updates.
Psychological Safety	People can take risks without fear of humiliation.	Team members openly challenge a leader's idea without backlash.
Purpose & Meaning	Work connects to a compelling purpose that matters.	Linking projects to sustainability goals employees care about.

PRINCIPLE	EXPANDED DESCRIPTION	EXAMPLE
Relative Goals	We measure progress relatively, encouraging continuous improvement.	"Reduce response time 20% compared to last quarter."
Self-Leadership	Everyone steers their own work and seeks feedback.	An employee requests a mentor to grow skills proactively.
Self-Organization	Teams decide how to achieve outcomes within constraints.	A team changes its meeting cadence without asking permission.
Stable & Semi-Stable Teams	We minimize churn so teams mature into high performance.	Keeping the same product team together for multiple releases.
Sustainability (Pace)	We work at a sustainable pace to avoid burnout.	No emails after 8 pm as a company norm.

PRINCIPLE	EXPANDED DESCRIPTION	EXAMPLE
Tell Why & What— Leave the How	Leaders provide context and intent, not detailed steps.	"We need to reduce churn; you decide how."
Transparency	We default to openness about goals, data, and decisions.	Publishing all meeting notes on a shared drive.
Trial & Error / Experimentation	We use safe-to-fail experiments to explore options.	Testing a new onboarding video with one team first.
Trust	We start from trust, granting autonomy with expectations.	Remote workers choose their schedules without micromanagement.
Visualization	We make work and risks visible with boards and diagrams.	A Kanban wall shows backlog, progress, and blockers.

THE AGILE PEOPLE MANIFESTO

Agile People created their Agile People Manifesto at a gathering in Smögen, in the summer of 2019.

I recall the inspiration for that initiative here:

"Why did I invite everyone in my network to join Smögen and craft the Agile People Manifesto with me?

Maybe because it had been ten years since I was introduced to agile values for the first time and was hopelessly convinced about the necessity of changing organizations accordingly. It had also been eight years since we created the Agile People brand in Smögen and started to build what would be a large part of so many people's lives a few years later.

It could be because I had a few extra minutes in my hectic travel schedule to send a Google invitation to my Agile People Slack workspace. But probably, like most things in my life, it was just a timely coincidence that a crazy idea hit me while preparing for a training session in some corner of the world.

The Agile People Manifesto sounded good to me, but I knew I would never have the time and energy to craft it by myself. After all, a manifesto should be something bigger and more important than something you stir together on a Friday afternoon, all alone. So, I turned to my global network of Agile People, who might be interested in co-creating it with me.

My network responded enthusiastically, and 19 people from 15 countries and five continents showed up at my summer cabin on a Thursday afternoon in June 2019. We kicked off the weekend with a Brazilian Portuguese barbecue we all cooked together. The following days were filled with fun, work, laughter, and quarreling. We completed a draft by Sunday and finalized the Agile People Manifesto a few months later during online meetings. It is our gift for everyone to use.

There is no universal solution for handling the pace of change, but agile is the way to work for the future. The agile mentality aligns with how the brain copes with high-level complexity in the world around us. Organizations can be more or less agile, depending on their unique structure, processes, culture, tradition, and leadership track. But one thing is sure - all kinds of organizations have to increase their business agility to stay competitive in today's world."

AGILE PEOPLE MANIFESTO: CORE COMMITMENTS[1]

- **Curiosity & Collaboration:** We commit to curiosity-driven collaboration to create innovative solutions that meet real human needs.
- **Diversity, Inclusion & Belonging:** We actively embrace diversity and inclusion to build communities where people feel safe and truly belong.
- **Connection & Human-Centric Culture:** We connect deeply with individuals, organizations, and society to nurture, value, and unleash human capability.
- **Purpose & Meaning:** We continuously pursue meaning and purpose to create a positive, significant impact in the world of work.
- **Experimentation & Learning:** We seek opportunities to experiment and learn so we can adapt fast and thrive in changing environments.

---

1   https://agilepeoplemanifesto.org

- **Transparency, Trust & Self-Organization:** We promote transparency across organizations and teams to enable trust, ownership, and self-organization.
- **Boundary Spanning:** We use boundary-spanning collaboration to overcome organizational barriers and accelerate learning and outcomes.

How will you use it in your organization? Translate each commitment into two or three observable practices (e.g., visible forums for ideas, inclusive decision rituals, and public learning reviews). Align people practices—hiring, growth, compensation, and leadership behaviors—to reinforce these commitments.

CHAPTER 1

The Birth of Agile

"Thinking is the hardest work there is, which is probably the reason why so few engage in it."
—Henry Ford

My goal for this book is to share how to apply Agile philosophies to an organization, small or large, new or established. I'll provide specific exercises and scenarios, share success stories of companies who are already enjoying the benefits of Agile thinking, and examine modern challenges and how to overcome them.

> We believe we can come up with a solution for every single thing that may go wrong. When those solutions are put into processes, everything is fine. HR is driven by hidden forces—mainly legal, finance, and management. Legal is especially prevalent in the U.S.
>
> —FABIOLA

THE AGILE DREAM

Martin Luther King Jr. didn't say, "I have a five-year plan." He moved a generation of individuals by saying, "I have a dream." It all starts with a beautiful dream; creating Agile organizations is mine. A dream has the power to unite a team, a department, or a whole company, and inspire people to work toward a common vision. You can run a company without a dream, but you'll never have passionate employees. If you're not clear on the organization's *why*, the employees won't be either.

The execution of strategy, which is how dreams are reached, happens every day between 8:00 a.m. and 5:00 p.m. (but with increasing frequency, people do their work after office hours and/or outside of the office). If employees are on board with an organization's *why*, they will choose to act and make decisions that lead toward the why, all day, every day. Decision making and innovation don't come from top-level management, or even the next level down. That doesn't mean that top management cannot be innovative; it's simply unwise to rely solely on the few at the very top or on a specific department for innovation.

> Very few people are in positions with enough power to implement changes that will actually build this kind of organization. Exceptional companies are identified in each country, usually from the "great places to work" lists, or something similar. They often have an owner who is so brilliant, they can make changes and build systems or organizations that they believe in. It might not bring the revenue in as quickly as they want, but they are building organizations in a lasting and organic way.
>
> —RIINA

Innovation happens everywhere, all the time, and we need to give people more space and time to be creative where they are. The best way to secure a company's future is by constantly innovating and designing new products and services for an ever-changing customer base.

The employee level is where things are done and where the work happens. The employees are the ones who realize the dream or the vision by doing what they do best every day. Therefore, management needs to be completely transparent, visible, and available to everyone. The whole organization should be asking, "What can I do to make our dream a reality? What steps need to be taken?" Everyone needs to have the authority to prioritize the right things as if it were a matter of life and death, because the reality is, it is. If we don't pay attention, we will be outrun by smaller, faster, and smarter players in no time.

THE WAY IT WAS

The workplace and the preferences of employees have changed dramatically over the last century, especially in the last twenty years. Power used to be a function of position within a hierarchical structure (and still is in many companies). A hundred years ago, most companies functioned as a machine. Employees were a big part of that machine. Management's challenge was to make their systems as efficient as possible. The emphasis was on standardization and logistics. People were resources; they were easily exchangeable parts within the organizational machinery. Most people were not required to think at all and, today, robots have replaced many workers.

One of the first business consultants, and a leading mechanical engineer during the industrial era, Fredrick Taylor, developed a scientific management system. His main objective was to improve economic efficiency and improve labor productivity.

Taylor's ideas and research impacted many famous benchmarks of efficiency, such as the processes adopted on the Ford factory assembly lines. Humans lined up and repeated the same task consistently, day in and day out. The workflow was analyzed, evaluated, improved, and standardized. His practices were highly effective for meeting the challenges of industrial manufacturing and logistics, and were largely responsible for the creation of the production line. People were not used for their brains, just their physical strength.

> As ordinary people, we haven't changed, but the context in which we are being brought up has disruptively changed. In the school systems today, we have a democratic situation where, for example, the student and teacher agree on targets. The students seem to have an accelerated level of power in terms of influencing their own development and learning. Today's students can have a different opinion than the professor/teacher and still get good grades. However, when these students graduate, they are tossed into organizations that are still run in a machine-like, bureaucratic, and Tayloristic manner. This leads to a big clash in their initial goals, since they more or less have to do what they are told. We hire people for their creativity and ideas, but in most cases, we still treat them as machines.
>
> —BJÖRN

Many photographs exist from this era: men in overalls on factory floors and women in neat lines with sewing machines or ironing boards. Their clothing, behaviors, and responsibilities were carefully dictated according to their rank in the manufacturing system. Senior executives determined an organization's strategy without input from employees or customers. Everyone reported to a boss. Tasks were assigned, not chosen.

Managers gave rewards for work well done, but employees did not reward one another. Compensation correlated directly with one's rank within the organization. Promotion was a measure of achievement and autonomy was uncommon. The few people at the top made all the decisions because they were thought to be smart enough to understand how work should be done. Hierarchies ruled and formal power, reserved for the chosen few, was a sign of success.

WORK LIFE TODAY

Today, the economy has shifted from industry—via knowledge—to the participation age, but remnants of industrial practices still exist. Our challenge now is to keep up with the pace of technological progress. To do so, we need to tap into the human potential for creativity, as opposed to placing people in rigid positions with zero flexibility. To remain competitive, we need to change and grow constantly.

> Today, we see only a few early adapters who are really changing workplaces and making a positive impact on how work is done, managed, controlled, and planned. I think we are just seeing the tip of the iceberg now. I believe, in the near future, we will see more products being sold that have substantially increased levels of technology, such as artificial intelligence and robotics that will basically disrupt the way people work. I'm not sure if the average working individual really understands this yet. I'm not even sure if I understand it. I just know something big is going to happen and change is coming really fast.
>
> —RIINA

The knowledge era demands freethinking and experimentation to survive. Lean is a powerful concept from Toyota, where the underlying principles of involvement and respect for workers are core values and essential for success.

Continuous improvement is still a theme, and it manifests through the acceptance or exploration of innovative ideas. It requires allowing people to fail (in order to learn), rather than just focusing on system efficiencies.

> In my experience, "workplace" nowadays is a fluid term. It's no longer a 9-5 environment.
>
> —LEILA

Increasing flexibility in the workplace means that people are less inclined to accept being told what to do or be a part of the machinery. Of course, there are still several structured organizations where every movement is documented and graded. McDonald's and other franchised restaurants are a good example. These establishments are managed using detailed checklists, processes, and systems. The work itself does not require any specific skill sets, creativity, innovation, or individuality. In fact, employees are hired specifically to follow instructions. Franchises are based on the factory model, which works fine for companies whose labor force is an expendable, exchangeable resource.

> We always design our HR processes for the worst possible scenario and person. We call it the Douglas Effect. Imagine Douglas is the worst person you would want in your workplace. He embodies all sorts of bad behaviors and character traits. Everything we do in HR is designed to help keep Douglas in check.
> —FABIOLA

THE HISTORY OF AGILE

In the 1970s, a project management system known as the Waterfall Model was widely popular. There are many variations of this approach but, at its heart, progress is measured in sequential stages. Development flows, like a waterfall, through the different project phases. Its roots are in the manufacturing and construction industries where it is costly—and sometimes impossible—to make changes.

> It started out as an IT thing. They had to come up with new systems and ways of working in fast-paced times when everyone depended on collaboration.
> —FABIOLA

Consequently, there is little room for flexibility or errors. Once a step is complete, the team cannot go back and make improvements. The Waterfall approach requires extensive preplanning and zero deviation from the plan. It is not terribly effective for software development, which is abstract and always changing. Five-year project timelines and rigid project phases don't allow for shifts in the marketplace or customer feedback. Once a project leaves one phase and enters another, there's no turning back.

Many people assume that finishing a step is a good thing. The problem, however, is the Waterfall Method presupposes that the world is predictable, which it categorically is not. In using the Waterfall Method for project management, many companies found that projects and feedback loops were stretched out over very long periods of time, often going way over budget and using far more resources than originally anticipated. It's an antiquated approach that doesn't suit the pace of change in today's world. The failure rate is extremely high because we cannot control change, and change is a reality. Real-time feedback is needed to develop the best and most useful products.

The Agile movement first started in the IT software development industry as a reaction to the Waterfall Model. There was a need for increased agility because things rarely go according to plan. Every day, people get sick or quit, managers leave, and projects fail. The only true reality is that we must adapt in order to survive. We have to assume that we do not know and cannot plan for what will happen in the future.

> Work has changed in the sense that one person cannot do the job without other people's help. I would say that's the most basic and biggest change. Very few of us can sit in a room by ourselves and get our work done without more and more networking, more and more communication with other people, and more and more collaboration.
>
> —RIINA

As a reaction against the Waterfall Model and the problems that came with it, a group of IT professionals got together in Snowbird, Utah, in 2001 to discuss a better way to work with change. Developers and project managers were frustrated with the traditional model. They wanted to improve IT development and implementation and be more flexible. Out of their gathering, the Agile Manifesto was born.[2]

> I think everything changed during the age of disruption, and obviously that doesn't stop because of HR, so there is a different talent contract in place. People have varying viewpoints on what they want to get out of work and how they want to be included in the way they work.
>
> —FABIOLA

---

2   https://agilemanifesto.org

MANIFESTO FOR AGILE SOFTWARE DEVELOPMENT

We are uncovering better ways to develop software by doing it and helping others do it. Through this work we have come to value:

1. Individuals and interactions over processes and tools

2. Working software over comprehensive documentation

3. Customer collaboration over contract negotiation

4. Responding to change over following a plan

That is, while there is value in the items on the right side of each sentence, we value the items on the left more.

THE AGILE PRINCIPLES

We follow these principles:

- Our highest priority is to satisfy the customer through early and continuous delivery of valuable software.
- Welcome changing requirements, even late in development. Agile processes harness change for the customer's competitive advantage.
- Deliver working software frequently, every couple of weeks to couple of months, with a preference for a shorter timescale.
- Business people and developers must work together daily throughout the project.
- Build projects around motivated individuals. Give them the environment and support they need, and trust them to get the job done.
- The most efficient and effective method of conveying information to and within a development team is face-to-face conversation.
- Working software is the primary measure of progress.
- Agile processes promote sustainable development. The sponsors, developers, and users should be able to maintain a constant pace indefinitely.
- Continuous attention to technical excellence and good design enhances agility.
- Simplicity—the art of maximizing the amount of work not done—is essential.
- The best architectures, requirements, and designs emerge from self-organizing teams.

- At regular intervals, the team reflects on how to become more effective, then tunes and adjusts its behavior accordingly.

The Agile Manifesto is the root from which all Agile principles and tools stem. You can always go back to the manifesto and get guidance, when in doubt. That's why we say that Agile is not a method, model, tool, or framework in itself. It's a mindset that resonates with the value structure from the Agile Manifesto.

WHAT WE NEED NOW: AGILE PRINCIPLES

When I was introduced to the Agile philosophy, I was immediately drawn to its values and principles. They made sense to me and seemed a superior way to approach work.

The emphasis of the philosophy is on satisfying the customer through continuous value delivery. What's more, the focus is on happy people rather than bureaucracy and rigid processes. IT companies and software startups have readily embraced Agile principles as well, but there is huge potential for organizational change across multiple industries and disciplines through Agile. The impact will be monumental for management and HR, especially in areas such as employee recruitment, training, motivation, engagement, compensation, development, and performance.

> A lot of people are talking about Agile HR. It's on the trending list at Deloitte, KPMG, and similar companies. Although they're all talking about Agile HR, very few people actually know what Agile is about. They don't understand where it comes from, why it exists, and the background on its complexity. It's too simple to talk about Agile HR and remodeling. In reality, it's not about that.
>
> —RIINA

We've already seen dramatic changes in the workplace as we've shifted from the industrial age to the knowledge economy and, now, into the participation age. There is tremendous room to grow, however. People need to be given the freedom to create and experiment so they can explore new heights and ideas. Despite this necessity, much of management's fundamental mindset is still rooted in the ideas of Fredrick Taylor and the old factory mentality. To keep up in today's world and be able to compete, management needs to change with the times.

Top-down, hierarchical organizations are no longer effective in today's workplaces. It is not practical or realistic to assume that an entire company can be managed from a control tower, far removed from the people who are doing the actual work. Decision-making power needs to be delegated throughout all parts of an organization. Authority cannot be relegated exclusively to the top; it needs to filter through all departments.

> From a long-term perspective, the workplace has changed, but I believe it looks the same as it did twenty years ago. Although there is a change in motion from the Agile perspective; the organizations that are easily changeable will be the ones that thrive.
>
> —BJÖRN

Ultimately, a company should be a network of self-steering nodes, instead of a top-down controlled organization. People need to be given the freedom to act locally, make decisions quickly, and communicate freely with other departments and customers in real time. When employees need to run every question or idea past a manager, invariably response time slows down. This will look different depending on the company and the industry, but essentially companies should function like a network, instead of a machine—always moving, changing, and adapting to the external world, customers, and environment.

Modern HR departments need to embrace a bottom-up approach to foster efficient communication and empower staff members to make decisions faster. Moving away from a bureaucratic structure simplifies operations. There are fewer processes, systems, reports, and checklists to gobble up management's time and energy, which means that time can be better spent on facilitating work within the team. Do they have everything they need in place to be able to perform in an optimal manner? Time can also be better spent aligning and communicating with other departments within the company to ensure smooth cooperation. The intention is to create a great work environment for employees and value for customers.

> I always say it's the business of disrupting HR because, at the end of the day, that's what it is. Everyone talks about the difficult times we have, or they say certain things don't work anymore. But, they don't have the courage or the stamina to say, "Okay, let's change it." They think there are easy fixes to huge problems, but we can't approach new problems with the old way of thinking.
>
> —FABIOLA

When happy people serve customers, we know that they will be more satisfied and loyal to our company. We also know that a satisfied and loyal customer is a profitable customer who can contribute to a profitable company. A profitable company can reinvest in employees and has a greater probability of reaching its long-term goals and realizing the company's vision. If management is wise, a substantial part of the profit should be reinvested in making sure that all employees have the prerequisites for engagement and great performance.

Another issue in today's organizations is the over belief in projects. Instead, organizations need to move away from project-based methods, where teams are put together to accomplish a specific task or goal. The people on the team are usually strangers. You can't expect a new team to perform well when it first comes together. It takes time, sometimes years, for them to get to know each other and find an efficient way of working together. If you break up the team at the end of the project, just when team members started to work well together, you will never reap the benefits from high-performing teamwork.

Organizations should move toward the creation of stable, high-performing teams, and this takes time. There is extensive research on team development and group processes made by Susan Wheelan (Integrative Model of Group Development, or IMGD), Bruce Tuckman (Norming, Storming, Forming, Performing Model) and William Schutz (Fundamental Interpersonal Relations Orientation, or FIRO). Their research shows that high-performing teams have to go through a number of phases before reaching the performance stage. Read more about these phases in Chapter 8.

When teams form organically in the workplace, they typically function at an elevated level. Those teams should be encouraged and rewarded for their output. They should be kept busy. If a team requires increased competency in a specific area, that competency can be developed within the team or added to the team through a temporary or permanent person, so the team becomes cross-functional and more varied in its capabilities.

One-dimensional teams usually represent departments such as HR or IT. They serve a single function within the organization. Instead, the functions within those departments should be broken up and dispersed to people with different competencies throughout the organization. This strategy allows for greater depth and fresh perspectives. This can be done in many different ways and the result is usually a matrix type of organization.

A task like talent acquisition can, for example, be carried out by a team consisting of multiple members from different departments and functions, each with a unique competency to bring to the table. Marketing will add their competency when attracting employees, the recruiting manager knows best what skills are needed, and HR will contribute with their people skills to make sure the candidate is a good match for the organization as a whole. Also, the team onboarding the new team member needs to be involved in the selection process. They should all work together to make the best decisions regarding new hires. Instead of only managers, only HR, or only the team making all the key decisions, everyone participates. The more people involved in the selection process, the better the quality of the new hire!

CHAPTER 2

Agile Organizations

> *"We can't be afraid of change. You may feel very secure in the pond that you are in, but if you never venture out of it, you will never know that there is such a thing as an ocean, a sea. Holding onto something that is good for you now, may be the very reason why you don't have something better."*
> —C. JoyBell C.

Organizational principles are different in Agile companies than they are in traditional businesses. In his book, *The Human Side of Enterprise,* Douglas McGregor, of the MIT School of Management, introduced two views of human motivation and management in the 1960s that he called Human View X and Human View Y. The theories represent opposing assumptions about what motivates employees. McGregor's research is highly regarded throughout organizational behavior and human resources circles, but it's not as well-known in other disciplines.

HUMAN VIEW X AND Y

In my courses, I refer to McGregor's theories as Human View X and Human View Y. The opposing perspectives examine assumptions about employees' overall attitudes, direction, responsibility, motivation, and creativity. Human View X presupposes that, in general, people do not like to work and they need to be forced into it. On the other hand, Human View Y assumes that people are interested in their work and enjoy it, under the right conditions.

HUMAN VIEW X

- People dislike work, find it boring, and will avoid it if they can.
- People must be forced or bribed to make the right effort.
- People would rather be directed than accept responsibility (which they avoid).
- People are motivated mainly by money and fear about job security.
- Most people have very little creativity—except when it comes to getting around rules.

HUMAN VIEW Y

- People need to work and want to take an interest in it. Under the right conditions, they enjoy it.
- People will direct themselves toward a target that they accept.
- People will seek and accept responsibility under the right conditions.
- Under the right conditions, people are motivated by the desire to realize their own potential.
- Creativity and ingenuity are widely distributed and grossly underused.

Most people more easily align with Human View Y than X, which is no surprise. However, there are still a good number of people in the world, management specifically, who believe their employees fall under the X umbrella. It's important to understand where various people within an organization lie according to this question, because what we believe about others forms our own behaviors. Behaviors are what drive companies, which is why this is an important distinction when assessing the overall "character" of an organization.

Could it be that the characteristics associated with Human View X are an assumption about those people? We assume they are a certain way and then they act accordingly. So, people *become* X people when they are treated a certain way. Whenever I ask people if they are X or Y, 99 percent of them say they are Y people. In that case, where are all the X people?

When a company transforms from one of the traditional models—which we'll review in detail shortly—to an Agile model, there is a marked mindset shift from X to Y. That mindset shift is critical to enhancing the human side of the enterprise.

> Most of the management and HR processes are built on distrusting people. They are built on trying to control everyone to ensure they are doing the correct things, instead of just trusting people to do the correct thing.
> —RIINA

TRADITIONAL COMPANY STRUCTURES

Traditional company structures are fairly easy to identify. They date back to the command and control model and the days of Taylorism, but they are still common today. As businesses evolve and become structurally looser, communication flows more freely between everyone. We'll take a look at company structures from the most structured, all the way to the most open.

> The truth is, we are working with an organic system, not a machine. Many organizations have tried to put management or work into a machine metaphor, instead of an organic metaphor.
> —RIINA

HIERARCHICAL ORGANIZATIONS

Most organizations today are, to some degree, a hierarchy. Hierarchies utilize a one-way, top-down, silo approach. There's little communication or collaboration between departments and the various parts of the organization. Decisions are made at the top and implemented all the way down the chain of command. There is no discussion or consideration for how those decisions will impact team members or clients. Typically, as companies grow and add more staff, they become more hierarchical. Increasingly, layers of red tape are added and there's less of an opportunity to make decisions or change courses quickly. The resulting inflexibility makes hierarchies poorly suited for the Agile approach.

> You need to evaluate the trend of centralizing HR functions. HR has been traditionally seen as a cost factor, rather than an entity that creates value. I'd prefer it if HR could be decentralized and cross-functional.
> —BJÖRN

FLATTER ORGANIZATIONS

Flatter organizations are similar to traditional hierarchies, but with fewer layers of red tape to cut through. The chain of command is minimized, so decisions are made more quickly. Communication, networking, and collaboration are possible across the enterprise. Employees are less apt to follow a particular order around decision making, which helps to remove barriers and free up communication. Flatter organizations are becoming increasingly popular, but not everyone thrives in this type of organization.

In Sweden, leaders commonly delegate authority to employees, which enhances the flatter structure to the degree that it is sometimes referred to as "the Swedish leadership model."

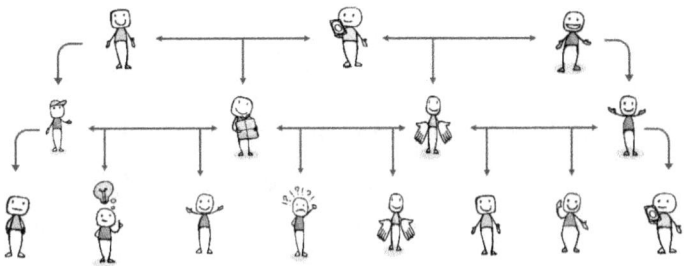

FLAT ORGANIZATIONS

Completely flat organizations are the oddballs of the world: they are manager-less. They represent true networks and employees have full decision-making mandates. This structure is typically seen in technology companies, startups, and a handful of mid-sized companies.

> Communication is the vital goal on all levels for companies. This includes virtual, face-to-face, and network communications. It needs to be a constant dialogue that you can support. Unstructured, decentralized communication in an organization is so important. We can only look at a biological structure and a responsive system that triggers better communications.
>
> —RIINA

In the modern business landscape, some small companies hire people without assigning them a specific role. For example, the American software company, Valve, hires according to the flat methodology. New employees are brought in to add value to the company; it's up to them what they do with the opportunity and what role they will play.

Valve's hiring philosophy clearly states, "When you give smart talented people the freedom to create without fear of failure, amazing things happen. We see it every day at Valve. In fact, some of our best insights have come from our biggest mistakes. And we're ok with that!" Since 1996, this approach has produced award-winning games, cutting-edge technologies, and a groundbreaking social entertainment platform.

In reality, communication flow cannot be dictated by an organization's predetermined structure, because it cannot be controlled. Communication has no regard for hierarchy. People will always talk and share ideas with each other, regardless of the managerial structure. An organization can be structured a certain way on paper but, in real life, communication flows like a network. If an organization is structured in a way that is more closely aligned with the way it "really" operates, it will follow a networked approach as opposed to a machine approach.

> If one or many of your units are going into digital business operation models, Agile HR is for those units. In corporations, we are working with digital services, digital businesses, and R&D, all of which are going into Agile operation models because they can't do it the old-school way anymore. It just doesn't work, which means you will have an industrial organization and an Agile organization in parallel. You need to be able to define Agile HR in order to support that unit.
>
> —RIINA

FLATARCHIES

Flatarchies aren't quite flat or hierarchical; they are a combination of both structures. They're amoebas that change shape as needed. It's not uncommon for flat organizations to organically form ad hoc hierarchies or break-out groups for specific projects and then disband. Similarly, the organization can have a loose hierarchy that flattens out when necessary and then returns to a loose hierarchy. Flatarchies are an adaptable model for organizations, which makes them conducive to the freelancer economy. Although it may be a fluid approach, it does require changes within the organization. Flatarchies are a suitable model for medium- and large-sized organizations that seek to blend both solid and loose structures.

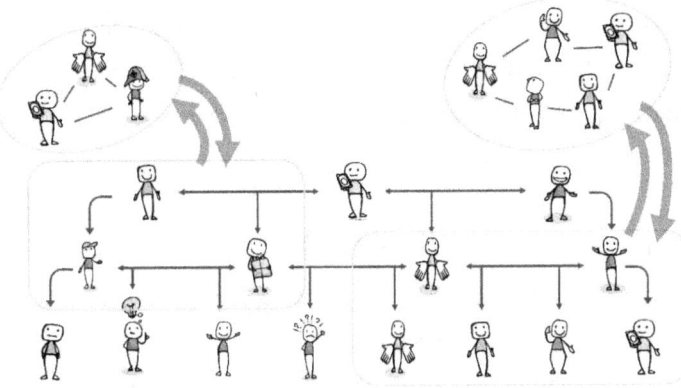

> We see organizations that have hybrid structures, so some teams run in an Agile way, and other teams are still more hierarchical, but those lines are disappearing. They are transitioning into a more structured network.
> —FABIOLA

HOLACRATIC ORGANIZATIONS

The Holacratic approach is based on a circular hierarchy. It provides a strict set of principles guiding how organizations should be run, how meetings should be conducted, and how tensions are "processed." Organizational roles are comprised of circles, each containing several people without any job title, indicating that each person may have several roles. The upper crop circles set the direction, priorities, and strategy of the organization, while the lower circles execute and perform tasks in a transparent and democratic manner. It's a model that defines the functions of each circle in great detail. Although the structure is quite loose in theory, in practice it has fixed guidelines.

Holacracy is a well-known concept, due in large part to its implementation at Zappos. The CEO and founder, Tony Hsieh, imposed Holacracy on his organization, which had previously been hierarchically structured. Initially, many managers resisted the change. Hsieh was determined to make Holacracy a success, so he offered anyone who was not on board the opportunity to leave with severance pay and take their noncompliant attitudes with them.

The move toward flat, self-management can be a hard one, particularly for large organizations that were built on different principles. After much trial and error, Zappos and Hsieh did effectively implement Holacracy, but it was not without its share of national attention and internal headaches. Judging by the transparency the Zappos culture blog offers, it seems they have weathered the storm.[3]

---

3   https://zappos.com/about

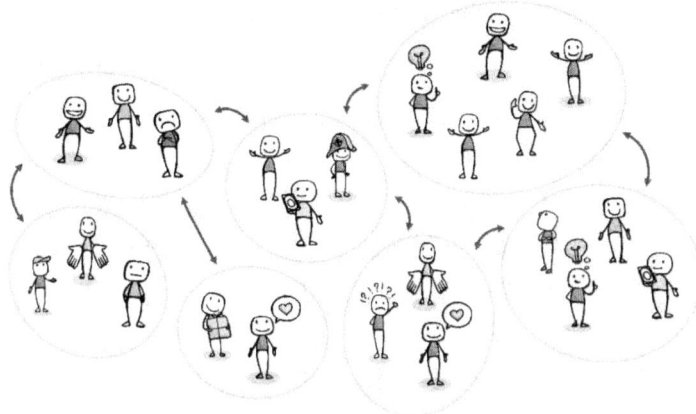

ORGANIZATION 3.0

Organization 3.0 is a set of principles that characterize modern organizations. They are globally distributed and have small, connected teams. They tend to be intrepreneurial, which means all the employees are empowered to behave like owners. Even if the company is large, it's made up of small teams that function both independently and cohesively, and it's able to adapt much more quickly than traditionally structured organizations.

Companies of the future are hyper-innovative and creative. Knowledge will soon be the only competitive advantage, so the companies that can learn and adapt fast are the ones that will survive. More women will move into leadership roles, storytelling will become the central emphasis of marketing efforts, learning will be visual and democratized, storage will move entirely to the cloud, and the focus will shift from profit to prosperity.

Overall, employees will take responsibility for their own learning, growth, and movement within organizations, rather than waiting for it to come from "above." As different aspects of a company's growth trajectory become important, the traditional employee/manager roles will change irrevocably. Companies of the future will embody Agile principles and practices more comprehensively.

> We don't expect people to stay in one company for their entire life. If they stay for another quarter, or if they stay for an extra six months, that's good. If we make the changes to do that just a little at a time, it's going to affect the rest of the company. We did some calculations to measure the change, and it is huge. If everyone stays for thirty days more, it's really going to affect how much money we earn.
>
> —CECILIA

In fact, the organization is a social system, not a machine. We have to move from viewing the organization as a machine that can be controlled and managed to viewing it as a social system. People are not cogs in a machinery, they have feelings, dreams, challenges and thoughts and cannot be controlled.

People are not robots. They are complex adaptive systems that work from intrinsic motivation. It means that we need to stop to see people as resources and view them as the living organizms they are, who we need to treat differently to work optimally. No standardization or boxing people with labels or grades anymore, just skills to understand better what makes each person tick. To create a wellfucntioning social system is a very complex task and we need to use a lot more experiemntation and trial and error for it to work. There are no recipes for success here and agile is not the silver bullet.

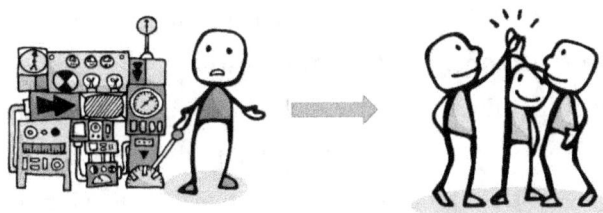

The organization is a social system, not a machine

OPOS: OPEN PARTICIPATORY ORGANIZATIONS

Open Participatory Organizations, or OPOs, are different from all the other previously mentioned company structures. It's a new paradigm. Essentially, it's a value structure that helps companies of all sizes think about a decentralized approach. Rather than offering an entire "package," meaning a fixed structure, OPO is a tool to shift conversations around the ways we conventionally think of organizations.

The founder of OPO is Bonnitta Roy, a writer and consultant, whose conviction is that there are better ways to work and run organizations. In the end of this book, you will find parts of an interview with Bonnitta, where she talks about the need for change and how you can create a new mindset about what work is.

THE STRUCTURE—CULTURE MISFIT

During my twenty plus years as a consultant, I have had the great pleasure of working with some of Sweden's largest international organizations and have seen them from inside, central positions. Mostly, they try to create structures to support the different parts of the business from the inside out. They also try to shape a new and different culture by creating values and frameworks of wanted behaviors using large and well-known consulting companies.

HR is regarded as less important to organizational success than, say, the CFO and the financial department. HR, which is responsible for the people and organizational development, represents the "soft skills"; it's viewed as less critical to success than "the numbers." It's illogical that the people who are responsible for creating the backbone and core structures, as well as the culture and the values the organization, are not as important as the people performing number-crunching activities, budgeting, and follow-up of quarterly financial targets. There is a large misunderstanding of what is actually important and at play within many organizations.

For any organization to be successful, you need to have a fit between the culture (values and behaviors) on one hand, and the structures (methods, processes, and systems) on the other hand. If not, you will experience confusion around what's said and what's done.

Regardless, if you value winning, money, status, competition, teamwork, higher purpose, whole people, and collaboration, you need to have a fit between the values you say you want and the structures that make up the business "way of working," which often consists of different tools, processes, and IT systems. Unfortunately, I've often seen the misfit in large companies. The kind of behaviors we say we want and need for success don't match the kind of behaviors that are rewarded and built into control mechanisms, processes, and systems. Instead, we say one thing and do another. Here are some examples:

- Let's say we value the importance of trust between people. Trust does not fit well with structures of control. If you really trust somebody, why would you need to control that same person by requiring detailed reports every week or month? If you trust somebody, you would give them the potential to succeed by providing the tools, the competence, and all other prerequisites that are necessary for that person to grow and perform. Then, you get out of their way and trust them to get the job; done.

- Imagine your company values are creativity and innovation, and then the structured, detailed job descriptions limit people by describing what they are supposed to do and not supposed to do. This is not a very effective way to create a foundation for innovation. If we use job descriptions and roles, we need to make them as wide and flexible as possible and let people go outside their role if it's what makes them tick. It's also a good way of knowing whether people are really thriving in their current role. Only when they are free to think and do, and not restricted by detailed instructions, can you release people's creativity.
- Let's say that cooperation is an important organizational value. But the performance framework rewards individual performance. If collaboration is important, you need to reward collaboration, not individual performance. One way to do that is to reward the team instead of the individual. If individuals need to be rewarded within the team for extraordinary performance, leave it to the employees to decide who should get the biggest part. They know very well who made the most effort, and this method of rewarding individuals will enhance cooperation.
- Imagine that the organization wants people and teams to engage with their whole selves for the greater good of the organization, but then they give them numerical

targets created by the management team. Instead, if you want employee engagement, let them create their own objectives and link their own measurements to the overall company targets.
- Let's imagine that equality is an important value. Then, the organization promotes certain people to better positions or gives them higher bonuses. Instead, involve the peers in the process of nominating managers and specialists. You will minimize envy, competition, and social pain.
- Let's say diversity is extremely important to the organization, but there aren't any women in top management. Where are the different ethnic groups that we see in marketing campaigns spread around the company?
- Maybe you value performance and want employees to exhibit the "right" behaviors. Then, you reward them on a scale of one to five in a formal performance rating exercise with a fixed distribution. "My manager says I did a great job last year, but there aren't any fives left, so I got a four." Guess who is disengaged instead of motivated?

These types of situations are contradictory and create a misalignment between what people hear the organizational values are (the wanted culture) and what is really happening in the organization (the processes and frameworks). The effect is a feeling of a social pain, which is just as harmful and real as physical pain. Plus, we don't achieve a better, more engaging place to work if the structure is not designed in alignment with the desired culture.

MINDSET SHIFT

Most organizations have two or more of the above-described organization forms, it's very rare to have just one "clean" organization type. And that's okay, as long as the organization type supports the purpose. I would like to see a move toward using more Agile structures because I believe these types of values in organizations are resulting in better performance, with happier employees.

For organizations to truly transform, there must be a seismic mind shift. We started to discuss this mind shift earlier when we referenced McGregor's X and Y theories. Essentially, his opposing theories are representative of what needs to happen in order to achieve organizational agility and remain competitive. Companies need to shift from thinking about profit to thinking about purpose. They need to move from hierarchical structures to networked structures. Management needs to switch from being controlling to being empowering, from planning to experimenting, and from privacy to transparency.

> You can't use the old-school industrial planning concepts anymore. You need to adapt iterative ways of working. Many people misunderstand the intentions of Agile. People think it is about a new kind of office. It's not about a new kind of office; that's just an enabler for Agile. Agile isn't about planning, but it's not about tossing plans away either. Yes, you still have to plan. You have to plan a hell of a lot, but you have to plan iteratively. It's a different way of doing work. For me, it is very irritating when lots of people talk about Agile without actually knowing anything about it.
>
> —RIINA

These changes need to be global across the organization, but they usually start with HR. As organizational architects, HR leaders set the intention to embrace a mindset shift. They make the initial decisions regarding organizational structure, change management, and leadership development. They set the stage for the change the entire organization will adapt to and embrace.

The shift to Agile will be unique to each organization, understandably. However, more traditionally structured businesses will shift according to the company's unique strategy and vision. They might acknowledge, "We are heading toward X. What do we need to do to get there? What specific roles and departments are necessary to execute on the vision and deliver value?"

Smaller companies or startups may already have Agile principles in place. The main difference in smaller, newer companies is that decisions usually come from the whole team. They might recognize that they need to enlist the help of HR to better adapt to Agile, which means they are pulling HR toward them, instead of pushing them away.

The team controls the need instead of management. The team seeks a solution, or a person with the competence necessary to provide the solution, either internally or externally. The team identifies the important issues, and they also drive the outcome. The best solutions come from working cross-functionally.

Self-organization is an important concept within the Agile approach. The idea of self-organization can be challenging for those from a traditional mindset. However, self-organization is part of our inherent animal behavior. Have you ever noticed that birds self-organize into flocks when they fly together, and fish organize into schools when they swim?

Similarly, humans tend to organize themselves effectively as well. Without being told what to do and who to group with, they naturally select who to team up with and what to work on; especially when they have a very clear *why*. The only prerequisites for self-organizing teams are clear goals and basic, simple values that the team receives from management or, preferably, develops themselves.

A company's organizational structure and overall mindset will directly affect every individual who works there. In order to empower employees to give and share their best solutions and ideas, it makes sense to give them the freedom to explore. Allowing for self-organization creates an environment ripe to benefit from specific Agile methods and tools.

Furthermore, in an Agile organization, HR's role, just like the organization's mindset, must shift. For Agile to work effectively, it's important that the company structure and culture match up. HR managers can hinder progress instead of help if they don't take the right approach.

> In HR, we have as much complexity, if not more, as the business side, because we're dealing with people systems. The events concerning change, adaptation, and iterative advances are essential. We can see HR isn't working. Many measures we've already tried are telling us that. Let's do something else.
>
> —RIINA

WHY HR NEEDS TO DRIVE AGILE TRANSFORMATION

It's been going on for some time now—the shift toward more agile, nimble companies that can change on the fly and adapt to the ever-changing environment. Organizations that don't manage to make the shift will slowly get weaker and die, and the ones that do transform to a new culture and structure, more adapted to the needs of today's and tomorrow's participation economy, will survive and flourish.

Small- and medium-sized companies can manage the shift pretty easily, since they have less top-down structures that hinder people from realizing their potential. The bigger the company, the more complex it becomes, with systems, processes, and structures that cannot easily be changed. You can try to change one (often functional) department of the company, but the problem remains in another. Since all parts are dependent on each other, the brave department that attempts to initiate change is typically forced to give up and return to the old structure, like a rubber ball after it's been squeezed.

There is one functional department in most large organizations, however, that can affect all the other parts at the same time: central group HR. This group, in most large companies, controls:

- Leadership programs and development
- Change management
- Organizational development
- Employee engagement and retention
- People development and learning
- Reward strategies and bonus systems
- Talent acquisition
- Long-term workforce management

All the above areas cut through the entire organization. They are the processes that support or stop the change to a more Agile future. It all depends on how we work with processes and programs. They can be developed in a way that limits performance and engagement, or they can optimize performance and employee satisfaction.

HR struggles with criticism of being organizational police that stop performance and engagement by implementing the very processes that were supposed to increase the same. This needs to change. HR has been sitting in the back seat for too long now. It's time to step up and take responsibility for change.

It's all about the people, the relationships, and the system in which the people live and work. If we can give the right prerequisites to people, they will take care of the rest.

The system needs to be managed, not the people. We don't need to do more things or implement difficult frameworks, methods, or models; we need to learn how to allow people to give their best effort to the company by providing the correct structures. It's a path of trial and error to find the best way for each company.

The Agile principles and mindset can serve as a guide. The tools and practices work sometimes, but not every time. The only way to move forward is through continuous learning. The companies that learn faster than the others will be the winners.

HR has the power to design the structures that either support people to perform or make it difficult to contribute in creative and innovative ways. If HR holds onto the old, traditional approach, the consequence will be rigid and fixed organizations chained to ineffective systems and processes.

HR can either support or hinder the change toward a more Agile organization, which is why HR needs to go first! By providing different structures and focusing on customer value instead of rules, HR can lead companies through change that no other department is capable of.

One of the contributors to this book, Leila, works as a People and Culture Whisperer at Snow Software. This is her description of their change journey.

We're in an interesting phase of seeing what is global and what is local. How can we ensure we have self-leadership all around the world? We don't want to push centralized corporate bullshit from one small corner into the vast world of business.

We do have local People and Culture roles who work in the bigger regions and countries. Mine is one of the biggest, so we have two small teams that work with cross-functional stand-ups. We meet and discuss different topics, depending on who is going to be involved. We're able to synchronize and redirect ourselves, depending on the changing environments, which is every week around here.

Our strategy is to be on top of things. We work with transparency and communication to effect rapid changes according to the needs of the business. We've created an environment that unleashes everyone's powers. We're working with our vision a lot. That creates a different demand on how we are organized and how we work together. We really need to work across borders.

—LEILA

LESS OF > MORE OF: ADAPTABLE ORGANIZATION

THE TRADITIONAL WAY	THE AGILE WAY
Top-down	Bottom up AND top-down OR Horizontally-Network
Upfront org. Design	Emerging org. Design
Communication via managers	Communication flow free between everybody
Sub optimizing	Optimizing for the whole
Machine metaphor	Network metaphor
Complex bureaucracy	Keep it simple
Project based	Based on stable teams
Functional teams	Cross-functional teams
Decision making by management	Everyone involved in decision making
Central control	Trust local variety
Human view X	Human view Y
Resource optimization	Flow optimization

CHAPTER 3

Modern Agile

"Make everything as simple as possible, but not simpler."
—Albert Einstein

The original Agile Manifesto was born in 2001. Although its four core tenets remain true to this day, the philosophy has evolved over time. True to Agile's nature, it will always change and adapt to remain viable and relevant in today's workplace.

According to Joshua Kerievsky, CEO of Industrial Logic, an Agile consulting firm, "The Agile Manifesto was great when it was first drafted. It had a wonderful lifespan and it is a distinguished part of our history, but it deserves an honorable retirement."[4] For example, Agile doesn't apply exclusively to technology departments anymore. Today, those same principles can be woven into an entire organization.

The four founding principles are:

1. Individual interactions over processes and tools
2. Working software over comprehensive documentation
3. Customer collaboration over contract negotiation
4. Responding to change over following a plan

Kerievsky cites limitations within the original four pillars. Specifically, he feels they fail to consider the entire ecosystem of a project. The manifesto should encourage ongoing experimentation as well as foster a healthy and vibrant work environment.

The end goal of any organization should always be to deliver value continuously, not just as it relates to software. To that end, Kerievsky proposed four new principles for modern Agile:

- Make people awesome
- Make safety a prerequisite
- Experiment and learn rapidly
- Deliver value continuously

---

4   https://industriallogic.com/people/joshua

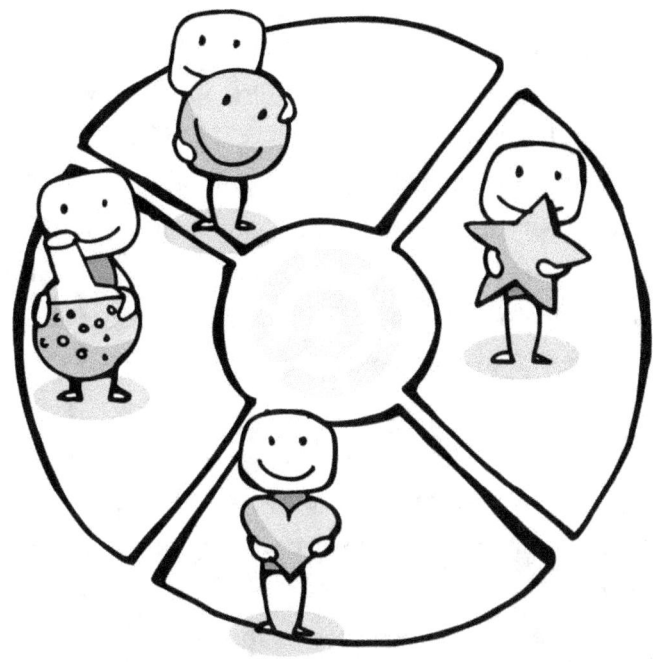

The new pillars are better suited to organizations as a whole. They're more specific to today's challenges and are inclusive. "Making people awesome" doesn't apply to customers exclusively. It applies to everyone in the entire ecosystem: the employees, suppliers, vendors, investors, owners, and partners. It includes all the stakeholders who participate in devising, creating, developing, buying, selling, marketing, and funding a product or a service. Everyone has value within the ecosystem and everyone needs to function at their personal peak.

"Making safety a prerequisite" means creating a culture of safety in order to unlock high-performance behavior. Fear is the greatest roadblock to creativity. The idea is to create an environment where people feel comfortable enough to make wild suggestions, to say what's on their minds, and to experiment without judgment or penalty. A psychologically and physically safe environment is a prerequisite for performance and engagement.

> Creating a safe environment is key for all employees within an organization. When you've created a safe environment, your brain will have a lot of energy left over to allow you to think in new ways. It's interesting. It's in the small things: How is the air in the office? How does it look in the office? How important is it compared to the bigger and more psychological things, such as how we approach each other when we have a difficult situation?
>
> —LEILA

Many organizations today are riddled with politics, backstabbing power struggles, and bureaucracy. People are afraid to speak their minds or share ideas for fear of punishment. Worse, they're afraid to step out of line in case a coworker has it in mind to throw them under the bus. The culture of fear needs to be abolished so that people have the energy and the brain space to focus on what matters, which is creating.

The Agile community has already been practicing "experimenting and learning rapidly" for years. It's a behavior that encourages people to take risks and learn from their mistakes. Often, mistakes lead to the greatest discoveries or inventions. We'll never be open to new experiences if we don't try them on for size and test the waters.

"Delivering value continuously" requires breaking work down into smaller pieces. Smaller pieces means delivering faster and creating value as early as possible for the customer. It might require learning a new approach to doing things. The idea is to focus on the outcomes to uncover better ways of getting amazing results, which is essentially the modern interpretation of the Agile Manifesto.[5]

The most important aspect of the Agile principles is that they are an overview of the rules today's companies should adhere to. They are like a lighthouse: they offer guidance and illuminate the path. The more the principles are practiced and absorbed, the better a company will function. There will always be obstacles, but when given the choice, it's preferable to speak face-to-face, rather than to communicate another way. It's preferable to trust coworkers and managers, rather than it is to live in fear of them. Likewise, it is better to try new things and see what works than it is to remain unchanged.

---

5   https://modernagile.org/

That being said, companies that use Agile principles don't follow a fixed recipe or prescription. There are no clear, best solutions. The principles can be used to the degree they are applicable in a given scenario. There are a variety of Agile tools that make the principles come to life, which I'll discuss in detail in the upcoming chapters. You can see a list of principles and tools at the end of the book.

HR'S NEW ROLE

> We have chosen to walk away from calling ourselves human resources. That is a very conscious choice, which reflects the kind of value we are actually creating. We are moving from HR to people in culture.
>
> —LEILA

Although Agile philosophies can and should be applied across departments, the real push should come from human resources. HR departments are the architects of organizations and their leaders need to take the wheel in the driver's seat. They need to lead the transition from traditional management practices to Agile, so that the company is prepared to compete in current and future business landscapes.

> It's not going to be about benchmarking and doing the same as Deloitte or some other large company. You have to be creative for yourself, and also for your organization's benefit. I like how HR is working in different organizations; it will be totally different from one place to another. Every company needs to tailor-make their own HR.
>
> —RIINA

When HR managers hold on to traditional ways of working, learning, developing, and planning, they are severely reducing the possibility for change. Those companies will be left in the old paradigm, which is rigid. Or worse, they will be outnumbered and outpaced by smaller, faster players in the market. Alternatively, if HR departments switch to a structure that focuses on customer value over rules and policies, they will be able to lead their companies through change in a way that no other department is capable of.

As the pace of change increases and competition becomes more fierce, the importance of agility increases as well. Companies that are lightweight and flexible have a better chance of survival than old, bulky clunkers with layer upon layer of policy and process to navigate. This reality is helping more and more companies to understand the value of Agile organizations.

> I try not to speak about HR processes. I don't succeed all the time, but I try. Basically, over the last three years, we have chosen the areas that demanded our attention and creativity. We communicated very clearly with the organization by saying, "This year, we're going to work with XYZ."
>
> —CECILIA

> I really try to move away from the focus of HR processes and move into the perspective of having the user in mind. By user, I mean the employee experience. Then, of course, we will have different parts of that journey that can be improved, but we're always striving for a better "people" experience.
>
> —LEILA

HR departments tend to lean toward tradition. Their processes are inherently slow and perceived as ineffective. The word "process" alone indicates control. However, certain functions within HR are purely transactional or administrative. Specific tasks, such as payroll, may require rigid processes. It's the kind of process that, if it does *not* work properly, people will be upset. However, it's difficult to perform the process better or worse—it either gets done or it doesn't.

> If we have a process and we implement it in an organization and nobody's using it, does the process exist? No, in my opinion, it doesn't. On paper, maybe it exists; perhaps in a PowerPoint presentation, it exists. But in reality, it doesn't exist.
>
> —RIINA

On the other hand, work tasks that involve creativity—such as performance management, goal setting, competency development, or learning—need to change as the world changes. Performance management and learning do not fit into a process. This is where HR managers need to shift their thinking. If a business demands change and adaptability to new customer needs, fixed processes are not the answer. Annual performance goals and ratings are often completely out of sync with Agile initiatives and goals. The dynamic creates internal conflict, especially within Agile IT teams.

The challenge, then, is for HR to adapt to systems and principles that allow for increased flexibility and autonomy. Agile is not a method or a formula that can be "implemented." It is a mindset, a way of thinking, and a collection of values around how work should be organized in a complex and ever-changing world. The key to its success lies in an organization's ability to adapt to change.

> Some industries are developing so quickly into Agile that, in HR, you just have to know how to support them. The same thing is happening in industries now with the IOT (Internet of Things). The IOT is going full-speed ahead, because if you don't have digital services to support your lamps, your cables, your roofs, your antennas, or whatever, you are immediately out of the game.
>
> —RIINA

Many of Agile's methods are derived from the manifesto and the principles that are linked to it. They also build on short cycles that involve frequent deliverables, continuous feedback, and cooperation throughout. By working this way, the products and services become better suited to the needs of customers and unnecessary work is minimized.

Running a business today is less about process than it is about people, teams, and relationships. There is a movement toward centralized decision making, which manifests through cross-functional, self-organizing teams. The principle here is that the people closest to the information and who have the most knowledge about the issue should be the ones who make decisions about it. They have the greatest competence and insight, and therefore should be empowered to operate in accordance with their best knowledge.

When team members are allowed a high degree of autonomy, they become more motivated. Motivated team members lead to high-performing teams that push themselves to constantly learn and excel. Within a sustainable system, work becomes both a challenge and a reward. Every day is an opportunity for individual team members to push their limits because the focus is on speed. Accordingly, teams start to adapt their behaviors and work more effectively.

AGILE HR

> Is there a crucial role and demand for HR in an ultimate Agile organization?
>
> —LEILA

HR's role is shifting from an administrative function to an internal contributor of high strategic value. Traditional HR focused on implementing standards, policies, and controls. Now the focus is on speed and internal customers. HR should foster flexibility, adaptability, and innovation to support management and employees. The goal is to help people be more competent in their roles, to work better with one another, and to make faster decisions closer to the customers.

> All HR does is make rules, tools, and processes telling everyone in an organization how things should be done. It would be better if HR offered a menu: "Dear leader, if you want to help your employees to grow, you need to do it in this way and have a dialogue around that."
> —CECILIA

The Agile HR Manifesto has been adopted from the Agile IT Manifesto presented in the previous chapter.[6]

AGILE HR MANIFESTO

We are uncovering better ways of developing an engaging workplace culture by doing it and helping others do it. Through this work, we have come to value:

Collaborative networks over hierarchical structures

Transparency over secrecy

Adaptability over prescriptiveness

Inspiration and engagement over management and retention

Intrinsic motivation over extrinsic rewards

Ambition over obligation

That is, while there is value in the items on the right section of the sentence, we value the items on the left more.

---

6   http://www.agilehrmanifesto.org/

Agile HR can be viewed from two perspectives: how HR should work internally and what HR should deliver to the business. We will discuss each of these processes and practices in depth in subsequent chapters. Because HR is the driving organizational force within businesses, our focus is on creating better workplaces through the development of individuals and teams across all disciplines. The trick is to start small where you are, and keep it simple.

> HR really has to get rid of all the stuff that is not core competencies, like the entire HR administration. Payroll could be done by finance. They're dealing with that stuff anyway. Legal should do legal documents, and HR needs to focus on the people.
>
> —FABIOLA

LESS OF > MORE OF: AGILE HR

THE TRADITIONAL WAY	THE AGILE WAY
Less of	More of
Develop policies, rules and standards	Support flexibility, speed and collaboration
Deliver programs & processes to customers	Involve customer in delivery
HR Specialists OR HR Generalists OR HR Admins	T-shape HR people who can take on many different roles
Individual work	Teamwork (cross functional)
Funtional HR/ specialist area	Value stream-based HR
Jobs & positions	Playing many different roles
HR Projects	Stable, high performaing teams
Promotions and bonus programs	Salary formulas and profit sharing (can be performance related)
Deliver programs & processes	Supporting the organization to perform
One size fits all	No-size fits all
Having the "HR recipe"	Experimentation
Human view X	Human view Y

CHAPTER 4

Performance Management

"Performance management isn't dead. The old way of thinking about it is."
—Anita Bowness

Bersin & Associates, the worldwide leader in talent management, developed a framework for performance management in 2011 used by HR professionals around the globe. In its entirety, it's a complex approach. I've chosen to highlight just a few of the most critical components necessary for reaching a company's vision.

THE NEW PERFORMANCE MANAGEMENT STRATEGY

The Bersin framework has four core pillars, or ongoing activities, that are vital to consider when striving toward improving employee performance.

- Set and revise goals
- Plan for development
- Lead, manage, and coach
- Follow up

Each of the four pillars is equally important, but how they appear and are realized differs from one company to the next. The best approach depends largely on where the company is in its growth cycle, what type of culture and climate exists, and which performance management strategy best suits the company.

The first step, setting goals (a mix of business and development goals is a good idea), is an area we're familiar with already. In the context of performance management, it requires thinking about what you need to learn or what competencies are necessary to reach those business goals. Then you make a plan to develop them. Daily activities should support the pursuit of the goal, and management should be there to support and guide the employee as needed.

How long will it take to achieve the goals? In most cases, the answer cannot be pinpointed. It could take two weeks, two months, or two years, depending on the nature of the goals. In general, it is preferable to establish several small goals that support "the big one." As discussed previously, this practice allows a company or team to change course easily when problems arise. When goals are split into smaller segments, it's easier to take corrective actions along the way.

HR's role is to lead, manage, and coach people toward their goals. When goals are achieved, the cycle starts all over again. The process adheres exactly to a Scrum sprint, which we will discuss in Chapter 12. The employee creates an "epic," or a user story, based on the product backlog. They set a sprint goal, work to achieve the goal, constantly reprioritize along the way, and then review the results in a retrospective with the team.

During the follow-up stage of the performance management process, the manager shares feedback and celebrates successes (equal to the sprint retrospective). During this stage, the employee and the manager reassess and plan for the future. Then, they hit the ground running again, building momentum and knowledge with each sprint.

The above way of working with performance management is just a first step in a more Agile direction for an organization that has worked for many years with a traditional approach to performance. In a more modern organization you may want to move straight to working with even more Agile methods, such as OKRs (Objectives and Key Results, see Chapter 5).

Case Study: Volvo

A few years ago, I was hired to work with Volvo as a consultant, responsible for the development of the performance management framework for the organization. The company offers a good study in performance management strategy. It's a traditional, but innovative company attempting to become more Agile.

At Volvo Cars, we produced a new framework for performance management, which looked at the overall picture and introduced an extended performance concept. The plan went beyond the development and measurement of goals. It incorporated several new ways of working that contributed to performance, such as goal setting, creating prerequisites for performance and continuous learning, and development of employees.

We started a cross-functional project team that operated across two departmental disciplines: talent management, and compensation and benefits. This was a way for internal

HR teams to be more Agile, flexible, and adaptable, instead of working in the narrow, confined silos they were used to.

Volvo's old approach didn't allow for opportunities of performance enhancement or employee growth on the individual or team level. Managers suffered too because they didn't control the process. HR dictated the compliance requirements and checked off boxes as steps were completed. In short, Volvo's entire process was not in alignment with the more flexible and empowered culture the company aspired to achieve.

After the new performance management framework was introduced, due to the integrated approach, Volvo managers are now able to focus on ongoing performance activities year-round. There is a new emphasis on empowerment, coaching, feedback, and continuous improvement, just as the Bersin framework suggested.

At Volvo, we decided that HR should not control how the manager and the employee work with performance management in detail. In a company with twenty-three thousand employees, it's impossible to have a "one-size-fits-all" approach. The framework needed to be taken down to a local level and adapted to the needs of the specific department or business unit. The overall recommendation was very "loose" and consisted of guiding principles for goal setting, performance, and development, rather than rigid rules and detailed processes. Each manager had a lot more freedom as to how he or she wanted to approach the performance challenge. Rather than directing how performance should be executed, it was about creating prerequisites for managers and employees to perform and be happy by providing a toolbox with references and guidelines for an improved way of working together.

> The biggest change HR made was to take away the performance review. In its place, we now have a totally new system of performance evaluation that's driven by the employees themselves. We put tools and methods in place for the employee to use, enhance, and be in charge of their performance.
>
> —CECILIA

At Volvo Cars, I did presentations for the management teams on all levels, even in the factories where I also collected input from management. At one of my presentations of the "New Performance Framework at Volvo," one of the factory managers raised his hand and said, "For years, I have been walking in kid shoes. Now, for the first time in my long career at Volvo, I feel like I can kick off my kid shoes and put on my adult shoes. I can finally take the responsibility to act as a manager who doesn't need to be supervised by HR. Thank you!"

BETTER PERFORMANCE MEASUREMENT

Talent and performance management encompasses all the processes that facilitate people's work within the business. We've already discussed some of the core elements that fall under the HR umbrella, but the full employee lifecycle includes

- Recruitment
- Setting individual and team goals
- Workforce planning
- Career development (succession management)
- Competency management and learning
- Compensation and benefits
- Leadership and management

Increasingly, companies are starting to understand the connection between work conditions and psychological balance. Traditional performance management systems have been proven to decrease performance. Many of them are built on a grading system where employee performance is rated on a scale of one to five, or some other similar measurement. This system is problematic on several levels.

> My opinion is that performance appraisals don't help the employee. Companies spend way too much time on this. I spoke with a company that has a presence in many countries and they were currently giving performance appraisals at the beginning of the year. It totally stopped every other aspect of productivity in the company. This is a dangerous process and hurts profitability. If you look at the performance appraisal, does the outcome change the revenue of the company? I believe not. It's a very old-fashioned and very industrial way of looking at performance.
> —CECILIA

Recent research at the NeuroLeadership Institute (NLI) examined the link between performance ratings and performance. A spokesperson for the organization said:

We've been studying this trend closely since 2011. Our interest in the topic was piqued when clients started to tell us how our research on motivation and the brain was explaining why standard performance reviews were failing.

In short, we found that social threats and rewards, like one's sense of status or fairness, activate intense reaction networks in the brain. This explained the intense reactions people had to being assessed on a ratings scale, and it also pointed to ways of designing better systems.7

It pays to focus on strengths instead of weaknesses when evaluating performance. The optimal praise to criticism ratio is 5:1, which is a ratio based on empirical data. Research into successful marriages shows the same ratio.

One of the problems with grading performance is it connects achieving fixed performance goals to rewards. When goals are tied to finances or status, sandbagging often occurs, which is the practice of setting lower goals so they can be achieved more easily (to get the bonus tied to goal fulfillment) when, at the same time, higher goals are demanded from management.

Within the traditional system, only the people with the highest scores will be happy. The people with average or below average scores, which is 70 percent of people, quickly become dissatisfied. Everyone wants to think their work is slightly above average, so, when told it's not, they become unmotivated and disengaged up to six months after the rating. They start to perform worse than they did before the performance rating; it's a counterproductive exercise. Even the employees who get the highest ratings will be less productive up to two months after the exercise.

---

7   https://hbr.org/2015/09/
    why-more-and-more-companies-are-ditching-performance-ratings

The lucky high achievers who receive a higher-than-average score on their performance rating oftentimes get a bonus, usually monetary. Bonuses breed bad behaviors within organizations. They create a scenario where people expect a reward, and it doesn't take long for them to feel *entitled* to a reward. If they don't get the expected reward, they will be unmotivated. The whole intention of enhancing performance through a reward actually shoots itself in the foot.

The bonus system also promotes self-optimization. People put their own individual goals ahead of the team or company goals. Scorecards and ratings create an unhealthy competitive environment. Cooperation and group efforts are not a top priority.

Grades and ratings sub-optimize motivation, too, as people work very hard until they reach their goals and then feel like they're done. They receive their rewards and then feel they don't have to work very hard—at least, until the next performance review cycle comes around again, usually in a year. Instead of rewarding continued hard work, the organization rewards laziness and complacency.

The only motivation one gets when working with bonuses tied to fixed performance goals is the motivation to get the reward and nothing else. We need people to be motivated to achieve more over a long period of time with sustainable results, rather than striving toward a reward.

Traditional performance management causes people to focus on all the wrong things. When people are promised something if they achieve X, Y, and Z, goals become too rigid. They are much harder to change because they are directly tied to the employee's finances. If there's an external change in the market or someone makes a new discovery, the organization is stuck. The more individualized the bonus system, the more damaging it is to the team because it isolates people and it puts a certain chosen few on a pedestal.

In addition to the documented psychological havoc annual performance reviews wreak on the staff, there are several additional negative effects that need to be weighed:

- No one likes them—employees or managers.
- They attempt to squeeze too much important data into a single conversation: salary, performance, goals, metrics, and development.
- There's too much emphasis on the past year and what went wrong, instead of looking forward and improving for the future.
- There is a lack of proactivity: the conversation should be centered on ideas and improvements, not on judging the past. You cannot do anything about the past.

- Is the manager the best person to evaluate the employee's performance? Has the manager been present for all individual and team activities throughout the year? Is the manager in the best position to give a fair and accurate assessment? The employee's teammates or customers may be better barometers of performance.
- By the time the conversation takes place, it's too late for change or to undo past mistakes. The timing is unproductive.
- Also, when you judge performance for a whole year, you tend to forget about the performance in the beginning of the year and focus solely on the performance that is closest to the discussion. Who can remember what happened in January, almost a year ago?

The traditional performance review system is antiquated and harmful to morale. It's based on the assumption that employees are driven exclusively by monetary benefits. It doesn't take quality of life, the camaraderie of participating in a team, the mental stimulation of being challenged, the passion for a fantastic company purpose, or the rewards of learning into consideration on any level. It also sets up the false dynamic that a single person—the manager—is equipped to appropriately evaluate and judge an employee's contributions and oversee their personal development. Who knows how the work is getting done better than the person who is doing it?

Additionally, there is no such thing as a "one size fits all" employee evaluation tool. The same system is not appropriate for everyone. Often, individual employees are evaluated on how the organization is doing. Very rarely does a single person have the power to affect how the whole company performs. It's a lot more complex than that. Relationships, situations, coincidences, and personal values all play a part that is too often overlooked by management. They strive to see the organization as a machine that can be optimized by adding the perfect parts that work perfectly together. Sometimes, they add a little oil to the machinery—otherwise known as team-building activities—to make things run more smoothly.

What can managers do instead of force the old-fashioned performance review conversations once a year? Here are a few suggestions:

- Make the conversation non-judgmental and open.
- Let other people, besides the manager, provide input on an employee's performance before, during, or after the conversation.
- Don't link rewards or salaries directly to feedback conversations.
- Focus on improvement for the future, rather than judging the past.
- Split conversations up into several smaller sessions throughout the year instead of one big one at the end.
- Make notes (if any) transparent to the rest of the team. Sometimes, this is dictated by your culture.
- Allow the employee to decide on the structure/agenda.
- Link the conversation to team retrospectives, if possible, and let the employee evaluate their individual contribution for each sprint.
- Don't call it a performance review/rating. Call it feedback or an improvement conversation.

AGILE PERFORMANCE TRENDS

When companies adopt Agile values, they will have new and more effective ways to measure performance. The most important factor is to recognize that motivation and drive come from within the individual. It doesn't come from a gold star or a red F on a report card. Teams are responsible for the outcome of their collective work because no one person is single-handedly doing all the work for the entire company. Shorter, more frequent feedback loops will lead to increased productivity and more engaged employees.

Peter Antman, a well-known Agile coach from Spotify in Sweden, advocates that companies should stop doing performance reviews altogether. In his book, *Tear Down the Pyramids (Again)*, Antman presents a better path forward. He says that instead of managers waiting a whole year to have a real discussion with their employees about performance, they should meet often, if not daily, to check in. Communication should occur as needed, in real time, not in accordance with some archaic schedule no one benefits from.

Further, Antman says that managers should enable and encourage frequent, informal, non-judgmental interactions. Emphasize the importance of taking responsibility. Employees need to know that, if they need something or have a question or an idea, it's their job to speak up and share. When you create a safe environment that supports communication and innovation, people are more inspired to come forward. Above all, Antman says stop using the phrase "performance management." It just makes everyone want to run and hide under their desks.

> Performance appraisals? Get rid of them. Agile ways of working take care of that. If you have a planning session where you go in with your stories, that's your goal. If you have teams, for instance, in the SAFE (Scaled Agile Framework) setting, PI planning takes care of that. Feedback and performance development and all that stuff are taken care of in other ways, and we have those interactions with people spearately so they don't tied to assessment.
>
> —FABIOLA

The value of ongoing conversations is immeasurable. A lean consultant who was working with the Swedish company, Scania, shared a story with me, and it nicely illustrates the power of frequent communication.

One of the managers the consultant was coaching at Scania told her he dedicated fifteen minutes for one-on-ones with each employee every week. She asked him why he did that. He explained, "Everything moves so quickly now. Having performance appraisals and development talks once a year doesn't work for us. Now we have those conversations thirty times a year and it works much better for everyone."

The lean consultant said, "What do you mean it's better for everyone? It must take a lot more time for you. Thirty times fifteen minutes equals seven and a half hours a year in review time for each employee, instead of two. That doesn't sound like the most efficient approach to me." Lean consultants typically look at ways to shave time. They're not always thinking about the non-linear effects of an action or process.

The manager responded, "I wasn't looking at it in terms of time efficiency. What I do know is that the problems we used to experience have decreased and the employee satisfaction scores have increased. We've only been practicing this system for a few months, but I have a lot more information about what needs to be improved and how to avoid problems."

The manager at Scania had looked at different ways to solve a problem and discovered that more frequent communication was the answer. He was flexible in his approach and willing to experiment, evaluate, and measure the results. The improvements he saw were not related to efficiency in the traditional sense, but, in essence, he was being more efficient with the employee's time, which led to greater happiness. He dared to trust, which is what makes the difference in most cases. Without any proof that the new, changed way of working would provide any value, he dared to plunge into the sea of letting go, which is a situation when very good things can happen.

> Just know that you don't know anything. What do we do when we don't know anything? We make small experiments. It's a fail-safe environment. Do small experiments and see if it works. If it works, do it again. Then do it a little bit bigger. Use it in different areas. Use it in different teams in different ways. Experimenting is a great way of working.
>
> —LEILA

Agile's alternative solutions to traditional performance management practices are transformative. When adopted, they have the power to change the entire landscape of an organization and everyone in it.

Introducing systems theory thinking and Agile principles and tools into an organization is sometimes a forced process. The suggestions are usually in direct opposition to existing practices and transitions are not always smooth.

> I don't know how many people I've asked, "Do you, as a leader, get good information from performance appraisals?" And they say no—every one of them. If you ask the employees, "Is that where you get the energy to be a better 'you,' and do a better job?" And everyone says "No," and asks, "Why do we have them?"
>
> —CECILIA

Theresa Welbourne is a researcher and the mother of an emerging trend known as the Role-Based Performance Scale (RBPS). This practice examines an employee's contributions outside of their original job description. It looks at how employees help one another and how they contribute to the development of the organization as a whole. This type of performance evaluation gives the organization a competitive advantage. It trains employees to look for opportunities to think outside of the box, and rewards them for stepping away from the confines of their job descriptions. The role-based evaluation model is easy to understand and benefits the whole organization over the individual.

In her model, Welbourne suggests that each employee has five roles within the company. The traditional job description is the anchor for the next four key competencies:

- Innovation: The employee's contribution to the development of new ideas, routines, and processes
- Career: How the employee develops new competencies that create value for the organization
- Organization: How the employee adds value to the organization as a whole when he or she is not operating within any of their other roles
- Team: How the employee contributes to team projects and development

Each of these roles can be measured and evaluated based on contribution. The central idea behind the approach is to remove limitations for employees. Don't push them into specific roles without growth potential. When organizations restrict movement and enforce fixed roles, they become increasingly dependent on specialists. They are vulnerable if someone becomes ill or has to deal with a personal problem. Freedom from fixed roles leads to a more flexible workplace and a happier, more thoroughly competent workforce. More T-shaped people will emerge as a result, which increases to presence of people with one or two areas where their competence is deep, resulting in a more broad, flexible, and general skillset to complete the T.

KING CRUSHES EXPECTATIONS

King, the company that developed Candy Crush Saga, has adopted an evaluation method almost identical to Welbourne's role-based reviews. They use what they call a "Role Expectations Cheat Sheet,"[8] which highlights different areas in which employees are expected to contribute. It is broken into sections according to each person's specific role, personal development, innovation for the team, innovation for the company, and contributions to the team. Matti Klasson at King is a management 3.0 facilitator colleague of mine. You can read the full interview with Matti at the end of this book.

8   https://www.linkedin.com/pulse/role-expectations-cheat-sheet-matti-klasson

The company is well-known for using Agile practices throughout the organization, also in regard to talent management and development. They use a creative approach to goal setting, which requires that each employee identify one big, personal goal. From there, they need to identify the quarterly ambitions that will lead them to their goal. And further, they need to identify the action steps they will take to achieve their ambitions.

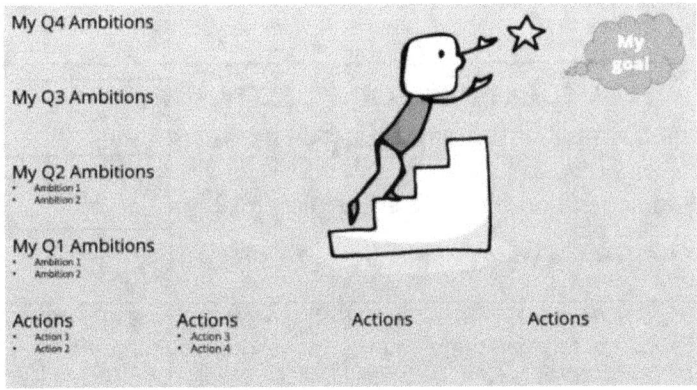

The ambitions document is in an A3 format. The developers work on it independently and then discuss it with their managers.[9] Every two weeks, they follow up together to make sure things are on track or to assess where and why they have gone off track. This process incorporates several effective Agile principles to enhance employee performance,

---

9   https://www.linkedin.com/pulse/ambitions-personal-plan-matti-klasson

development, and achievement: clear goals, visual analysis, short feedback loops, and flexibility for changing direction.

On top of King's effective system for goal setting and evaluation, they have also put together a list of questions for managers to ask employees when they meet for progress check-ins and project retrospectives. This is a common practice, especially for companies that have incorporated frequent goal reviews and OKRs.

GUIDELINES FOR FOLLOW-UPS ON THE ONE-ON-ONES (BI-WEEKLY)

Suggested duration: Fifteen to thirty minutes

- How are your ambitions progressing?
- Have any conditions changed or are there any hindrances preventing you from achieving your ambitions?
- Do you need any support or guidance?

GUIDELINES FOR RETROSPECTIVE AND PLANNING MEETINGS (EVERY QUARTER)

Suggested duration: Forty-five to sixty minutes

- What do you think was your greatest achievement?
- What do you think was your biggest mistake?

- What do you think you need to change (or continue doing) to stay motivated and perform?
- How do you think you have progressed toward your ambitions?
- What could I, as your manager, have done to support you better?
- What are your ambitions for the next period?

When the HR executives at Microsoft learned about increased performance due to more regular manager/employee check-ins, they changed their policy. They switched from annual reviews to bi-annual reviews every February and September, and one-on-ones at least once a month. This change required a major overhaul of the organization because there were too many employees per manager.

The importance of performance management as related to employee growth is well documented. By adopting Agile practices and philosophies, businesses will be better prepared for the uncertainty of tomorrow: celebrate frequent and open communication, collaboration, and ditch the grades. The results will be transformative.

> You should have performance appraisals on a team level rather than on an individual level. Compensation and development need to be separated.
>
> —BJÖRN

FROM→TO FOR PERFORMANCE MANAGEMENT AND GOAL SETTING

PRINCIPLES FOR INCREASING PERFORMANCE	
Less of	More of
Annual appraisal and rating	Continuous coaching and feedback
Forced ranking	No ranking
Annual goals and process	Quarterly or monthly goals with regularly check-ins
Annual talent reviews by managers	Continuous talent reviews by peers and manager
Recognition by manager	Recognition by peers, manager and team leaders
Career plan for promotion and HiPos	Career plan for everyone with open movement and career mobility
Focus on miving up or out	Focus on moving across, up, down and around
The manager evaluate performance	Everyone evaluates themselevs (OKR:s)
No transparency in goals	Total goal transparency
Rating linked to results	Rating (if any) linked to learning and growth and continuous improvement

CHAPTER 5

Goal Setting and OKRs

> *"Ideas are precious, but they're relatively easy. It's the execution that's everything."*
> —John Doerr

Productivity is ideal when people work with goals and measure themselves and their improvement. Clarity leads to optimal energy output from individual employees and teams. When there is confusion or uncertainty around the direction of the organization, frustration and disengagement ensue. Productive energy is transformed into wasted energy because people put their efforts toward trying to understand what they're supposed to be doing instead of actually doing it. An organization needs absolute clarity around *what* it is doing and *why* it is doing it to *function well*. When they focus on the *why* and the *what*, companies can meld their structures and cultures accordingly. In the absence of clearly articulated goals, the ship is heading out to sea without a compass or a destination.

WHY AND HOW TO SET GOALS

One of the problems with traditional HR is that it's based on a certain worldview about how things need to be done. It's stuck in a structure that doesn't allow for the pace of change we're seeing in today's economy or the flexibility necessary to remain competitive.

> We are trying to shift to an iterative performance flow, but we streamline the methodology so we'll have iterations on all new performance cycles. Goal setting takes place in the teams and in the themes of teams, and we decouple it from HR and HR systems.
> —FABIOLA

Setting goals once or even twice a year is not enough to meet the ever-changing pace of business. Oftentimes, the goals are no longer relevant in a year's time. Modern Agile organizations need to set goals quarterly, at minimum, to remain competitive.

> Our environments change so quickly, which makes working with annual goals really hard. However, when we work with quarterly goals or shorter time periods, our goals are more easily met. From that perspective, we look at what needs to be done. We look at it as a group, and everybody puts their appreciation and estimates on the table. We work on different things during a specific period of time, and we meet up after a while to look at what's happening. Then, we create new goals.
>
> —LEILA

Creating customer value is a central Agile principle and it should be a guidepost for decision making. Without customers, there will be no business. To step toward the future, build a goal model centered on creating customer value in everything the company does. Take a good look around and ask, "What activities or roles can be eliminated because they are no longer adding to the customer's value?"

Building a goal model is a visual way to identify what the organization wants to achieve. It forces the team to ask the hard questions that lead to the higher purpose. When executed correctly, the goal model is a stacking ladder with one goal leading to the next and then the next, until the overall company vision is articulated, along with the prerequisites and activities of getting there. As soon as the overall company goal is set, people further down in the organization need to think about their own goals and determine whether they need to change as well to contribute to the overall company goal. The goal-setting process results in a web of interconnected goals that ultimately lead in the same direction.

Once organizational goals have been established, HR professionals can focus on their own immediate goals. HR's goals lead to team goals, which then inspire individual employee goals. Everyone's goals should support the main company goal at the top of the pyramid, and they all need to be re-evaluated and reprioritized frequently, when top priorities change.

The top-down and bottom-up processes of setting goals can take place at the same time. Employees do not have to wait to start setting their own goals. They likely have an idea of what their own goals will be. Once they know which direction the company wants to move, every employee can draft a set of their own goals.

> When you have something to work toward, you don't need micromanagement or someone controlling your work processes, because you already know what you're going to do. I don't need to double-check your work. If you have transparency and every piece of information I need is fully available and visible, we both know the progress you're making. At set intervals, you can provide me with what you're doing.
>
> —LEILA

For goals to be effective, they need to be inspiring. This is a critical detail that many companies overlook. They're so focused on the endgame that the steps necessary to get there become pure drudgery. If you want engaged employees and a culture of exploration and experimentation, the goals must have some pizzazz. For example, consider this team goal: "As a team, we will increase our sales by 10 percent next quarter." Does that goal make you want to jump out of bed in the morning and sell, or does it make you want to hit the snooze button five times? On their own, numbers are rarely inspiring. Goals need to convey a sense of excitement and purpose.

Consider now the previous goal remastered: "As a team, in the next quarter, we will close the largest deal we have ever made—and it will definitely increase our sales by more than

10 percent!!! We will do this by great teamwork and use the strengths of every team member."

The revised version is far more inspirational than the dry first attempt. One of my clients suggested that a goal should be so powerful and fun that you can't get it out of your head. It's a great place to start. The goals need to appeal to each employee at their core, or they won't be motivated to reach them.

THE GREAT UNIFIER: OKRS

Business leaders and managers have been looking for techniques to improve employee performance since the 1950s, if not earlier. Peter Drucker was one of the early pioneers in the management world. He introduced the concept of Management by Objectives (MBOs)—a process by which managers and employees define and agree on goals and what it takes to reach them. In the early 1980s, key performance indicators (KPIs) and SMART goals (specific, measurable, actionable, relevant, and time-based) became popular.

In 1999, John Doerr presented the idea of OKRs (objectives and key results) at Google. Since then, Google has become one of the most successful companies in the world. Doerr learned about OKRs when he was at Intel and, today, OKRs are one of the most popular tools for creating direction for individuals, teams, and companies. The most cutting-edge companies in the world use or have used them, including LinkedIn, Spotify, and Zynga.

As organizations evolve and transition from the old ways to the new, the emphasis has shifted from SMART goals to OKRs. The "A" for "attainable" changes to "aspirational," and the aim is constant evaluation and improvement. Instead of everyone moving along their own path independently, OKRs help to unify the whole company toward one common direction. The new goal criterion promotes unification and Agile principles by being connected, transparent, progress-based, adaptable, and aspirational.

Connected means that the goals should have vertical or horizontal alignment. To work with transparent goals, ensure the whole company knows what every other part of the company is working on, so you don't have to reinvent the wheel twice. This approach breeds communication and collaboration.

Check in frequently, follow up, and measure to assess whether you are on the right track or whether anything needs to change. The goals need to be adaptable to accommodate shifting business needs. Finally, an aspirational goal is one that should not be too easy to reach. There should always be space for further improvement.

When using OKRs, it's important to understand that the objective needs to support the company's vision or top priorities. The objectives should be qualitative, *not* measurable. They should be ambitious, time-bound, and actionable. It's okay if the objectives make people a little uncomfortable. They should fall under the realm of *stretch goals*, in that they will be (very) difficult to achieve. They require stepping outside of the comfort zone. For maximum effectiveness, everyone in the organization should create one to five new objectives on a quarterly basis.

The "key results" portion of the formula also has some guidelines. The key results should be quantitative. Managers should give employees objective evaluations. Ideally, each objective will be supported by a maximum of four key results. This helps to keep people focused. Each key result should be based on outcomes, not tasks, and they should focus on where the employee is now and where they want to be in the future.

The key results are, unlike the objectives, extremely measurable. Objectives are not replaced by key results, because the results could lead in any direction. If you're not on the best path, you need to change to more efficient key results that will increase your objective in a better way.

So, let's say you set a simple objective, for example, "get fit within three months." Once the objective is determined, it is then connected to the desired results. So, the key results might be,

- Be able to run 3 km in 20 minutes
- Be able to do 50 push-ups
- Be able to do 200 sit-ups
- Objective: Get fit within 3 months

Instead of working with activities, you work with outcomes—what you are trying to achieve. You don't know in advance whether the key results will take you toward the objective, which is why the key results have to be changeable, should you see that you're not moving in the right direction. Focus is on improvement in a given direction. The key results should be set as a challenge and not be too easy to reach. It should be an honest assessment—if everything works out really well, I *might* be able to hit that target!

In an organization, the process is meant to be iterative, instead of top-down. In fact, most OKRs emerge from the bottom up. Ideally, every facet of the organization will have its own OKRs: individual employees, teams, and the company as a whole. Each unit's OKRs will have an "owner" who is responsible for following up on the team's goals.

Once an employee's OKRs have been established in agreement with their manager, the evaluation process should be repeated every quarter. During the evaluation, each key result is graded on a scale of one to one hundred, or one to ten, and then the average is calculated. There's no science behind the grading system; it's simply an honest assessment. The whole evaluation should only take a few minutes.

If we use our previous example of an OKR, this is what the evaluation process looks like:

BE ABLE TO RUN 3 KM IN 20 MINUTES	75%
BE ABLE TO DO 50 PUSH-UPS	50%
BE ABLE TO DO 200 SIT-UPS	80%
OBJECTIVE: GET FIT WITHIN 3 MONTHS	68%

Getting a perfect score of 100 percent is *not the goal*. If the score comes back higher than 90 percent, it means the objective was too easy to obtain and there's no room for improvement. If the score is lower than 40 percent, it was too difficult. However, low scores are not failures; they are learning opportunities. People should shoot for scores in the range of 60 to 70 percent and remember that the scores are not as important as the pros of experimenting and learning. The key is to clearly communicate the nature of stretch goals and understand the threshold for success. It's not about reaching the goals, but about continuously improving and learning what works. If all employees work in this way, with continuous improvement linked to company goals, there is a fantastic power that unleashes from the joint effort.

OKRs create learning and collaboration opportunities throughout the entire organization. They are *not* used for appraisals or bonuses. If you link OKRs to monetary rewards, the concept of trust and honest conversations about what *could* be possible will be spoiled. Instead, they help to show that everyone needs to contribute and be engaged in the company for it to function optimally. They create transparency and establish prerequisites for cooperation and learning. Someone once said, "The distance between your dream and reality is called action." OKRs are the action steps to reach the company's vision by realizing employee potential.

I've worked with several banks where they implemented OKRs as a replacement for more traditional systems of goal setting and performance management. From my experience, it pays off when you stick to the method and don't quit during the first year. When people feel it "in their bones," it tends to create a lot more value than the traditional performance mindset.

> Of course you need to measure your progress and you need to look at results, but the best results will come if you do the right things.
>
> —CECILIA

CHAPTER 6

Agile Rewards

"Paychecks can't buy passion."
—Brad Federman

Salaries and financial differences between employees have always been a sensitive subject. People think about the word "fairness" when it comes to money, and defining what that actually means can be a slippery slope. What is fair for one person is not fair for another. While one person thinks it's fair to reward extraordinary performance with an extra "something," another person may think everyone should have exactly the same pay if they have the same role, work experience, and education.

How can we talk about rewards and compensation in a more productive manner? How can we make them less competitive and secretive, and more centered on real contribution and participation? It starts with recognizing the differences between the traditional way of looking at compensation and the Agile way of looking at it.

> Regarding bonuses and commissions, I don't think you should connect a compensation or bonus plan to an employee's motivation to do the work, especially if you want to create Agile teams. That could be devastating, because you need to think about which behaviors you're encouraging.

> For those people who really are motivated, at least to some degree, by external motivators—seeking everything from healthcare to money—you need to ask yourself, "What do I want to contribute to? What kind of behaviors do I want to push with this motivator?" Don't create individual bonus plans if you want to create effective teams. That's contradictory. It's not pushing in the right direction.
>
> —LEILA

SALARIES

Most companies tend to focus exclusively on the topic of money when discussing performance rewards. A person's salary amount is important and it should be perceived as "fair," but it's not the only thing that matters. Research shows that salary is not, in fact, a primary motivator for most people. To make the issue a "non-issue," salaries should be market based and fair as a general rule. You need to pay enough to get the issue off the table.

> If we come back to the topic of IT—your coders and your technical staff—they're usually more introverted people, so they're not very good at negotiating their own salary. Transparency takes that away, so it's not about individual negotiation power. The system kicks in and that helps them do their job, so the more transparency the better. It's not just about salaries. It's about the contribution.
>
> —FABIOLA

There are several Agile organizations that have adopted creative approaches to handling salaries. The software company, Buffer, is a famous example.[10] They are at the forefront of several groundbreaking Agile practices.

Buffer introduced a transparent method for compensation by offering salary formulas on the website. The potential employee plugs in their skill set, location, and credentials, and then the formula calculates what their salary will be. This information is available in advance of the interview process. When the company introduced the salary calculator, there was an immediate flood of people who wanted to work there. They were able to know their income even before they started working. It eliminated the salary negotiation phase of

---

10 https://ravio.com/blog/compensation-examples-buffer

the hiring process. Even better, the company is 100 percent transparent about *everyone's* salaries, from the CEO on down.

Aside from their salary innovations, Buffer is also 100 percent virtual. Every single employee works from home. There's no central office, not even for headquarters. The employees use Slack, Zoom, and other communication tools to share information throughout the day. The workforce is entirely autonomous. These types of virtual companies are getting more and more common in today's work climate.

The nursing company, Buurtzorg, is similarly experimental and transparent about salaries. Every year, all the teams perform individual evaluations based on a competency model and employee experience. Through this practice, Buurtzorg has been able to unearth some inconsistencies or discrepancies across countries and cities and make adjustments accordingly. The salaries vary according to the cost of living and the specific job market.

The Morning Star Company, a leader in the tomato product and services industry, was built on a foundational philosophy of self-management.[11] The company is deeply committed to salary transparency. In support of that initiative, they

---

11   https://www.morningstarco.com/exploring-morning-stars-mission-focused-self-management-model/

practice "self-set" salaries with feedback from an elected salary committee. Every employee writes an annual statement expressing what they think their salary should be and why. They need to include feedback from their colleagues, along with supporting performance-related criteria.

The elected salary committee provides feedback. They provide guidance as to whether the salary request is too low or too high. Most of their employees set fair salaries for themselves. If the company has not been profitable enough that year to accommodate increases, employees are guaranteed to receive an upgrade in line with the cost of living.

Another example of self-management through salary transparency occurs at W. L. Gore, a multinational manufacturing company in Delaware. Employees rank the colleagues they work most closely with throughout the year. They use a system of peer review to determine salaries by rating each employee on two statements:

- This person is contributing (a lot) more or (a lot) less than me (on a scale from negative three to positive three).
- This person has a good knowledge about my performance (on a scale from one to five).

A simple algorithm calculates the results, which determines where the employee falls on a scale of fixed salary intervals. It's a simple solution and is perceived as extremely fair.

The AES Corporation, a global power company with over nineteen thousand employees, also practices self-management for setting salaries. They have a peer advice process in which employees ask each other for help to determine their salaries. This means that each employee takes full responsibility for their own contributions as well as their coworkers'. People are accountable to each other, as well as dependent on each other, which fosters teamwork and respect. Semco Partners, a venture capitalist firm in Brazil, uses the same peer-to-peer salary process as AES.

Björn Lundén (BL) Information is a small Swedish company with about ninety employees. They help other small companies run their businesses through their proprietary software. To determine salaries at BL, each employee writes down what he or she thinks everyone else should be paid. Then, the company tallies the results, and determines salaries based on the average of the consensus. Almost all the company's decisions are made this way. The system clearly works because only eight people have left in the twenty-eight years it has been in business.

These companies are proof that the salary discussion doesn't have to poison the water at work. When the secrecy surrounding the topic is removed, there is a universally positive impact on trust, motivation, and culture.

Everyone has a different approach to salaries. Jurgen Appelo's Management 3.0 Salary Formula is

- Develop criteria for what is important to reward.
- Weigh all the factors against each other. What is more important than anything else?
- Develop a formula to calculate a salary that is fair for everyone (or as many as possible).
- Do not use salary as a reward for evaluation of performance.

SALARY EXERCISE

1. Consider all the variables.
2. In your opinion, which variables should influence compensation?
3. What should be the weight of each variable in compensation?

EMPLOYEE VARIABLES

EXAMPLE	WEIGHT
*Rate each 0 (no!)...3	(important)
Gender	male
Job Category/Title	designer
Job Level	senior
Tag/Responsibility	team leader
Age	43
Years of employment	5
Prior Work Experience	15 years
Relevant Education	4 years
Special Achievements	design award
Performance	NPS = 85%
Family size	3 children

The more transparent HR can be, the better. Of course, we have certain things in HR that are confidential, and there's a limit to what we can reveal. For instance, we consider salary packages confidential. They don't need to be confidential. Of course, you must be organized and have your salaries well documented before you pubically publish salaries, but you can still be transparent. In fact, you should be transparent about your salary system. But, how do you approach it? The more transparency you can have up front, the less it becomes an issue. You don't want to discuss salaries when someone threatens to leave, because then you've already lost. If you can publish all the salaries, that's fine, or at least have a salary formula where you say, "That's the way we make our salary decisions." It's better, because then you get rid of discussions. Another great benefit is that people know their salaries are fair, or at least consistent, and it doesn't matter how good you are at negotiating your salary.

—FABIOLA

REWARDS

As a Management 3.0 facilitator, I've used the reward principles from the Management 3.0 framework in trainings and in my client assignments when giving advice on how you can get the most impact with rewards. Rewards are so much more than just money. In addition to being transparent about salaries, it's also important to give employees *unexpected rewards*. I discussed the many problems with the traditional bonus system in the previous chapter. The human tendency is to concentrate on the reward first. The goal is to keep employees focused on their work and tap into their inner motivation and drive, instead of dangling a carrot in front of them. Unexpected rewards help to keep people motivated all the time, as opposed to when they think they might get something in return.

Big rewards and bonuses have been proven to decrease performance and increase stress. *Keep the rewards small* and distribute them often. The effects on the brain are the same as when the reward is large.

Everyone in the organization should understand what behaviors and achievements are rewarded. Therefore, *celebrate accomplishments in public* instead of behind closed doors. Let everyone know who did what and why. It's not just about results and data. Sometimes people take shortcuts to achieve results, so focus on attitude and approach instead of just milestones.

Make it easy for coworkers to *reward each other*. Giving recognition for a job well done should not be an exclusive managerial responsibility. Create an environment where employees invite each other to lunch, stock the kitchen with stuff that is free for employees to grab and give to each other (like a case of wine bottles) or otherwise to applaud team member successes.

> Acknowledging people has to come from peers inside the organization. It makes a positive difference in the working environment and culture when it's not only management who congratulates an individual, a team, or an entire department. But it is up to management to provide the award and other compensation.
> —FABIOLA

Whenever something has been accomplished, regardless of how large or small, it should be accompanied by a *celebration*. It serves to reinforce learning and good practices, and it gives people a sense of belonging and togetherness. In any environment, people should look for reasons to celebrate small victories. Ask questions: What did we learn? What did we do well? How did we move forward?

Jurgen Appelo once shared a story: "One of the offices I worked in had a ship's bell hanging in the central common area. Whenever something interesting had happened in our organization, we would celebrate it by ringing the bell, getting everyone in the office together, sharing the story, and eating cakes or cookies."12

Even in failure, there are things to be learned, which is cause for celebration. In fact, failure is a great way of learning.

For a company to engage in reward conversations and practices, there must be profits. If the company is doing well, and everyone is on track with their goals, OKRs, sprints, and retrospectives, introduce the concept of merit money. Unlike other rewards, merit money is *only based on performance as determined by one's peers.* Who knows better how you have performed than the people that you work with every day?

There are many ways to incorporate performance-based peer bonuses. Some companies create a virtual currency that is made up of hugs or points. Everyone has a budget of credit to give to their teammates over the course of a month. Then, at the end of each month, they convert the accumulated currency for cash or other benefits.

---

12 https://www.slideshare.net/jurgenappelo/agile-management-authority-delegation

> We were able to listen more to what the employees wanted and could reward them accordingly, based on their input. This was of more value than having management decide to give everyone the same award, regardless of the tasks, efforts, or roles. Most important is to reward employees who are engaged in their work rather than just giving them perks that were nice to have, but didn't fit in with the employee's personality or preferences.
>
> —CECILIA

The Agile reward system emphasizes teamwork and de-emphasizes money. Financial rewards are great on the surface, but they don't tap into people's intrinsic motivators. Rewards should be used to optimize individual behaviors, strengthen team performance, and foster a culture of continuous improvement.

> The amazing thing about Agile is when you see a change in behavior, you feel the atmosphere change immediately. It doesn't take months or years for things to change. They can change very quickly, and I think that's also the power of Agile. It's important to show people that they are unique and are appreciated because of who they are and what they do. We know that people will react differently, and that's how you can learn about new behaviors.
>
> —FABIOLA

FROM→TO FOR REWARDS

THE TRADITIONAL WAY	THE AGILE WAY
Salary is a motivator	Salary is a hygiene factor
Only managers give recognition	Everybody gives recognition
Seldom	Often
Big rewards	Small rewards
Reward privately	Reward publicly
Reward results	Reward behavior
Unfair salary distribution	Fairness is the most important aspect
Teams/individuals are not involved	Teams/individuals can set their own salaries
Salaries are secret	Salaries can be transparent
Bonus	Profit sharing
Budgets and plans	Comparison with previous period

CHAPTER 7

Agile Recruitment

> *"Hire for attitude; train for skill."*
> —Unknown

Recruiting is a topic that could fill volumes of books on its own. HR professionals and individual organizations usually have their own unique strategies, practices, interview questions, and hiring processes. Whenever I interviewed someone for a position at my company, GreenBullet, the most important question in my mind was always, "Why do you want to work with us?" And perhaps, more importantly, "What does your value structure look like? Does it correspond with our company values and our real culture?" I say, "real culture," because many companies have nice values framed all over the walls that don't mirror their *real* culture.

> I still think that "hire for attitude, train for skill" is very, very valid. If we do that, we are Agile in the way we recruit. I also think we need to use the organization much more in recruiting, whether the recruitment is done by a leader, by HR, or by a recruitment specialist. Employees are the ones who really know who will best fit in with the organization.
>
> —CECILIA

Employees need to be devoted to the company's core values, even before they start work. You never want to hire someone who is "just looking for a job"; you want to work with people who are passionate about what your company stands for. Hiring people in a smaller operation is, of course, a lot easier. In a small, tight-knit team, everyone can be involved in the hiring decisions. Look for people who will complement your company and who will fit in with your team.

Larger organizations tend to get mired down in bureaucratic red tape and nonsensical hiring criteria. It's possible and advisable to utilize a small team approach to hiring, even in a large company.

HR RECRUITING TRENDS

A common belief among HR professionals and hiring managers is that you can't judge a candidate's strengths or weaknesses by looking at their resume. Some feel the best way to assess a candidate's potential contributions are to ask a series of situational questions to gauge how they would handle hypothetical scenarios. Others say that what people have accomplished in the past has little to no bearing on how they will perform in the future. They argue that what really matters is what the candidate hopes to accomplish down the road.

How can a recruiting manager feel confident in their hiring decisions? How can they predict how a candidate will perform in the future? How can risk be minimized? Would you prefer to embrace a fixed and proven skillset to attract and retain motivated employees? Most big companies follow prescribed templates for each position within the business. They hire exclusively within a predetermined list of qualifications and characteristics. However, with the right attitude, people can learn a lot (although not everything!). It might be more important to look for drive and passion than the right competencies. In some cases, motivation is the most important skill. There are certain jobs where skill can be more easily taught if the candidate has the right disposition.

> The Agile mindset for recruiting has two parts. One part is how you can gamify your recruitment process, or how you can recruit in the digital age. Talent management, or recruiting, starts long before you have to fill a position. That's why you have to interact with people beforehand—you have to work with them before you actually need to fill a position. The second part is onboarding. Quite often, we lose that time between people signing the contract and actually starting to work. The only communication you often have is just through some legal paperwork. It's actually a valuable time, because people are never more engaged than when they just sign the contract.
>
> —FABIOLA

In my dream world, I would like to work with someone for at least six months before making a decision about hiring them onto the team. I want to get to know them to see if they're a fit and will be productive. Rarely do we have such a luxury! Someone can be a star player in one organization and a complete dud in another. Everything, especially performance and behavior, depends on the context of the situation. A person will show a certain behavior in one particular situation, but when you put the same person in a different situation, he or she could exhibit entirely different behaviors.

However, even the most rudimentary line of questioning can help to determine whether someone is the right fit for your team. "Can you do the job?" identifies someone's strengths and weaknesses in terms of qualifications. "Will you love the job?" indicates what precisely motivates someone, and "Can we work with you?" examines whether the person will fit in with the team and the company culture. Which questions to ask and what traits the company is hiring for varies from one operation to the next.

THE AGILE RECRUITMENT MANIFESTO[13]

We are always uncovering better ways of hiring people and helping others to hire better too. Through our work, we have come to value

- Individuals and interactions over processes and tools
- Quick, quality hires over comprehensive documentation
- Customer collaboration over contract negotiation
- Responding to change over following a plan

Do these values sound familiar? They are the same core tenants of the original Agile Manifesto.

---

13 https://www.ere.net/articles/the-agile-recruiting-manifesto

THE AGILE PRINCIPLES OF RECRUITING STATE:

- Our highest priority is to satisfy the customer through early and continuous delivery of quality hires.

- We welcome changing requirements, even late in development. Agile processes harness change for the customer's competitive advantage.

- Deliver quality hires frequently, from a couple of weeks to a couple of months, with a preference for the shorter timescale.

- Internal customers and recruiters must work together daily throughout the project.

- Build projects around motivated individuals.

- Give them the environment and support they need, and trust them to get the job done.

- The most efficient and effective method of conveying information to and within a recruiting team is a face-to-face conversation.

- A quality hire that is on time and within budget is the primary measure of progress.

- Agile processes promote sustainable employee development.

- The sponsors, developers, and users should be able to maintain a constant pace indefinitely.

- Continuous attention to professional excellence and first-class service enhances agility.

- Simplicity—the art of maximizing the amount of work not done—is essential.

- The best requirements, processes, and hires emerge from self-organizing teams.
- At regular intervals, the team reflects on how to become more effective, then tunes and adjusts its behavior accordingly.

The Agile principles of recruiting embody what companies should strive for when hiring. Think about your own organization. Are your practices aligned with the principles? Do the principles seem achievable or far-fetched from your perspective? Many corporate recruiting companies are still several miles away from adopting the Agile approach, but through my work and research with many well-known international companies, I have found the approach to be both effective and mutually rewarding.

AGILE RECRUITING TRENDS AND TOOLS

> I started in the recruitment industry many years ago. And for me, the skills I have from my old days in recruitment are totally invalid, because there's been a total game change.
> —CECILIA

Most HR professionals are familiar with a multi-tiered approach to attracting, hiring, and retaining employees. In

Agile, we start by simplifying the process, and focus instead on the people.

Recruiting should be a part of everyone's job, not just the HR team. The reason for this is straightforward. A cross-functional team that encompasses marketing, HR, and the other disciplines the new hire will interact with are essential for a broad and differential perspective of the candidate's breadth and adaptability.

> You might have the best player in the market, but if they don't really match with the team, nothing good will come out of your new hire. So, the question is, "How do you include the team in the decision-making process; and, at the end of the day, how do you make sure it's the team that decides? It's not the manager and it's not HR, because the team has to carry that person. As you and I both know, only the team can ensure that the new person is successful. So, the decision, the hiring decision, and the final decision, has to involve the team, and you have to include the team in the selection process.
> —FABIOLA

Recruiting is also an activity that should occur all the time, not just when a specific position is open. If an employee from your organization encounters someone who embodies the company values, that person should be brought in to meet the team and assess how they can contribute to the company. HR professionals refer to this practice as "always recruiting." It means the company is always on the lookout for people who are the right fit for the organization.

The first step in the recruiting process is attracting candidates. Attraction starts with branding. How is your company positioned in the marketplace? What is its reputation as an employer? Recognize the relationship between consumer branding and employee branding, because the two are directly connected. Anyone you come into contact with across any channel contributes to brand perception. Be transparent with information on the company website and make it easy for people to learn about what you stand for and value.

> You need to show that you have a company that connects with the applicant's values and has something to give. It's easier when you have an Agile approach. I would say that's impossible if you don't have it.
> —CECILIA

How can your company best interact with and create relationships with candidates? The traditional routes such as job fairs and advertisements through the company website are still viable, but recruiting via social media channels is a fast-growing trend. Almost all recruiting today involves a

LinkedIn search and a spin around the candidate's Facebook profile. Social media is frequently used to attract, recruit, and vet candidates.

HR professionals have started visiting candidates where they are, which is online. Internet sourcing is no longer a competitive advantage; it's a must. Finding the right niche and social forum is now a crucial component of hiring.

Make use of your talent networks—both through accumulated and curated online social activities and through your existing internal team. Your employees are usually your best resource for finding other great people. The likelihood that they have access to other people who share the same values is very high, and if they want to recommend your workplace to someone else in their network, it means they are engaged and motivated.

A simple and flexible approach to the hiring process is ten times more effective than a rigid, step-by-step program. Finding the right people for the organization is an internal responsibility. It's not appropriate to outsource this critical company function to an external agency. Recruiting and attracting quality staff requires an intimate knowledge of how the company operates; it cannot be trusted to an outsider.

> Transparency is key. Having the team involved is key.
> —LEILA

Hiring is a time-consuming process and one that should be handled carefully. There needs to be a lot of dialogue and interaction with the candidates in order to get a true sense of how they will adapt to the team environment. The goal is to get to know someone's real character; not just the buttoned-up persona people tend to put on when they're interviewing for a job.

Invite candidates to spend a day with the people they would be working with. Allow them to speak with a variety of people throughout the organization to get a real sense of its character. You want the new hire to feel empowered to speak up and bring their best selves to the table. Communicate openly and often. Good candidates will not sit on the shelf for long. The competition will snatch them up if you don't move quickly.

> From time to time, adjust the process—or at least how you prioritize tasks within the process—based on the current situation and need. It's best to keep recruiting in-house, because that competency is brilliant when it comes to internal talent sourcing and succession planning. Team involvement is key. The recruiting manager should only help out with administration work.
> —BJÖRN

Sometimes people are hired to join a company but they're not hired for a specific role. Perhaps the person is a specialist in one area, but has broad competencies in a variety of areas. In Agile, this type of person is referred to as a specialized generalist or a generalized specialist. They're usually hired based on team fit over a position fit. We call them T-shaped, which means they have broad general knowledge with a deep specialist competence in one or more areas.

Agile recruiting is centered in one central mantra: hire for attitude, train for skill. Instead of evaluating a candidate on their apparent competence, the emphasis should be on whether the person is a cultural fit for the organization. Has your organization identified and articulated both the values and the culture that define it? Without these two ingredients, the person won't be happy at the company and will not function at a high level. The candidate and the organization must be in alignment with values.

> We have to change the questions to assess whether someone is a cultural fit, and whether they will fit in with the team. We need to back those actual values, like collaboration, trust, honesty, and respect. If we embrace that into our processes, then, yes, it can certainly enhance the recruiting process.
> —FABIOLA

HR professionals determine a person's values through the interview process or they can use a personal profile test. My personal favorite assessment is the Reiss Motivation Profile, which clearly identifies an individual's sixteen primary driving motivators. It's an invaluable tool to determine if there is alignment with organizational values.

Without assessment tools, we usually only see what's on the surface of someone's character. Personality profiles help us get to the much larger foundation below. I think of it as an iceberg: How can we best chip away at the outer shell to determine *why* people do what they do and find out *what* drives them?

One of my favorite activities for recruitment is to use a Kanban Board, which is a visual way of making the recruitment procedure visible. You can read more about Kanban in Chapter 11. Ask the team, What steps are needed to recruit the right people in our company? Each step should be represented by a column on the board. Once you have a handful of candidates for a position, lay them all out on the Kanban Board to keep track of who is where in the process, as well as the team member's impressions of each person. This is a visual way to track hiring decisions and keep the team engaged. Hiring teams can also use a Trello Board (a digital Kanban Board) to track recruitment steps. As candidates move through the process, the cards are moved to illustrate where they are.

Spotify is well-known for using Agile recruitment processes and tools. As a rapidly growing company, they're always on the lookout for new employees. They actively practice visual recruitment exercises and run retrospectives to learn more about their candidates.

When building a high-autonomy, high-alignment work culture, as Spotify is, hiring is a priority initiative. They want to get people in place who will thrive in their environment and contribute to the overall company mission. One of the company principles is "don't hire jerks."

At Spotify, there must be a balance between the ability to work independently and an alignment with corporate initiatives. They need people who are self-directed *and* collaborative. To filter through their candidate pool, they scrutinize how people communicate about work they've done in the past. They talk about what they've accomplished on an individual level, as well as team achievements.

There is a delicate balance between alignment and autonomy. It's important to hire people who are capable of leading in a way that releases motivation in others so they can function optimally. The goal of hiring managers should be to bring people in who thrive in a culture of aligned autonomy, which means high autonomy (people decide *how* to reach the goals) and high alignment (people are moving in the same direction, not in different directions). Ideally, that means hiring people who are motivated, take responsibility, and who love the organization's goals.

There must be diversity in the talent pool. Don't make the mistake of hiring people who are all exactly the same. Even though it's challenging to work with people who are different, the results are stronger when there are more perspectives and ideas. And diversity on the inside just may be more important than diversity on the outside.

Agile HR teams are not just in touch with their own values, but the values of each person on their internal teams and how they interrelate. We must all be aware of each others' differences so they become easier to accept and we can perform productive work together.

> This is what we're doing for our client who is doing mass recruiting: we are getting rid of the CVs and applications altogether. We thought about how to make the recruitment process leaner, and decided to get rid of the CVs and applications because they were not useful.

Instead, we ask a couple of questions up front for screening purposes: Can you work on weekends? Here's a situation, what would you do in this circumstance? How far do you live from the place where you would work? Then we ask a few more questions. We prescreen according to these questions and let about 60 percent pass, and then we do online assessments for their IQ, their EQ, their service motivation profile, and all that. Those three tests give us a very high probability of finding a candidate who is a good fit.

After the prescreening process is completed, we then have a short list of people we will ask to do a video interview. They record their answers, which takes about five minutes. For the manager, going from reading two hundred CVs and application letters, which give you nothing, to looking at maybe five video interviews for a maximum of four to five minutes is a huge time saver. Knowing these applicants have been prescreened to fit according to their EQ and IQ service-mindedness, and making us aware of whether they're willing to work on weekends enhances the interviewing process. All applicants have been screened so managers can choose five to ten viable candidates from the short list of people.

—RIINA

FROM→TO FOR RECRUITMENT

PRINCIPLES FOR AGILE RECRUITMENT	
Less of	More of
Evaluate competence	Evaluate value & cultural fit
Just HR	Cross functional teams/ different roles
When needed	Always
Job boards & advertise	Social media
Detailed process with fixed steps & responsibilities	Simple and flexible flow with Kanban
External supplier	Internal responsibilties
Standardizatiob = low diversity	Time-consuming, careful selection with a lot of dialogue
Only traditional Interviews	More practical selection techniques
Recruiting into fixed roles & positions	Poeple find their roles
Recruitment same old roles with the same experience	New sources of talent - disruption

CHAPTER 8

Learning and Development

"We now accept the fact that learning is a lifelong process of keeping abreast of change. And the most pressing task is to teach people how to learn."

—Peter Drucker

One of my favorite HR anecdotes involves a brief conversation between two executives. A CFO was worrying about the budget for internal education. He thought it was a poor investment for the company and said to the CEO, "What happens if we invest in developing our people and then they leave us?" The CEO looked at him for a minute and replied, "What happens if we don't and they stay?" The exchange nicely summarizes the divide I often see in organizations when it comes to continued education for employees.

Learning and competence development is a critical component in the employee value proposition. Many people want to be in an environment where they can learn and grow—both are vital ingredients for employee attraction, engagement, and retention.

> This is a shift where you are made aware of some employees who still expect that the company will tell them what to do to develop, whereas others feel like they have a lot of possibilities. They think, "It's just up to me to create them and take on those challenges."
> —LEILA

The whole organization benefits from nurturing a talent pool of people who want to better themselves. Building internal knowledge and skills leads to faster innovation, which is necessary for survival. When continuous improvement and development are key pieces of an organization's fabric, the likelihood of realizing the company's vision and accomplishing the mission increase dramatically.

> In Agile, we talk a lot about empowering people and letting them make decisions for themselves, and that empowerment has translated to HR. The question is, How do we showcase empowerment, or, how do we empower people as employees, when it comes to their learning and development? Are they in the driver's seat? This is going to have a huge impact, and it will change the way leaders interact with people as well.
> —FABIOLA

ORGANIZATIONAL LEARNING MODELS

The 70:20:10 Model is a popular and easy-to-understand training formula.[14] Its premise is that 70 percent of a person's knowledge is learned or developed through experience, which includes on-the-job learning. Another 20 percent is learned through coaching, mentoring, or relationships with other, more experienced people. The final 10 percent is learned through structured courses or formalized programs. The 70:20:10 Model dates back nearly thirty years, and there have been several notable developments on the topic since.

The individual approach looks at learning and development for the sake of enhancing one's future employability. The team perspective examines technical aspects of team learning

---

14 https://www.ccl.org/articles/leading-effectively-articles/the-70-20-10-rule/

to improve cooperation, communication, problem-solving, and conflict resolution. When people learn as a team, they have the opportunity to reach group goals faster and easier. The organizational perspective argues that, through learning, the organization is stronger and more competitive. It has the ability to adapt to new circumstances or changes in the market with greater ease. The opportunity to become an industry leader or groundbreaking innovator increases through continuous organizational learning.

> For me, talking about leadership, it's about what we all have inside of ourselves. There's a possibility to develop, to be accountable, and to discover more insights about how we are affecting our surroundings.
> —LEILA

A 2015 *Harvard Business Review* article, titled "Why Businesses Don't Learn," presented an interesting viewpoint about organizational resistance to learning.[15] The writers, Francesca Gino and Bradley Staats, argue that there are four main reasons why businesses fail to take learning seriously, despite best intentions to the contrary.

---

15 https://hbr.org/2015/11/why-organizations-dont-learn

The first reason is that organizations are afraid of failure. They are biased toward success and avoid the realities of failure at all costs. The concept of failure triggers anger, pain, and fear. Most businesses try to sweep failure under the rug and avoid the negative feelings instead of embracing it as a learning tool. Experimentation involves failure and lots of it. To be truly innovative, businesses need to focus less energy on trying to achieve perfection and more energy on accepting mistakes.

Second, most companies have a bias toward action, and they neglect to engage in the important practice of reflection. What went wrong? What can we do better next time? How can we improve? What other competencies are needed on the team? Shorter work cycles and project retrospectives are an effective strategy for overcoming the fear of action.

Third, there is an unproductive tendency toward conformity. Many companies are afraid of rocking the boat in their industries. They want to fit in and they have the false assumption that "sameness" is attractive to an existing client base. They don't dare to be different and, as a result, they end up in jeopardy.

Finally, Gino and Staats argue that big businesses rely too heavily on the guidance of outside experts or consultants. The best source of information is from the people on the ground, who actually do the work. What does an outside consultant know about the inner workings of team dynamics and project experimentation? External "help" simply adds an unnecessary layer of complexity to a fairly straightforward solution: involve frontline employees in brainstorming and decision making. They are in direct communication with the customers and they are the most precious resource.

Many companies fail to recognize the economic value their employees bring to the organization. It takes time to see a return on talent investment, but doing so requires an awareness of the employee lifecycle.

> I know some companies do virtual reality for their onboarding process, and the candidates actually wear the headgear glasses and see their workplace surroundings. They can walk through the office and simulate an entire day there, so you can take it pretty far.
>
> —FABIOLA

There's a period of time in the early stages of a new hire relationship when the organization invests in the employee. As soon as new hires transition to the onboarding process, they begin to acquire knowledge. They go through training and begin to acquire new assignments, while learning and gathering information. At that point, they begin to have value. The organization starts to benefit from that employee. HR professionals who work with employee engagement and management strategies are able to recognize and increase employee value in the return zone. The more engaged the employee, the higher their return.

Peter Senge, a leadership and sustainability professor at the MIT Sloan School of Management and founder of the Society for Organized Learning, wrote a book called *The Fifth Dimension*. In it, he explores five indicators of organizations that prioritize learning.

The first is an emphasis on personal mastery. This means the organization supports individuals who want to continuously enrich their personal vision. Specific mental models represent deeply rooted ways of thinking, and people learn best through pictures, which affect how we understand the world and how we act. To promote shared vision, pictures are used to increase engagement and acceptance. Team learning starts with dialogue and the capacity of team members to enter into genuine thinking together. The goal is to stop making assumptions and interact on a real level. The fifth discipline, systems thinking, is the basis for Agile. It views organizations as dynamic systems in a state of continuous adaption and improvement. This creates an open environment, where experimentation is encouraged, making mistakes is acceptable, and different viewpoints are welcome.

"Fail fast" is a core mantra in Agile. It indicates that failure is simply a part of constant learning. We need to dare to try, and make it easy to try. Thomas Edison famously said, "I have not failed. I've just found 10,000 ways that won't work." He was well ahead of his time and in touch with the role failure plays in discovery and continuous learning.

> HR has to make sure we have access to technology but, then, empowered people need to take care of their own development by pulling information and working with that. For instance, HR can create platforms for communicative practices and can pull information.
> —FABIOLA

LEARNING TRENDS

Fifty years ago, learning was relegated almost exclusively to the formal education periods of one's life: high school, college, and, for the intellectually advanced, graduate school. Today, continuous changes through technological advances means we need to always be learning. It's a never-ending process. Most organizations provide basic training and company-specific information, but, to remain viable and competitive, employees need to take the lead on their own education.

Traditional learning methods are becoming outdated. Our brains work differently than they did in the past because of all the new stimuli coming at us. We process information faster and need to find new ways of digesting and processing it. Modern companies understand that simply sending their employees off-site for a course in a certain subject is no longer sufficient. A single training intervention isn't going to close a performance gap.

Courses have been replaced by learning experiences in which various activities are spread across time and space to maximize absorption. We are limited only by our imagination as we move into the future. We need cross-functional, interdisciplinary, continual, self-directed formal and informal education.

> Learning is the only way to adapt. The problem or challenge in an Agile or organic system would be how to direct the learning to a valuable place, or how to create cross-organizational learning, across borders such as location boundaries.
>
> —RIINA

Knowledge has been democratized through the Internet. All the information in the world is available all the time to anyone who wants to learn. Information is everywhere: wikis, blogs, online forums, YouTube, books, seminars, TED Talks, podcasts, apps, and more. In fact, the volume of information can feel overwhelming and exhausting. There is no shortage of content or vehicles for digesting it, and it's increasing at an exponential rate. We've reached a state where there is too much content and too little time.

A new trend for industry-specific information is minimum viable courses. In the past, organizations held back on releasing training materials or how-to manuals until they were completely finished. These days, they release information as it becomes available in smaller modules. Minimal viable courses contain the least amount of information possible, while still providing knowledge value. Employees can start the learning process sooner, and the company can maintain its competitive edge.

A lot of newer businesses have successfully turned their education cost centers into profit centers. Through minimal viable courses and other delivery mechanisms, knowledge has become a commoditized product. By selling proprietary research, methods, or processes to company suppliers, vendors, customers, and even the competition, information is now an income stream that generates direct cash flow.

Another corporate learning trend is the expansion of gamification, which has become a valuable tool for product and team development, as well as problem solving. Through interactive games, companies make complex problems accessible to the entire organization, instead of relegating them to the developers and engineers. Anyone who is interested or curious about creating solutions can participate, including clients. A company called Folditrecently solved a complex problem that scientists had been working on for ten years. By making the problem widely accessible through gamification, they had a solution in just three weeks.

> Some aspects of problem solving come from social learning, blended learning, interactions, and brown bags. That's why you have to embrace all those new ways of learning.
>
> —FABIOLA

In the coming years, we can expect to see a greater reliance on social learning activities through peer-to-peer and online learning. Additionally, learning in real time will take precedence over precertified specializations and degrees. Eventually, these newer approaches will completely replace in-house, supplemental training courses.

Although other learning mechanisms are on the rise, degrees still carry a lot of weight. These days, it's simple and affordable to get an online degree in any subject matter. SPOCs are small, private online courses, which have more credibility than MOOCs, which are massive, open online courses. MOOCs tend to have high attrition rates, while SPOCs offer small classes that use blended learning techniques. Typically, they are made up of a video lecture, followed by a question and answer session that allows for interaction with other students. SPOCs are gaining popularity because of the personalized approach and direct access to the professors.

> We're trying out artificial intelligence with employee engagement by having weekly drop-ins from a virtual assistant who checks in with each individual on our teams. This virtual person interprets what you're saying and tries to figure out if it's positive, neutral, or negative, and then the results are aggregated in a portal, which is open for the full team to view. It's a very transparent process and everyone can see the results. Then we'll look at the results in a group and figure out what we want to do in terms of improvements.
>
> —LEILA

Crowdsourced learning is also gaining popularity. From T-shirt designs to technology issues, people are crowdsourcing design solutions with increasing frequency. It's a means of leveraging the expertise of the masses at a very low cost.

There are several examples of crowdsourced learning initiatives. Global Learning XPRIZE develops scalable, tech-based solutions to improve education in resource-limited countries. MentorMob is another learning initiative where knowledge experts in a certain subject field curate resources of articles and videos for others. Wikipedia uses crowdsourcing to translate their articles into different languages, and CourseHero provides online crowdsourced study documents, expert tutors, and customizable flash cards. The trend is growing quickly and resources are becoming available to wider audiences.

> Give the people the freedom to learn from mistakes as long as they are small. Intuitive, adaptive learning by creating the possibilities for mistakes and the safe space to make them is how people learn. As they learn, they will take steps forward if you just enable that opportunity.
>
> —RIINA

A discipline called "adaptive learning" is also on the rise. This is when eLearning tools are personalized to a learner's proficiency. It's designed to advance as the student does, and matches lessons and information according to the user's interests. Adaptive learning is effective because it allows people to learn how and what they want, and at a speed that is appropriate for their developmental level.

> If I was in HR in the role of the Chief Human Resources Officer, ongoing learning and constant development would be the most important processes, because I'm thinking in systems. I'm thinking self-adaptive teams and self-organized teams. I'm thinking they should be microlearning in their environment all the time.
>
> —RIINA

AGILE LEARNING

> Dare to experiment more and set the organization up in that mode. There are no given solutions as to how an organization should act. We do have good practices, but there is no best practice. Experiment and learn in cross-functional teams.
>
> —BJÖRN

Agile is built on the understanding that people learn most effectively in small amounts. We've touched on this concept several times because it's at the heart of the Agile approach to work. Employees process smaller pieces of information quickly, instead of focusing on a large, comprehensive overview of everything.

The success of Agile learning initiatives is dependent on the shift of responsibility from the manager to the employees. They design their own schedule, to-do list, goals, and education. In order to make the shift, management should focus on creating environments that invite people to communicate and mingle.

FROM→TO FOR LEARNING

Less of	More of
A couple of days/year in total	A couple of days/month in total
Several days of training in sequence	A few hours in sequence
Using an external supplier	Colleagues share knowledge
"One size fits all"	People learn in different ways
Individuals learning - self studies	Team leaning - We learn together
Required and controlled	From intrinsic motivation
Sequential	Iterative
Planned long in advance	"On demand delivery"
Genreral content	Selective - dependent on peoples needs
Using best practice from others	Experiment to learn whr works
Mainly books	Other knowledge sources, including Google and AI

Agile learning is geared toward the creation of T-shaped people, or people with both breadth and depth of skills. People with these types of competencies are also sometimes referred to as generalized specialists or specialized generalists. On an individual level, T-shaped people are those who develop a broad and general competence base with deeper knowledge in particular areas, depending on what is of interest to them. Developing T-shaped people can be achieved by active rotation between teams and departments throughout the organization.

It's a constant process of trial, error, and learning. Employees test what fits, where they perform the best, and how they can most effectively contribute to the organization and their own growth.

From the team perspective, T-shaped people mean increased flexibility because they are able to swap tasks and try on several different hats. They are able to work together in small, shifting, and evolving teams, which decreases bottlenecks. It also helps to save jobs because people are skilled in multiple areas. Even though someone may have one special skill, they are still able to provide value across several departments or teams, due to their broad, general competence base.

Standard job descriptions are viewed as archaic and limiting. It is generally believed that job descriptions are boxes for standing on, not living in. They should serve as the foundation for growth instead of a restriction. Job descriptions are a starting point. People need to feel free to develop in any direction they find interesting, challenging, and rewarding, as long as it benefits the whole organization.

The emphasis in Agile is that learning should be easy. Instead of using benchmark figures and best practices, employees should be given the freedom and flexibility to experiment and absorb new information. Best practices are probably the best at someone else's place, so they have to find their own way, and it's different for each company.

"Lunch and learn" is a practice that facilitates quick learning. The phrase was born from the notion that people should be able to use their lunch hour to exchange ideas and try new things.

> Best practice is dead. Of course, you can benchmark and learn, but what you should be learning about is why some organizations have decided to do something. So, you learn about the underlying mechanisms and the decision-making points, instead of the processes and tools themselves.
> —RIINA

The concept of "pairing" at work is another popular practice, which is when people pair up to design, test, manage, or simply explore new ideas together. It's based on the idea of the buddy system. Having a partner helps to make people more accountable to themselves, their buddy, and the company.

Even in a partnership, self-reliance and self-development are critical in Agile learning. It's the starting point for everything that comes after. If *you* don't take a vested interest in yourself, your education, and your own happiness, how can you reasonably expect anyone else to?

The esteemed scholar and writer, Isaac Asimov, said, "Self-education is, I firmly believe, the only kind of education there is."

If you aren't open to learning, you won't learn; you will be left behind. One of my favorite cartoons is a drawing of two people trying to push a wagon with square wheels up a hill. Someone else is standing on the side of the road, holding a round wheel and waving at them. He's saying, "Hey guys, I have an idea! I know how you can get up the hill faster!" The two laborers scoff at him and respond, "Buzz off! We're busy working here. Don't you have anything better to do?" This cartoon reminds me of some of the people I work with who tell me they don't have the time to improve. They say they can't find room in the budget for education, and all their employees are already working at capacity.

> Agile doesn't differentiate between working and learning. You have your retrospectives, you have your daily stand-ups, you have your teams that jump in and help you out, so you learn and constantly improve.
> —FABIOLA

THE FOUR PHASES OF TEAM DEVELOPMENT

Susan A. Wheelan, a professor at Temple University in Philadelphia, Pensylvania, has studied work groups and their development for almost thirty years. She transformed the way people understand team development and dynamics from a psychological perspective. Wheelan's extensive research into group development led to the discovery that teams go through four distinct phases of evolution.

In the first phase, teams are heavily dependent on the manager for decision making and direction. The individuals within teams are typically extremely polite to one another and tip-toe around controversy and disagreement. Basically, they're not being themselves.

In the second phase of development, team members start to squabble. They question management and each other as they try to find their roles. Conflict is to be expected. By the third phase, people start to calm down because they've found their roles and understand their place in the team. They can relax and focus on working productively. By the fourth phase, team members are 90 percent focused on productive work. When the team has evolved to this level of functionality, the manager joins the team and becomes one of its contributing members. By phase four, the team is considered high performing.

In order to fully mature, it is necessary for a team to move through all four phases of development. The process takes time and cannot be forced. It must be an organic transition from one phase to the next. Some teams never move past phase two or three, but the goal is always to get to phase four where the need for management decreases dramatically.

The degree to which management is necessary depends on both the maturity of the team and the structure of the organization. There may not be a need for a formal management structure in all types of business. Whenever there is a group of people, structured or not, there will always be those who slip into an informal leadership role. This leadership role can change whenever the team's goals change. In Agile, the people who have extensive knowledge in a particular area are considered an "informal leader." When team goals change, so does the informal leader.

Corporate leaders and managers need to put the energy into making their organizations sustainable now if they hope to see the future. Tomorrow's companies embrace continuous learning and development as an investment. What is the focus for your company? Are you in it for the long haul or are you only concerned with short-term gains? Agile is about creating an environment where people can thrive and grow and give back: to each other, to themselves, to the company, and to society. The best way to achieve that goal is through continuous learning and development.

PSYCHOLOGICAL SAFETY AND LEARNING

I believe in psychologically safe workplaces. The fact is that nobody wants to go to work and look stupid or incompetent. We all want to look smart and helpful. We don't speak up if there is a chance that we will be backstabbed or a chance what we say will be misinterpreted.

Sometimes we don't speak up because everyone is sitting quietly, even if there is a question in the air that needs to be answered. Most of the time we are too busy managing impressions, instead of saying what we really think or asking the questions we need answers to. There are many situations where, if people felt psychologically safe and asked the right questions, mistakes could be avoided.

Professor Amy C. Edmondson from Harvard Business School has conducted important research into psychological safety in the workplace and how it affects people's learning ability.[16] Her research shows that the higher the degree of psychological safety and motivation/accountability, the higher the degree of learning is in the workplace.

---

16 https://www.youtube.com/watch?v=LhoLuui9gX8&feature=youtu.be

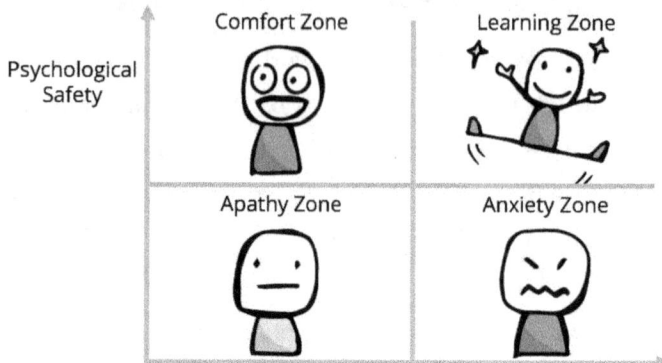

How do you build psychological safety if you're a manager? How do you create an environment where people feel free to speak up and admit errors and mistakes so that everyone can learn from them? As a leader, admit that there is enormous uncertainty and interdependence facing the organization. If you're in an uncertain situation:

- We can't know what will happen and we need everybody's brains to try to figure out the best way forward.
- You must acknowledge your own fallibility—you are not perfect. Create the necessary safe place for speaking up when something is not right.
- Ask a lot of questions to show that you don't have all the answers.

If you do the three things above, you can maximize your learning by making it okay for people to ask questions before and after they make mistakes (preferably before), so that the entire organization can learn faster, which is the goal.

In the future, the only competitive advantage that remains is knowledge, continuous learning, and innovation. The company that learns the fastest and transforms that learning into new products and services (that the customers want and need) will have the competitive advantage.

CAREER PATHS AND SUCCESSION MANAGEMENT

> In an Agile setting, there are no clear career paths. Instead, you have a network and a web of opportunities that need to be open for all employees.
> —BJÖRN

Career planning has been HR's responsibility forever and so has planning for successors of important managers and specialists. The difference between career planning and succession is how high in the hierarchy your role sits. For the most important positions in a large company, there will be around one hundred people that HR considers to fill the position and who will be taken into account as soon as there is a vacancy in a high-level role. The process is often surrounded by secrecy and nobody can know who is a candidate to replace the top positions—in most cases, not even the candidate.

It's a waste of talent in my opinion, as there are so many competent people in international organizations who never get the chance to be considered for positions, simply because nobody knows about them. In any case, the discussion becomes superfluous in an Agile company and the expression "succession planning" disappears in smaller- and medium-sized organizations. It's a concept that comes with hierarchy and management positions. When management roles change, so do these processes.

> The old ways of working with succession planning or career planning are not that interesting anymore. They are hard to apply when roles are expanding beyond the originally prescribed scope. The career path nowadays is not made up of fixed steps you take to secure a management role. First of all, not everyone is interested in management positions anymore. Second of all, from an organizational perspective, we don't need as many specialists. We need to create teams that are less sensitive, and we need to have a wider view on competencies and skillsets in general.
> —LEILA

A first step for a traditional company that wants to become more Agile is to make it possible for more/other candidates to be considered for leadership positions. The selection process needs to be transparent and, ideally, employees will have the opportunity to vote for their own leaders—not unlike how it's done in the political system. Why is democracy not practiced in business when it works quite well in politics?

> Careers need to be more flexible but, of course, we all still use a traditional career path framework. For example, we say a developer eventually becomes a senior developer. Probably 80 percent of people will go down that path, but that doesn't mean it's the exclusive option. Perhaps you come in and say, "I would really love to go into marketing, and I think I have a knack for it." Then we'll see if we can make it work. If not, we'll help that person find something else in the organization or outside, but it has to be more open, more flexible, and more accommodating. It can't be a career killer to say, "I want to reduce my workload." Work is not your only role, and it must equal the amount of time and effort you are willing to put in.
> —FABIOLA

A lot of effort has been dedicated to tailor a person's future path in a company and to find the right career opportunities for different roles in the organization. Often, there are fixed steps that mean taking on some kind of management role. But some people may want to take a horizontal step and learn new skills (broaden their competence) or they may want to deepen their skills in a specific area. They may also want to take a step down for a while and focus on their children or a sick relative. If career paths are needed (which is not obvious), they should be as flexible as possible.

Instead of moving up or out (as in the old days) it should be possible to move up, down, out of the organization, and then back in again, to another function, around, or on any other path that fits with the particular employee for the circumstances in his/her life at a given point in time. After all, it's about developing a person's competence and growing in a way that optimizes satisfaction and performance.

> What we're doing is something we call "grow talks." We're focusing on strength-driven competence development. We're not really talking about your weak areas that need improvement or rating you according to a specific scale. We think using that kind of lingo or ways of working creates a threatening environment. It's not a growth mindset, and it's not what we want to create systematically.

We focus on positive outcomes, and since we've just started with this, it's in the pilot stage. I hope we move even further toward strength-driven development to make sure we're working with those things that create motivation and happiness. We want our people to feel eager to go to work the next day because somebody cares about their strengths. We strive to help them stop focusing their thoughts on negative things that don't really give them energy.

—LEILA

FROM→TO FOR CAREER PATHS AND SUCCESSION MANAGEMENT

THE TRADITIONAL WAY	THE AGILE WAY
Strict career paths, up and/or out	No strict career paths
Purpose: Get a better title and more money	Purpose: Competence development
Predefined titles	Set your own title
Managers decide about succession	Let employees nominate future managers
Non-transparent process	Transparency in who will replace who
A few candidates in an excel sheet	All people in the company can be considered

CHAPTER 9

The Reiss Motivation Profile

> "Values, of unconscious psychodynamics,
> drive the human psyche."
> —Steven Reiss

To even better understand the Agile mindset, I want to dedicate a chapter to a framework called the Reiss Motivation Profile (RMP), which is a model to better understand yourself and others. It highlights primary motivations so that people can interact more efficiently with their team members and be aware of areas where conflict may arise.

Motivation is commonly, and erroneously, categorised into two types: intrinsic and extrinsic. The flaw here is to speak about "extrinsic motivation". External influences are merely triggers for behaviour that is deeply rooted in intrinsic motives. All motivation is, in fact, intrinsic.

Several motivational theories describe what drives people's behaviour (e.g. incentive theory, reinforcement theory, expectancy theory, and even Herzberg's two-factor theory). Upon closer inspection, you will find that all of them indicate that people's (re)actions are based on internal desires and exhibit internal responses to external influences.

The Reiss model affirms that behaviour is a reaction or expression of internal motives to the environmental factors. Intrinsic motivation is naturally driven by personal satisfaction or interest. It typically provides energy, purpose and engagement, without external rewards.

As per the Reiss Motivation Profile, it is based on fundamental life motives or needs, which vary in intensity between individuals.

Every person has individual needs, stimulated by distinct triggers. This is why we can generalise that behaviour is the function of personality (internal motives) and environment (external factors). Depending on different settings, the mood we are in, the intensity, etc., the same external stimulus will provoke a different reaction in us. And of course, different people will react differently in the same circumstances, based on their own motives.

Leaders often misunderstand this and are falsely convinced that they can "motivate" (i.e. convince) people in the organisation to follow them, purely based on external factors. They believe everyone shares the same intrinsic motives and that "rational" arguments, social norms, expectations, organizational pressures or rewards such as money, grades, and recognition will persuade employees. When they fail— and they will, in the long run—they blame the people.

Furthermore, satisfying result-driven external demands can be effortful or conflict with intrinsic desires. It is perceived as energy-consuming, so people are more likely to seek ways around it, instead of embracing it. Some will even devise avoidance strategies, simply to meet their basic desires.

In other words, extrinsic triggers function as catalysts or as an invitation, but the real drive must come from within a person. Leaders and change agents who understand this, focus on inspiring reflection, supporting autonomy, and connecting goals to personal meaning—thus helping others naturally find motivation, according to their intrinsic needs and desires.

Shaping the organizational environment to make it easy for employees to act in alignment with their motives, will determine how individuals invest in work, learning, or personal growth.

Everything we do to make people happy and feel good, is just an extrinsic trigger, intended to fulfil intrinsic needs. And we know that happy people, will be a far greater driving force in the organization.

> Trying to "motivate" others to pursue our goals and share our own desires, is a futile endeavour, because the most we can do, is to try to inspire others and hope that this will awaken their own intrinsic motivations.
>
> - ALEX

In summary, the Reiss Motivation Profile reframes motivation as a set of intrinsic life motives that drive all behaviour, including responses to external factors, while also recognising varying intensity and individual differences.

DR. STEVEN REISS AND THE ORIGINS OF THE RMP

The Reiss Motivational Profile is the result of Dr. Steven Reiss' empirical psychological research between   and   . The idea for the study came to him when he was in the hospital recovering from a liver transplant. While he was lying in bed, he started to think about why all the nurses were so nice to the patients. He wanted to know what motivated them to behave so kindly. They seemed to have an endless amount of patience. They always smiled and tried to do their best, even though some of the patients behaved terribly in response.

Dr. Reiss vowed to himself that, if he survived his hospital stay, he would devote the rest of his life to researching

human motivation and why people do what they do. The liver transplant granted him another fourteen years and, true to his word, he devoted those years to the study of human motivation. Sadly, Steven passed away in October   , leaving a dream behind that everyone should take the Reiss Motivation Profile to better understand their unique motivators.

The psychology of personality and what makes humans "tick" has been a subject of fascination since long before Freud came along. There are several different methods of trying to figure out how people think and why they behave the way they do: Myers-Briggs and DISC are among two of the better-known and widely used personality tests.

The difference in Reiss' approach is that he believed people are motivated by their basic needs that show their values to different degrees. Reiss believed that behavior is the result of someone's innate inner values:

> *The sixteen basic desires may have a genetic origin. They have been demonstrated by using samples from four continents (North America, Europe, Asia, and Australia), and in multiple cultures. Further, a number of them can be observed for animals. Animals raise their young (indicating a desire for family), defend themselves (indicating a desire for vengeance), have sex (indicating a desire for romance), show fear (indicating a desire for tranquility), display dominance (indicating a desire for power), eat (indicating a desire for food), and exercise (indicating a desire for muscle exercise).*
>
> *This is not to say that culture and upbringing play no role in determining the strength of the desires; certain desires may be encouraged in some cultures or families and suppressed in others. Two teachers, for example, might encourage their children to start reading at a very early age, while two athletes might encourage sports participation. Parents in a very small apartment might discourage uninhibited running around. Such differences in upbringing, especially*

in the early years, may strengthen or diminish the natural desires with which a child is born.

Culture and upbringing also likely play significant roles in determining how people go about managing and gratifying their basic desires. People everywhere are motivated by hunger, power, curiosity, and so on, but they differ widely in the food they eat, how they go about satisfying their ambitions, and what they spend their time learning.

Since our basic desires have a genetic origin, we tend to have the same basic goals throughout our lives. People do not change much in what they fundamentally desire and intrinsically value. Curious children tend to become curious adolescents, who become curious adults. People who have strong appetites tend to struggle with their weight all their lives. People who like to organize and plan things when they are adolescents probably will continue to enjoy organizing and planning when they are adults. I suspect that the underlying genes that influence these desires do not change much as we grow older.

—STEVEN REISS[17]

---

17 Steven Reiss, "The Reiss Motivation Profile: What Motivates You?", IDS Publishing Corporation, 2013

Unlike the ideas behind Myers-Briggs and DISC, which are rooted in the teachings of Carl Jung, Steven Reiss studied motivational researchers. Four generations of Harvard University psychologists, William James (– 1910), William McDougall (1871–1938), Henry Murray (–) and David McClelland (–) suggested that psychological needs are the central organizing themes of behavior.

Typically, psychologists develop theories and then do research to prove their theories. Dr. Reiss went about his work from a different angle. His approach was not based on theory; it was based on fieldwork and collecting information. He interviewed a large number of people and asked what motivated them. He wanted to know what made them happy and what motivated their actions and behaviors. He gathered responses from thousands of people and then cross-referenced his findings with more people from all over Japan and Europe.

All of Dr. Reiss' research was collected through interviews. Through his analysis of over six thousand people, he concluded all humans are motivated by sixteensixteeen basic needs. This is the first empirically tested and validated research regarding human desires. A person's RMP is like their fingerprint. No two people have the same one.

BASIC NEED: WHAT IS IT?

Most people don't wake up in the morning and think about who they are and where they're going in life. They simply wake up and go about their daily business. Many of the people Dr. Reiss interviewed said they felt automatically propelled into their actions and decisions.

Everything we do is motivated by our basic needs, which show the deepest values we hold inside. Our inner motivations show us that we need to have values-based happiness in our lives, which is ideally long lasting and sustainable. Our innermost needs occur with varying degrees of self-awareness and intensity. Some people are highly in tune with them, while others never give them a passing thought. People get so caught up in day-to-day activities, they forget to look at the bigger picture of who they are, why they do what they do, and where they're headed.

When you know what drives someone, that person's behavior is easier to predict. Of course, people are skilled in adjusting behaviors for various situations and reasons. The RMP helps us to see what values that person is most naturally inclined toward, or where they are happiest.

Today, over   people from   countries have rated the   statements that make up the web survey that result in the Reiss Motivation Profile—and drastically improved their communication with others as a result. Although our priorities vary in strength, the one thing everyone has in common is the sixteen basic desires.

The intensity, or lack of intensity, of those sixteen motivators is what Reiss found to be of particular inter- est, especially when it comes to our understanding of ourselves. Everyone is guilty of trying to increase the importance of their unique values at one point or another. We convince ourselves that "what is best for me is also best for everyone else." This rationale leads to trying to impose your own values, or primary drivers, onto other people; a practice Reiss referred to as "self hugging" and "everyday tyranny." Your own basic needs and the degree to which you experience them are unique to you and you alone. They cannot be imposed on others, although we try to do that all the time. When we become aware of our differences, we can stop trying to change other people's value structure, since it's practically impossible.

The real question is, What is the intention of my actions? The responses in the RMP are either weak or strong, and they never change. They are genetically unique, like DNA, and they cannot be chosen. They

- Occur automatically
- Motivate all of your actions
- Reveal your deepest values

- Show what you need for basic happiness
- Occur with varying degrees of self-awareness

The RMP is administered electronically. It takes about fifteen to thirty minutes to evaluate   sentences, answer-ing issues such as

- What is your intention?
- What are your intrinsic motivations?
- What rituals are important to you?
- What do you believe in?

Our rituals and beliefs stem from birth and the culture we grew up in. Our skills, knowledge, and behaviors are affected by everything around us, such as our country of origin and the type of family we were raised in, but the sixteen core values are shared by all of humanity.

Dr. Reiss came up with a grading system to measure the intensity levels of each drive. It's easy to visualize where people fall on the spectrum, from extremely strong to extremely weak. Those who fall on the outer edges are more special, unique, or strange. We can use either pos-itive or negative language to describe each drive and the lack of it, but what really matters is how you describe yourself in relation to other people. You tend to describe your own strong and weak needs in a positive way, and the more someone differs from your scores, the more negative your description.

Let's look at the desire for "independence" as an example of what the score indicates. If you happen to fall in the middle (neither strong, nor weak), then you are someone who can make a situational decision about independence. You may be okay making independent decisions, and you're fine when others make decisions too. It's not that important to you whether you do or not.

If your rating is very strong, there are no emotional alternatives. A strong rating indicates you are extremely autonomous and you don't enjoy working together with others. It also suggests that you don't like to be helped or ask for help. However, if you are both fiercely indepen- dent, but also extremely extroverted, you may be okay working with others most of the time. You simply want to work with them *your* way.

It can be challenging to relate to people who are very different from us. Conflict is caused because of the variances between our primary motivators, no matter how hard we try to find common ground. Those who fall in the middle have an easier time understanding both sides.

I love introducing people to the Reiss Motivation Profile because it helps us to see ourselves how we really are— not how we perceive ourselves to be and not how others perceive us to be. Living in accordance with our values and our drives leads to the greatest possible happiness and fulfillment in life. When we learn about our own values, we are able to see ourselves, primarily and finally, in the light of our own intentions. Those intentions are almost always invisible to others, and sometimes even to our-selves, but the RMP brings them to the surface.

THE SIXTEEN BASIC HUMAN DESIRES

In order to better understand yourself and the people around you, let's examine each of the sixteen motivators. I'll walk you through how each motivation manifests in someone's behavior, depending on whether the drive is strong, weak, or neutral.

1. POWER: THE DESIRE TO INFLUENCE AND LEAD OTHERS

People who score high on power like to be in control in all situations. Some say that high power people are manipu- lative of others, while others say they're ambitious. They enjoy influencing others and assuming leadership roles.

When someone is low on power motivation, it means they're more service-oriented and enjoy working directly with people. They are non-directive; they want to support other people's decisions more than they want to lead. Low power people prefer to stay in the background and avoid the spotlight.

The world needs all types of people, and it's very helpful to understand where people fall on the spectrum. A good friend of mine who I work closely with is very high on power, but our other coworker is very low. Personally, I lean toward the middle to low range, so I'm considered "average." We complement each other *because of our differences*.

2. INDEPENDENCE: THE DESIRE FOR SELF-RELIANCE

This motivation specifies whether someone is good at working alone or if they do better in a team setting. Those with a high drive for independence prefer to be autonomous and would rather not rely on other people. Sometimes, highly independent people create emotional distance between themselves and others so that they have an easier time being alone.

In my family of six people, three of them rate high for independence. The three of us who lean low on the scale sometimes have a hard time relating to the others. We want closeness and consensus, while the others prefer to make their own decisions without consulting the group.

Personally, I like being attached to others and having close emotional relationships. Interdependence is important to me, so I like working with people on teams and making group decisions. There is no right or wrong way to be, but knowing where others are coming from helps us to get along better. Typically, people who like Agile values, are low on the independence scale. Imagine the problems that can arise when working with someone with the opposite values. As always, awareness of differences helps people to understand.

3. CURIOSITY: THE DESIRE FOR KNOWLEDGE AND THINKING

Those who are high on the curiosity scale have a strong need to understand how things work and operate. They tend to be professors or researchers or gravitate toward careers that require deep thinking. They enjoy engaging in discussion and debate on different topics. Dr. Reiss, it should come as no surprise, was very high on the curiosity scale. He enjoyed thinking about things in new ways and coming up with innovative ideas.

Those who are low on curiosity are practical and tend to be doers as opposed to thinkers. They prefer action or routine to a deep understanding of how things work. These are the people who want to move ahead without too much planning up front.

4. ACCEPTANCE: THE DESIRE FOR INCLUSION

Those who value acceptance want to be recognized by others as an important member of the group. They need feedback and compliments. They need to hear positive affirmations all the time, and if they don't, they start to feel quite low. Have you ever met someone, or are you the type of person, who needs constant reinforcement? You may need to hear things such as, "I love you. You look fantastic. You are so smart. Keep up the great work."

On the flip side, people with a low desire for acceptance are more self-confident and have higher self-esteem. They don't put a lot of weight on what others think of them. Consequently, they are able to handle tough and con- structive feedback as a means to continuously improve.

5. ORDER: THE DESIRE FOR ORDER, ORGANIZATION, AND STABILITY

People who crave order tend to need stability and struc- ture to feel at ease. They like planning in advance and to stick to schedules. This could manifest itself through orderliness in the home, or general tidiness. The people who lean low on order are spontaneous and flexible. They like to be free from plans and they "wing it" when it comes to decision making.

I have direct personal experience being out of balance with order. I was in a project management role, which required order and organization. It required a lot of planning ahead, schedule making, and follow-up. I needed to be in control of what people were saying and doing at all times. On a professional level, I needed to be highly ordered. However, as I later learned, my inherent motivation for order is quite low. I prefer to be free of tasks and I need flexibility, spontaneity, and improvisation. When I discovered Agile, I was thrilled. It gave me a way to run projects in alignment with my basic needs. I didn't have to struggle with the ordered approach anymore. Working as an Agile project manager suddenly made me enjoy work a lot more.

6. SAVING/COLLECTING: THE DESIRE TO COLLECT THINGS

Saving is the accumulation of things. Some people are unable to throw anything away. They hold onto every single scrap of paper or piece of memorabilia they've ever encountered.

Collecting can be seen in people who insist on storing, fixing, or mending everything they've ever purchased. They are wed to the sensation of owning and maintaining things. People who feel strongly about saving might refer to themselves as economical or sustainable.

On the other side of the spectrum are people who don't want to hold onto anything. They want to be free from property and the burden of ownership. Things have little or no importance to them. They tend to be quite generous, but have the potential to border on wasteful.

Agile people are more often on the low side of saving than on the higher end. They want to share information and knowledge and help others succeed. They often have a tendency to give, rather than hold things in.

7. HONOR: THE DESIRE TO BE LOYAL TO ONE'S PARENTS, MORAL VALUES, AND PRINCIPLES

Honor relates to how we conduct ourselves. If honor is important to you, you have a high regard for all of your principles, morals, and ethics. High honor people value tradition; they're truthful, loyal, and upright. For honorable people, the *how* tends to be more important than *why*. Therefore, the *way* things are done might be valued more than the end result.

Those who do not put a lot of stock in honor tend to be more goal-oriented. They focus on doing what is possible and necessary to meet the end result.

I am very low on the honor scale, which means I don't like to wait. I just want to get to the end by the quickest means possible—another word for it is expedience or purpose orientation. People who fall in the middle are usually able to take either a principled or a purpose-oriented approach.

8. IDEALISM: THE DESIRE FOR SOCIAL JUSTICE

Idealism is tied to social justice, altruism, and fairness. High ideal people think of others—not just the people close to them, but people everywhere in the world. You might find them working with the poor in different parts of the world. They want to improve society as a whole and make the world a better place.

Those on the low end of the spectrum are more realistic. They take responsibility and usually put themselves first. They are not overly concerned with others and can easily look the other way if they see someone begging for money on the street. Some Agile people tend to be a little high on idealism.

9. SOCIAL CONTACT: THE DESIRE FOR COMPANIONSHIP

Some people have a strong desire to spend their time with others, being social and extroverted. The introvert or extrovert characteristic is common in psychological testing. It comes up in Myers-Briggs and DISC as well. Some people simply cannot stand to be alone. Alternatively, there are those who value their alone time above all else. They even go so far as to schedule it into their calendars.

It's nearly impossible to avoid interacting with other people altogether, and there are a handful of entrepre- neurs and inventors who only interact with a select few. Then, there are those who cannot function or feel at ease unless they are surrounded by large groups of people at all times: in meetings, at parties, while traveling, or at meals.

10. FAMILY: THE DESIRE TO RAISE ONE'S OWN CHILDREN

Increasingly, more people are choosing not to have children or get married. The traditional concept of family—although still strong—is changing. Not everyone prizes having a family or sees it as the end all, be all.

There are vast differences between those who highly value family and those who don't place as much importance on it. They may see family as a burden or a threat to their freedom, and those who are committed to family can't imagine life any other way. Very few people have a "take it or leave it" attitude toward starting a family.

I've worked with many people who have a low drive for family, but are parents regardless. When I ask them why they have children, they explain they did it for their spouse or their parents, or because of pressure from their peer group—not because they particularly wanted to have kids. It's obvious to see where their heart and head lies when looking at the RMP results. A lot of people don't live in accordance with their basic drives.

11. STATUS: THE DESIRE FOR SOCIAL STANDING

Status is related to the need to feel slightly elevated above other people. Those high on the status scale like to spend time with other important or famous people, and they place a lot of emphasis on material possessions as outward symbols of their status. For example, they may own a flashy car, live in a big house in a posh neighborhood, or wear the latest style of clothing. They likely enjoy having important titles at work and getting respect from others.

People who are low on the status scale are more down to earth. They are informal and happy to be just like everyone else. They don't covet certain brands or buy their clothes in a special store. They're okay making a little less money and driving an unassuming car. They approach transportation as a practicality, not a status symbol. Agile people are more often lower than higher on the status scale.

12. VENGEANCE/WINNING: THE DESIRE TO GET EVEN AND WIN

Those high on vengeance value competition, aggression, and conflict. They find arguing necessary and refreshing. High vengeance people have the tendency to go beyond an attitude of "friendly competition" and become fixated on being right or winning. If someone has done something to get on the wrong side of a high vengeance person, they need to look out! That person will not let the wrongdoing slide and turn the other cheek. They want to get back at the person who did them wrong. This is the same drive that propels successful athletes who are driven to win at any cost.

People with a low desire for vengeance prefer harmony to conflict. In fact, they try to avoid conflict. Low vengeance people look for common ground in arguments and seek win-win solutions. Agile people are often low on the desire for vengeance.

13. BEAUTY: THE DESIRE FOR BEAUTY

Most artists and other creative types have a deep passion for beauty. They appreciate aesthetics and natural scen- ery.

Beauty-lovers may spend a lot of time decorating their homes or visiting art museums to admire sculpture, paintings, drawing, and other rare artifacts. Those who do not value beauty look instead at how things function; they are interested in the mechanics of things and operations over outward appeal.

14. EATING: THE DESIRE FOR FOOD

Some people think about food all day long. They start thinking about lunch the minute they get to the office, if not the night before. They plan what they're going to have for dinner four days in advance. They're mentally walking down the aisles of the supermarket and making lists of things to buy. They enjoy thinking about, preparing, and ingesting food.

When food is not a priority, it's viewed as little more than something that must be taken in for fuel. These people view food as an energy supply, or they are very picky about what they eat.

In a work environment, it's easy to underestimate the power food has over certain people. For example, meet- ings that are scheduled near the lunch hour can cause real anxiety for people who highly value food. They worry that the meeting will run late and they will be deprived. When they enter the meeting room, if there are no snacks or coffee provided, their bellies start to rumble and they'll do whatever they can to speed things up.

15. PHYSICAL ACTIVITY: THE DESIRE TO EXERCISE MUSCLES

Some people cannot be happy unless they go for a five- mile run or work their body to the point of exhaustion. I am one of those people, so I can easily relate to others who get out of sorts when they are denied their daily exercise. I'll start to climb the walls if two or three days go by and I don't break a sweat.

The desire for movement and physical activity is just as powerful as the desire to be sedentary and inactive. Those who detest physical activity dread it with as much energy as others look forward to it.

16. TRANQUILITY: THE DESIRE FOR EMOTIONAL CALM

Those who have a strong desire for tranquility are sus- ceptible to the dangers of stress. They need security and peaceful surroundings as much as possible. They prefer predictability to spontaneity and avoid taking any unnecessary risks. They like stable environments and want to know of any changes long in advance.

Low tranquility people are not afraid of challenges and are known to embrace the unknown. They are "cool" in stressful situations; most entrepreneurs are low on the need for tranquility. It's not uncommon for very cool people to like extreme sports, like skydiving or fast motorcycles. Or, they could be huge risk-takers when buying and selling shares on the stock exchange.

THE VALUE OF THE RMP IN RELATIONSHIPS

An individual's combination of basic needs is what creates complex personalities. Everyone has different motivations, which can't be seen on the outside. We can see how others act and behave, but we have no idea the degree to why or what makes them tick on the inside, so the reason for their behavior is hidden.

When your drive is used in the right way, your life can be dramatically improved. My world cracked wide open when I first took the Reiss Motivation Profile and the results were explained to me. A second time (the first time being when I first encountered Agile), I understood why I had been struggling so mightily in my project management position. I was in a role where I was expected to behave in direct opposition to my natural inclinations. I was essen- tially at war with myself. The descriptions of high and low drive toward "order," in particular, resonated with me. I thought, "Aha! At last! I finally understand why I've been so unhappy at work." This was yet another piece of the lifelong puzzle to understand myself. It strengthened my self-image as somebody with an Agile personality.

When I was faced with the truth about myself, I was able to put the information to practical use in both my career and personal life. I often ask, How can I best use my strengths for this particular situation? What is it about this dynamic that makes me uncomfortable and why? How can I be in a situation that best fits my personality?

The RMP is a framework for living your life. It's not an anecdote or a prescription for change. It helps you to live your best life in alignment with your deepest values. Agile, combined with the RMP, helps you to understand everyone's unique differences and unlocks unimaginable doors. It celebrates all the different styles of working and makes room for everyone.

When people are able to identify certain motivations in others, it fosters collaboration and appreciation. Sud- denly we're able to understand why other people do the things they do. Prior to the clarity the RMP provides, we may have just assumed someone was strangely power hungry, or an unusual loner, or whatever other extreme personality trait fit the bill.

The RMP is used in businesses to increase individual engagement, but it is also an invaluable tool for team development. All groups are made up of people with different drives, needs, and goals. The RMP helps to reduce stress and discontent through heightened awareness. Increased awareness of one's own drives as well as others improves cooperation and strengthens relationships. It helps to clearly and visually identify team motivations and resolve conflicts in values and behaviors between team members.

The RMP is also quite useful in personal relationships. As mentioned earlier, I must have physical activity or I go stir crazy. My partner is the polar opposite. He scores extremely low on physical activity. Instead of letting this difference drive a wedge between us, we are able to acknowledge it and meet each other in the middle. I don't expect him to jump out of bed at : a.m. and join me for a run every day, but I know that if he joins me occasionally on the weekends, he's making a gigantic effort to make me happy. This is a simplistic example, but it works for larger issues as well.

When it comes to marriage or relationships based on love, the profile can give you guidance as well. The more similar your profiles, the easier your life together will be. "Birds of a feather flock together," as the saying goes. To avoid any later conflicts, the best would be to know about your basic needs before getting married, which is, of course, easier said than done, since love obviously doesn't care about basic needs when you meet someone you fall in love with.

The Reiss Motivational Profile is extremely valuable to help teams
- Know what motivates individuals and how to provide what they need
- More easily solve conflicts with the knowledge of the profile differences
- Understand why people behave in non-Agile ways (for example, if they are highly independent) or don't buy into Agile values
- Have a powerful tool for values-based recruiting
- Ensure they have the value structure necessary to reach team goals

People do not come with instruction manuals, but the RMP is the closest thing I've found to one. Many people think that success is about accomplishing goals, but it's really about feeling happy and at peace. The best way to go about having those happy feelings is to respect yourself and others as the unique individuals we all are.

CHAPTER 10

Agile Leadership

"You manage things; you lead people."
—Admiral Grace Hopper

Agile leadership differs from traditional leadership in almost every conceivable way. Most notably, it doesn't follow a hierarchical, top-down approach. The goal of Agile leadership is to delegate as much power as possible to the employees, which means allowing them to take responsibility for their own engagement and performance. In that regard, Agile leadership takes a bottom-up approach.

> It has to start in the leadership. We've put a lot of light on leadership in the last few years. Maybe the most tangible thing we did was stating we're an IT consultancy firm, and the consultants are our heroes. We all need to know much more about what it is to be a consultant. Every leader needs to either sell our services, be a consultant themselves, or both—and this goes for the CEO and the whole organization, including me as an HR director.
>
> —CECILIA

Instead of focusing on control, the intention of Agile leadership is to motivate people to contribute to the greater good of the organization. To promote motivation, leadership is informal and communication flows freely between everyone. There are no closed-door meetings or secret policies. Agile supports complete transparency. Everyone is involved in decision making, not just a select few at the top.

Agile thinking is similar to systems thinking in that it looks at the whole picture. We cannot predict what is going to happen or when. It all depends on the relationships, the people, the systems, the structures, the processes, and the organization itself.

REINVENTING ORGANIZATIONS

Many people think organizations have been stretched to their limits by the way they are run. In study after study, executives and business people have expressed the opinion that their workplaces are plagued with fear and a lack of enthusiasm, and lack the passion or purpose that drive some of the younger organizations. The disappointment is pervasive: we've heard it from government agencies, nonprofit organizations, schools, and hospitals.

> They need to understand what is going to change and how we will implement those changes. Quite often, especially leaders, will say, "We have to do things differently. I want a different culture." That's very nice, but how are we going to approach that? What's our first step in creating this new culture of collaboration?
> —FABIOLA

The negative feedback about the workplace doesn't stem exclusively from people who work at the bottom of hierarchies. Behind the facade of success, many top-level leaders are tired of the power games and politics of traditional business structures too. Despite an outward display of overloaded calendars and busyness, they feel a vague sense of emptiness. Everyone is yearning for a better way to work together. We long for more soulful workplaces where our skills and our talents meet our deepest desires.

In his groundbreaking book, *Reinventing Organizations*, Frederic Laloux inspired the next stage of human consciousness by changing the conversation about work. He shifted the dialogue from what's broken to how we can fix it. The book has driven thousands of organizations, corporations, nonprofits, schools, and hospitals to adopt radically more purposeful practices.

Laloux examines the history of organizational structure, beginning roughly ten thousand years ago. He invented a color-coded system to represent various time periods and characteristics of those structures. He starts with red organizations, which are focused on power, structure, hierarchy, and processes.

The leaders of red organizations used their formal power to keep the masses under control. Laloux uses a wolf pack as a metaphor to describe these groups. In today's society, the mafia is an example of a red organization. They use their power to dominate subordinates and they breed a culture of fear. If people with power want something, they take it. When people don't do what the leader wants them to do, they are punished. This type of leadership does not require a lot of planning or strategy because the groups are run by force.

The next tier Laloux focused on was amber. Thousands of years ago, the emphasis was on order, stability, and predictability. There was a growing emphasis on conformity, influenced by the Catholic Church. It was thought that non-believers were doomed to hell.

Laloux uses the Army and the Indian caste system as metaphors for amber organizations. It was believed that everyone had their place in the pecking order of the hierarchy. The central question was, How can we use our power to keep everything exactly as it is? There was only one way of doing things. Right and wrong were directly linked to roles. The person wearing the priest coat was always right.

An amber organization is not forward thinking. It functions under the belief that whatever worked in the past will always work. It is the right way and if you disagree, you will be an outcast. People in these types of organizations or societies are highly suspicious of others and fearful of competition and change. Often, they already have a monopoly and the competition has been squashed.

Ambers are hierarchical organizations built on formal reporting lines. The thinking is done at the top. Planning and execution are separate areas. All of the work and operations are taken care of by the lower tiers. Typically, people are viewed as lazy, dishonest, and in need of discipline. Innovation is of zero importance, and information is only shared when absolutely necessary among the most relevant parties.

Compared to the restrictions within a red organization, amber organizations have slightly more freedom. People have to do what they're told, but they don't have to plan or think. Amber companies are like the early days at Ford Motors; the factory took care of everything for the workers. If someone was fired, they didn't just lose their job, they lost their housing, access to food, their social network—everything.

In Laloux's color-coded breakdown of organizational development, orange comes after amber. Instead of hierarchical or top-down management, the key focus in orange organizations is success. It represents the time period from World War II to the present day. The big question in orange organizations is, How can we win? Many of the big-named companies from the twentieth century fall into this category, such as Walmart, Nike, Coca-Cola, and IBM.

Laloux uses the machine as a metaphor for orange organizations. One of the key concepts is the self-made man. Success has to be earned and hard work always pays off. The harder you work, the more you are recognized. Overconsumption is the norm. People believe that anything is possible and those with special skills or knowledge are considered heroes.

Orange is associated with capitalism, materialism, and maximizing shareholder value. People are focused on the future, not the present. They are process and project driven. They are heavy on marketing and research and development, which became new areas of focus after WWII.

Cross-functionality exists in orange companies, but expert consultants are brought in to enhance communication and increase shareholder value. Management focuses on financial objectives, budgeting strategies, key performance indicators (KPIs), strategic planning, and pay for performance. Several different diverse consulting methods and management tools have been developed during this time, for example, Capital Budgeting, Balanced Scorecards, Business Process Reengineering (BPR), and Six Sigma. The problem with these methods is that they only address a part of the problem. The problem probably depends on many different and complex factors and circumstances and we cannot control the process of "fixing it." There are dependencies and relationships between the different functions of the organization. We need to use good practices and trial and error to manage organizational issues.

Whereas amber organizations ruled with the whip, orange organizations utilize the reward system. There is a push-pull dynamic: decisions are delegated to give birth to innovation and motivation, yet managers fear the loss of control. They aren't quite ready to relinquish power and they don't entirely trust the employees. Management continues to make decisions that should be made further down the chain of command.

In management-heavy organizations, there is a tendency toward a practice Jack Welch refers to as "sandbagging" in his book, *Winning*. Sandbagging is when employees establish low-performance targets so they can more easily meet their goals and receive a bonus. On the flip side, management attempts to establish high-performance targets in order to eke out the most work from the staff. Sandbagging fosters a culture of mistrust. Employees do as little as possible and management squeezes them to death. Nobody wins because people are not empowered, so they don't work to their full potential.

Orange organizations represent the era when the philosophy was that anyone could be a CEO if they worked hard enough. Obstacles to power, such as sexual orientation or gender, are decreasing, but still, rational behavior is valued above all else. People are encouraged to wear a professional mask and suppress their feelings. Displaying weakness or vulnerability is highly undesirable, particularly in the workplace. Achievement and skill are valued both socially and financially. People are viewed as resources to be optimized. They are part of the machinery. The orange mentality is still the most common type of work environment today, although change is coming.

Since the beginning of the 1900s, green organizations have been evolving alongside the orange organizations. Green companies more closely align with Agile than any of the other paradigms. They concentrate on people, relationships, consensus, cultures, and values. The metaphor Laloux uses to describe green organizations is family, and the central question is, How can we give people more power and delegate more responsibility? Because of this thinking, the early part of the century saw the civil rights and women's movements.

Relationships between people are more important than results and the leaders have a service mentality. Empathy is becoming an important part of the social and cultural fabric. Companies such as Southwest, Google, Apple, and Spotify have paved the way in social responsibility and stand up as leaders in stewardship.

There's been a large-scale movement toward decentralization and team-driven decision making. Managers are increasingly chosen by the team, rather than appointed by executives or other managers. The focus is on total stakeholder involvement—the customers, suppliers, and employees—not just the shareholders. The external and internal environments are weighted equally and the focus is on the big picture.

Finally, Laloux turned his attention to the organizations of the future, which are teal. Teal organizations are a big buzzword in Agile circles. Since they are just evolving now, we don't know exactly what the characteristics are, but it looks like they will be primarily self-organizing, decentralized networks.

A few companies have already embraced the teal concept. Yvon Chouinard, the founder of Patagonia, chronicled his own evolution toward becoming a partially teal organization in his book, *Let My People Go Surfing: The Education of a Reluctant Businessman*. There are a few other pioneers testing the waters too: most notably, Burtzoorg in the Netherlands and The Morning Star Company in California.

The central question in teal organizations is, How can we find a purpose that changes and develops us? Life and work are integrated. They focus on the whole person instead of just the work persona. The number of hours that people actually spend at work or doing work is not as important as the amount of time that people spend developing themselves and becoming better. Employees are more accountable to their colleagues than they are to a department head or a manager. Peer pressure is a powerful motivator in both teal and Agile organizations.

> So many companies say, "People are our biggest asset, and our people are at the core of our business," but then, when you look at the day-to-day functionality and company goals, you realize that statement is not true.
> —FABIOLA

People often ask me if it's possible for orange or amber organizations to evolve into a green or teal organization. The answer depends entirely on how people choose to behave. If over 50 percent of a population decides to get behind something or someone, the tide will turn in that population's direction. If the majority of employees within an organization decide what direction to head, I am hopeful that leadership will heed the call and listen to the staff. Change is certainly possible in theory, but it's another story in practice.

There is a growing curiosity about change because the old ways no longer work and people are frustrated. HR managers have started to look for solutions and explore new ways of working. When leaders and managers start to behave in accordance with Agile principles, the employees will follow suit and slowly, the entire organization will become more Agile. Its principles will seep into the culture.

THE NEW CEO

Executives and employees are craving more meaningful work environments, so what's the problem? How can we get everyone motivated to create these types of organizations?

The biggest challenge to allowing people to take responsibility for themselves is the culture of control that pervades so many organizations. It's a catch-22 because more control does not lead to better companies. In reality, control is demotivating. The more we try to control, the more we increase negativity, stress, and anxiety. Additionally, when the culture encourages instruction, approval, and reward, it actually discourages individuals from taking responsibility for their own behavior and performance.

If you're in a leadership role, how do you approach your position? Are you trying to keep tight reins on your employees? Do you control what they do and how they do it, or do you lead by explaining the *why*? Do you emphasize methods or intentions? What kind of results do you see? Are your people engaged in their work and consistently meeting or exceeding your expectations, or do you feel like you are herding cows through a tiny gate?

> If you talk about power, yeah, you can work with influencing. That's the way to work with power from an Agile leadership perspective. But what you need to let go of, which is often correlated with power as well, is control.
>
> —LEILA

"Control less; enable more" should be the new mantra of leadership. By enabling your staff, you foster collaboration toward a common agenda. Every leader needs to facilitate an environment where people are motivated to work toward shared goals. One does not need to be controlling to get the best out of people. An effective leader is one who inspires others to perform to the highest of their abilities, while also making them feel good about the work they're doing.

Innovation is about creativity and coming up with new solutions. It can only flourish in a safe environment, where people aren't afraid of the repercussions of failure and they trust their coworkers. With the rate of change in today's workplace environment, there is a constant need for new approaches.

The Chess Media Group in San Francisco compiled a list of the ten core skillsets tomorrow's leaders will need. That person

- Is a leader—not controlling, organizing, overseeing, or supervising.
- Follows from the front—removes roadblocks for employees, while empowering them to work in a way that makes them feel engaged.
- Understands technology—on top of what is happening in the world of technology.
- Leads by example—engages with employees, shares content, listens to what is going on in the organization, and is present.
- Embraces vulnerability—has the courage to show up and be seen. There can be zero innovation without vulnerability, which is about being human and connecting with other people.
- Believes in sharing and collective intelligence—taps into the wisdom, experiences, ideas, and knowledge of teams or the company as a whole.
- Is a fire starter—questions old truths all the time; experimentation is a manager's best friend.
- Gives real-time recognition and feedback.
- Is conscious of personal boundaries and encourages open access.
- Adapts to the future employee—instead of the other way around.

Leadership within organizations must change to accommodate the prevailing and increasing expectations of the workforce.

My generation, which grew up during the 1960s and 1970s, was made up of people happy simply to have a job out of college. Our goal was to get into a solid company and work our way up the food chain over time. As Bob Dylan said back in my day, "The times, they are a-changing."

> I think the most important trait of an Agile leader is to be able to know and apply the values, not the methods. Agile encourages a team focus instead of a very individual focus. Agile means not getting stuck in processes when you feel there are other needs from the people who are involved. For a leader, being able to work with higher-level goals and not getting into details is paramount, because you know that it's up to the team to handle the details. As a leader, I will provide guidance to help you reach your goals and desired solution.
>
> —LEILA

The standards for work are significantly higher than they were even fifteen years ago. Today's workforce has completely different expectations of employment. They will only work if the job gives their life meaning, and they expect constant feedback from their peer group. People new to the job market prefer unemployment to menial jobs. The labor force is younger and connected to each other globally through mobile technology. Plus, the workplace is more specialized.

Teams are increasingly virtual, so communication is even more important.

The new CEOs are able to accommodate the incoming workforce's expectations. They make quick decisions and cultivate a culture that supports flexibility, high-performing small teams, transparency, and access to information when needed. They're in a constant state of development and embrace change.

LEADERSHIP MATURITY FOR SELF-ORGANIZING TEAMS

Jonathan Reams is a teacher and researcher on leadership development at the Norwegian University of Science and Technology.[18] He's an expert in leadership maturity and has worked with a variety of organizations and individuals throughout the U.S., Canada, and Europe. He spoke at an Agile conference I organized recently and presented a unique leadership assessment method.

During an interactive exercise, Reams handed out ten cards. They were not in any particular order and they each contained random statements related to leadership. He asked each participant to put the cards in order from least mature leader

---

18 http://jonathanreams.com/about-me/

to most mature leader, according to the statements. I've saved you the trouble of having to do that on your own and present Reams' cards to you here, in the proper order.

Leadership Maturity #1

Q: What makes a good leader?

A: A follow-the-leader.

Q: What does a good follow-the-leader do?

A: Gives you a turn.

Q: Why is that good?

A: I like to be the leader.

Q: What do you like about being the leader?

A: I get to go first.

Leadership Maturity #2

Q: What makes a good leader?

A: I have a good wilderness club leader.

Q: What makes him a good leader?

A: He's really nice. He takes us camping and we do fun stuff. I got two new badges and I learned how to tie some cool knots.

Leadership Maturity #3

Q: What makes a good leader?

A: You mean like my coach?

Q: Yes. Is your coach a good leader?

A: Yes, mostly.

Q: What makes her a good leader?

A: She's a really good athlete and she bosses us around just the right amount.

Leadership Maturity #4

A good leader always tells the truth and has strong values. She always does what she says, and she does that so people will trust her. People like a leader they can trust.

Leadership Maturity #5

A good leader is someone who really knows his stuff. He's an expert and also knows how to get other people to do their best with decent bonuses for people who are the most productive.

Leadership Maturity #6

A good leader knows how to work with people, not just tell people what to do. This means he has to understand what makes different people tick so he can help them to do their best. There's a lot of give and take.

Leadership Maturity #7

A good leader knows how to balance the needs of the company with the needs of the employees. A good leader can find an optimal solution by listening to all perspectives and weighing alternatives.

Leadership Maturity #8

A good leader understands her organization's system. She knows all the people in her organization are part of that system. The best way to keep the system healthy is to get everyone on the same page. This means lots of dialogue and openness.

Leadership Maturity #9

A good leader can look beyond the present or a particular problem to see events from a broad, almost global perspective. He or she can stand outside of the system to view a problem from multiple perspectives.

Leadership Maturity #10

A good leader is a highly knowledgeable and an enormously competent servant to his or her organization, which he or she sees as a complex web of human beings whose activities are all directed toward the same mutually beneficial goal.

Leadership Maturity #10 represents the highest level of maturity possible. Its sentiment is in alignment with Bonnitta Roy's philosophy regarding Open Participatory Organizations (see interview with her at the end of the book). OPOs are united by common goals and values. All the rest takes care of itself when people are permitted to self-organize and self-manage.

> I think a lot of companies and organizational cultures, including lots of individuals, have a very strong feeling that to retain their power they have to keep everything to themselves, rather than sharing that information or power with others.
>
> —LEILA

The team discusses how they will reach goals. They select their own leader(s) for various initiatives, or they may choose not to have a leader. They may also choose to follow a lot of rules or not have any at all. The beauty of self-organizing teams is they decide how they will reach their goals that ultimately will lead to the fulfillment of the company vision.

Being in touch with one's own strengths and weaknesses breeds empathy in others and gives them the opportunity to lean in or fall back, depending on where the need is. I suggest true employee engagement, which comes from being recognized for who we are and appreciated for how we contribute based on our unique strengths.

> Employee engagement depends on moving away from micromanagement and moving toward engaging and empowering leadership. They need to be that engaging leader, and they must be learning, constantly improving, and adapting themselves as well. It's not enough that they just want to help their people get better. They have to strive to get better themselves first.
> —FABIOLA

One of the most underutilized approaches to creating high-performing teams is to provide an environment of psychological safety. We have already touched on the topic, but it deserves to be repeated. Few leaders recognize that psychological safety is just as important as physical safety, and therefore it is often overlooked. If the environment at work isn't one that feels safe for employees to share ideas, make suggestions, or address uncomfortable and outlandish notions, innovation will suffer. No one wants to make a wrong move or risk being laughed at. If the culture doesn't support openness and people behaving in full accordance with their primary motivators, there will be a drought of fresh ideas.

The different tendency toward a concern with physical safety over psychological safety struck me on a recent visit to see my brother, Olof, in Hong Kong. He is the project director for several large bridge projects around the islands of Hong Kong.

Olof brought me to work with him one day to show me what he was working on. Before taking me up on the bridge, he gave me a helmet, protection glasses, a neon-colored life vest, steel-toed shoes, and gloves. All of this was for my physical protection and all the workers had similar outfits. While most organizations are primarily concerned with physical safety, psychological safety should be treated with the same measure of caution and protection.

Charles Duhigg, the author of *Smarter, Faster, Better*, wrote an article for the *New York Times* called, "What Google Learned from Its Quest to Build the Perfect Team."[19] In it, Duhigg

---

19 https://centre.upeace.org/wp-content/uploads/2020/09/7.1-what-google-learnt.pdf

makes the argument that the most important precondition for high-performing teams is psychological safety. The teams that managed to provide it were the most effective and they outperformed the other teams in terms of results.

Organizations have traditionally built a wall between employee's personal lives and their business lives. Today's companies recognize that trying to separate the two is unrealistic and even harmful. We spend most of our waking hours at work or working on work. Work and life are constantly evolving and changing. The best and most rewarding approach to handling that change is to strengthen our resiliency and ability to adapt. By helping one another follow our hearts and using the strengths that make us each unique, there's greater collective appreciation for our accomplishments. At work and in life, you get what you give.

> We will always find heroes; we will always be fans of somebody. We will always find the ones who we look up to, who we will allow ourselves to be led by, who we think are amazing and believe in. That's in our biology.
> —RIINA

FROM→TO FOR AGILE LEADERSHIP

DIFFERENCE BETWEEN THE MANAGER AND THE AGILE PEOPLE COACH	
Traditional formal Manager	Agile People Coach
No or low competence in lean/agile	Deep comptence in lean/agile
Deep skills in some specialist area	Deep people skills
Process driven	People and purpose driven
Fixed mindset	Growth mindset
Command and control "I decide"	Empowerment and alignment "I facilitate"
Focusing heavily on numbers	Focusing more on people
Artificial harmony	Healthy conflict
Telling what to do	Story telling to inspire action
Judging employee in ratings	Coaching employees to perform
Local optimization	Global optimization
Deciding career paths	Mentoring growth
Carrots and sticks	Dialogue about intrinsic motivation
decision delay	Faster decentralized decision making
Speaking and proposing	Framing, probing and listening

CHAPTER 11

Agile Management

> *"Management is about human beings. Its task is to make people capable of joint performance... Management is the critical, determining factor."*
> —Peter Drucker

There is a tendency in the business community to blur the lines between leadership and management. The terms are often interchangeable in a hierarchical structure, but there is a clear line of demarcation. In traditional business models, "leadership" indicates the executive suite or the real decision makers. Management tends to represent the group of people who are responsible for ensuring that everyone else does what they are supposed to do to keep the wheels spinning.

> Many managers have been managers for several years and some people really didn't like the change. We were quite frank about that and said, "This is not going to fit all. If it doesn't fit you, maybe you should be somewhere else." We didn't put it that harshly, but that was definitely the message.
>
> —CECILIA

There is a distinct difference between leadership and management in Agile environments as well, although there is less rigidity. Both leadership and management must embrace the Agile principles of being flexible and adaptable, while motivating others to follow their lead. Both leadership and management roles are earned and not appointed. Agile leadership is about people: empowering them, letting them take control of decision making, choosing effectiveness, doing the right thing, and setting the direction.

We discussed Agile leadership practices in depth in the previous chapter. Now, I'd like to shift the focus over to Agile management, which focuses on tasks, speed, efficiency, good practices, and helping teams direct their energies and activities productively.

> We are facing a shift in paradigms toward a more transformative leadership where we have an interdependency and equality between manager and employee.
>
> However, administrative duties are weighing heavy on leaders' shoulders, as we have reduced the number of secretaries and administrators and put their tasks into an IT system that managers have to handle. The result is an overloaded manager, with little time to lead.
>
> —BJÖRN

There is often a big divide between what managers think matters to people and what actually does matter. Old management styles focus on bonus-driven systems based on performance metrics. Often, teams work in competitive environments that encourage winners and losers. Agile management focuses on work elements that resonate with employees, such as a shared vision and purpose, recognition, trust, and autonomy. These are the factors in a work environment that touch people at their core. However, everyone does not share values that resonate with the Agile mindset (see Chapter 9 for more information about individual values).

> The question is, Do we need a leader here? If this is an Agile organization or one moving toward Agile, do we need a leader? If yes, then why? Do your homework very thoroughly before just hiring a leader. The other thing is that I think it's ineffective to make these leadership traits or role model management rules. You create the leadership role of a company, but then you go away with the executive team and ask them, "What is a good leader?" That is the stupidest process I've ever heard of for finding good leaders.
>
> The second stupidest thing is to ask the people what kind of leaders they want. You will get a bucketful of requests close to Jesus. I've just done this with twelve people, and the list was four pages long. This is what we want from a good leader. No person can live up to that. It would be better to assess the good leaders who actually exist within the organization—in that context.
>
> —RIINA

According to Jurgen Appelo, the creator of Management 3.0, the origin of the verb "to manage" can be traced backed to the Italian word *maneggiare*, which means to handle and train. It was historically associated with horse training, which is appropriate because, traditionally, the role of management has been to take care of a living system. The great Austrian management consultant, educator, and author, Peter Drucker, said, "Management is critical for organizations to survive, but learning how to manage is not exclusive to managers." Everyone on the team must adopt a management mindset to take care of the organization and make decisions that will have the best possible outcome for it.

Drucker's observation is applicable to testing in software development. There are specialists who are experts in testing methods, but everyone in development needs to adopt a testing mentality. The same can be said for management. Everyone on the team needs to think and behave like a manager. It's not reserved for a select few. Managing is everyone's responsibility.

MANAGEMENT 3.0

Management 3.0 is a movement of innovation, leadership, and management. It is redefining the definition of leadership with management as a group responsibility. It's about working together to find the most efficient way for a business to achieve its goals while maintaining the happiness of workers as a priority.[20]

---

20 https://management30.com/learn/

Appelo says, "Management is too important to be left to the managers!" This sentiment emphasizes why management needs to be evenly distributed between everyone on the team. Instead of less management, as some theories advocate, Agile and Management 3.0 call for *more management* so that everyone in the organization can take on more responsibility.

Appelo's theory suggests that management, and by that he means everyone within the organization, redirects his or her energies to a few core competencies. To illustrate those competencies, he unveiled an illustrative tree named "Marty, the Management Monster." Its design is inspired by Marty Feldman, the 1970s British comedian and actor, who was famous for his large, bulbous eyes.

The first branch on the Marty tree is to *energize the people* because people are the most important part of an organization. Managers need to focus their activity on keeping people actively and creatively engaged and motivated. Many organizations say they do this, but in practice, they don't. It sounds nice to say, "people are our most valuable asset," or, "our people mean everything to us." They may have the best intentions to adopt that mindset, but their behavior doesn't support the statement. Actions speak louder than words, so energizing people is a behavior that should be modeled until it infiltrates the organization and everyone naturally behaves in a way that energizes others.

To promote the action of energizing people, Appelo recommends an exercise called "Moving Motivators." It's a simplification of the teachings of Daniel Pink, author of *Drive*; Richard Ryan and Edward Deci (selfdeterminationtheory.org); and Steven Reiss, creator of the Reiss Motivation Profile. The exercise involves a card game, in which the participant works with ten cards, each with a value statement on them, and then organizes them in order from what is most to least important to them, personally.

The second core competency in Management 3.0 is to *empower teams*. As discussed, in Agile supported workplaces, teams begin to self-direct and self-organize. In order to do so, people must feel free, which means they are in a trusting environment where they are empowered to act in accordance with their natural strengths and interests.

For example, when Ford owned Volvo from 1999 to 2010, it operated by the same tried and true processes and procedures Ford is well-known for creating. The systems were locked down tight, and there were checklists, processes, systems, and reporting structures for every function and deliverable within the business.

When Volvo was sold to the Chinese and Ford took their systems and structures with them, the employees and managers went through a few years of chaos as they struggled to regain their footing and figure out how to best to function and perform. They went from total order and structure to the opposite end of the spectrum. They didn't know how much structure they should have, what the limitations were, or how to find a balance between the lack of structure and the need for direction. Gradually, Volvo implemented just enough structure and found a balance that was appropriate for the organization. There is a word in Swedish, *lagom*, which means "just right" and is appropriate in this context.

A company can thrive when it has just the right blend of structure and chaos, which is in between over-structured and complete disaster. A little bit of structure is necessary to focus on productive, creative work, but too much structure stifles creativity. The balance is crucial and different for each company, depending on the nature of the business, the culture, and the people who work there—just to mention a few variables that would affect the "sweet spot" for a particular organization.

> You create boundaries and a clear vision of where we want to go. You are very clear on the kind of resources available, and you give people the freedom to learn.
> —RIINA

The next branch on the Marty tree is to *align constraints*. This relates to the importance of setting goals and rules to improve performance. Employees need to understand the *why* behind what they do, and they also need to know what the rules of the game are. Most organizations have goals, and each individual should have them too. Aligning constraints is about recognizing the boundaries around those goals and devising a cohesive way to cope with them. It's a clear way of communicating that says, "This is what we want to do, this is how far we need to go, and these are our limitations. How can we get where we need to go, given what we've got, and with the rules that apply in our reality?"

The practice of aligning constraints is necessary to protect people and the resources they share. It gives everyone a clear purpose with defined goals and parameters. How they choose to operate and behave individually and as a team within those borders is determined according to the dynamics of each group.

It's important for managers to focus on *developing competence*. Teams cannot achieve their goals unless its members are capable enough to complete the necessary tasks and experiment to find solutions. Therefore, managers need to ensure everyone learns what they need to learn to succeed. This could mean making certain courses or conferences available to team members or sharing other educational resources. Discussing each individual's need for the necessary competence development is time well invested for a manager.

Growing and nurturing the structure of the organization is another branch on the management tree. Many teams operate within the context of complex organizations; therefore, corporate structures that enhance communication are encouraged, especially within fast-growing companies.

Finally, the last task on Marty the Management Monster's tree is to *improve everything all the time*. It may sound like an overwhelming assignment, but managers should always look for ways to get better across all channels. Continuous improvement requires continuous learning and the opportunity to experiment and make small, calculated mistakes.

> Leadership has to change, but if the expectations, the systems, and the structures around leadership aren't changing, leadership is not going to change.
> —RIINA

THE SEVEN LEVELS OF DELEGATION

In Agile organizations, the goal is to spread management responsibilities as much as possible to team members. To do so effectively, people need to take on responsibilities that are typically associated with management positions. It's about taking ownership and sharing in decisions, and, according to Management 3.0, there are seven different levels of management delegation:

- Tell: Telling someone what to do falls under the traditional umbrella of management. The manager makes the decision and then tells others what it is. There is little room for debate or negotiation.
- Sell: This is when the manager attempts to convince others that the decision he or she is making is a good one and, therefore, they should buy into it.

- Consult: Consulting is when the manager collects input from the team before making a decision.
- Agree: Agreement implies there is consensus about the decision between the manager and the team, or the decision is made together. This is the most difficult of the seven levels because it requires the most time.
- Advise: This is when the manager influences the decision made by the team.
- Inquire: Once the team has made the decision, the manager asks for feedback and insight into the decision.
- Delegate: The manager has zero influence on the decision. It is made entirely by the team.

These seven layers of delegation are fundamental for understanding the techniques organizations can use to practice more effective delegation.

To help determine what level is appropriate for every key decision, play Delegation Poker from Management 3.0. It's briefly described in the next chapter, but you can also read more at management30.com.

> We have to unlearn jumping in and telling people what to do. We have to stop dictating what people are supposed to do, and instead, work on empowering them.
> —FABIOLA

FIND THE BALANCE

Keep your eyes open to opportunities for improvement and encourage downtime. There is a famous story from Google, which has always celebrated an 80/20 approach to work. They advocate that 20 percent of someone's time should be used for relaxation or exploration. One of their employees invented Gmail during his 20 percent time away from work, and, since then, the concept of rest or exploration time has spread to many other organizations. Today, they have abandoned the 80/20 approach in favor of new and better ways of working; all in the spirit of always experimenting and improving.

The Gmail story proves that good things happen when you allow people to relax into their creative headspace. It's a more productive approach than having employees fill out forms, adhere to checklists, and constantly report on their progress. When there is trust, there is no need for constant reporting anyway. The only reason for all the reporting is to maintain control, and in Agile management, control is distributed. When people are given the opportunity to take responsibility for themselves, they are empowered and don't need to be monitored every five minutes.

Agile is useful and productive for finding the balance between too much order and not enough. I recently worked with a company that fell onto the chaos end of the spectrum. Casumo is an online casino founded by two Swedish guys with offices in Malta. Founded in 2012, the company is still relatively young. When I was first contacted, the HR department informed me they didn't have any processes or structure. They approached project flow in an ad hoc manner and there was no accountability. The lack of control was too extreme to foster an environment of productivity.

Casumo needed to find a way to evaluate the work they were doing from a retrospective viewpoint. Most of the companies I work with are too orderly and need to stop certain behaviors. Casumo was too loose and needed to bring structure to their workflow. Using Agile principles and tools, we were able to find the right balance to get the company into a more productive, operational flow.

> The leadership can't adjust and adapt before the expectations are adjusted. Those expectations come from the owners.
>
> —RIINA

Jurgen Appelo contends, "Managers let self-organization (anarchy) do useful work while steering the system toward valuable results."[21] How do we grow a self-organizing system? Kevin Kelly, author of *Out of Control: The New Biology of Machines, Social Systems, and the Economic World*, expands

---

21 https://www.slideshare.net/jurgenappelo/agile-management-authority-delegation

on this idea. He says complex systems are more than the sum of their parts. Everything happens at once across all channels and can't be governed by a single, central authority. Therefore, governance must be spread among all the parts.

> You think if you micromanage people, they will improve, perform great, and everything will be fine. It's hard to let go of that old pattern. The new pattern is trust, and trust is very hard. They say, "Okay, yes. We trust people to do the right thing," but then, of course, we have all these HR systems, reporting systems, legal systems, and finance systems in place that force managers to be micromanagers. They think they must report information in a specific way, but they work around budgets, so we're not really helping them to become engaging leaders.
>
> —FABIOLA

When Agile is introduced to managers, they fear they will become powerless if they surrender authority. Managers who fear powerlessness fail to understand they are not dealing with a zero-sum game. Business organizations should not be run the same way as judicial courts or elections. Holding onto an "I win, you lose" mentality does not serve the greater good of the team or the company.

Managers become *more* powerful once they give power to others, or delegate responsibility. When power is distributed, we all win. We need to adapt practices that best serve the social networks, free markets, and teams we're a part of, because there is a place for everyone. We should not be in competition with each other when we're all working toward the same goal. Work is not about the individual; it's about the team.

> I think sometimes it's harder for top management to change, because they've done something one way for many years and they've done it successfully. They are bright people who have been working in successful companies doing their thing, and it has always worked. Now, suddenly, they are asked to do something new. It's extremely hard to keep making changes when you're used to doing something another way. We know that improvement depends on change, but it's still very hard.
>
> —CECILIA

Whenever I introduce different Agile tools and principles to an organization, I become more powerful in the eyes of the people who are learning about it. Top management likes the practice and can easily see the results, and therefore, my value goes up from their perspectives. I've introduced a tool that has the power to change the organization in a powerful way. Even though I am not personally driven by power, getting some is a side benefit of sharing knowledge. In a non-zero-sum game, powerful teams cause managers to look more powerful.

The fundamental anchor of a strong team is trust. Without it, there is no confidence within the team and people second-guess themselves at every turn. A manager needs to work on creating trust in order to foster strong teams. Managers are the key ingredient to creating strong, self-organizing, high-performing teams.

> I can give you an example of a telecommunication company. They wanted to run in an Agile way. It was a group of sixty people, so it gave us a couple of nice-sized teams. The way we did it, we put them all into one room. We had management there to explain to them what was going on, and why we were doing it. Then, we explained the specific guidelines of what each team would cover. We told them the types of skills we needed to have, and we created a maximum number of people that would comprise each team. We developed a list of needed skills, each member's capabilities, and the main goal of that team. They wanted to know why we created a specific team and what they would be doing.

We told them, "It's self-organizing. You organize yourself. We're going to come back in thirty minutes and see what you have." Guess what happened during that first round? Nothing. They were like, "We don't know how to do this," so we explained the exercise again and left again. When we came back for the second time, they had organized themselves. The interesting part was it was an international team. They were all at the same location, and they had certain teams that formed their own language and culture, which was very interesting.

Management was very worried that people would just get together, but that's not what happened. People really had a dialogue. They said, "I would really love to have you on my team, but because we have the same background, maybe it's better if you go to a different team and we can liaise." They had an honest discussion and moved people around. The result was just fantastic.

We didn't tell people before we did the exercise why they were doing it, but it was a team-building exercise. We said to the manager, "If you had to put the teams together, how would you do it?" Eighty percent of the teams were exactly the way management would have structured them, and some of them were surprises. But when people explained why they put the teams together, management was impressed. "That's really cool. We wouldn't have thought of that." It was a good thing, because people decided for themselves to change the team. It was not management coming in and directing them. They decided that for themselves.

—FABIOLA

CHAPTER 12

Agile Tools

> *"Agility is the ability to both create and respond to change in order to profit in a turbulent business environment."*
> —Jim Highsmith

Agile is about being able to adapt to change—specifically, the changing needs of the customer. The company must understand what creates the most value for the customer and strive to deliver it above all else.

> I would start with some kind of organizational and transparent communication channel, such as Slack or Yammer, to support people and the network. A vehicle of this nature would allow everyone in the organization to talk, learn, and share information.
>
> —RIINA

Rather than rely on a fixed set of rules, Agile relies on its own principles[22] as the guide. A company can choose the degree to which the principles apply to the organization. There are also a series of tools and frameworks that can be used to identify company priorities, workflow, and create more customer value. This chapter examines some of the most popular Agile tools.

Note: If you already know about Agile tools, you may want to skip ahead.

> We need tools and we need structure, but the most important element is to simplify the tools we have and use. The tools the HR manager implements should make it easier for the employee and the leader to do their job. All too often, we implement tools because we want to control, for example, performance appraisals.
> —CECILIA

SCRUM

Scrum is one of the oldest and best-known Agile tools, though it is losing in importance as new, more modern methods are gaining attention. However, I like the simplicity and the straightforward, clear approach of Scrum, and still find it very useful. It emphasizes the implementation of short, iterative

---

22 refer to Chapter 1: The Agile Principles

development cycles. The idea is to reduce complexity and focus on building products and services that directly meet the customer's needs. Providing value for the customer is the primary goal and transparency, evaluation, and continuous improvement is built in in the form of daily stand-ups and retrospectives.

> The role of HR is a catalyst instead of a central, decision-making, control function because many traditional HR tasks are actually taken up by the teams, the coaches, and the Agile process. You don't need once-a-year-feedback discussions anymore, because you have ongoing feedback in the sprint cycles. You don't need to implement target setting once a year anymore, either, because you have ongoing target setting and iterations in the sprint cycles.
>
> —RIINA

Like everything within Agile, Scrum was born from software development practices, but it has much wider applications as well. The focus is on working in short sprints, which minimizes risk and expenditure. Short work cycles ensure constant improvement, quick learning, and encourage listening to and utilizing customer feedback.

Tip: To evaluate the experience of recruiting an applicant, you can get their view and take on it, which allows you to build and improve the process. For example, I've used it in onboarding. You can see the onboarding period as a sprint; and, if that onboarding period is about four months, after those four months have gone by, you have a measurement to evaluate the experience of the onboarding process. You can, of course, do the same thing while recruiting.

—LEILA

Ideally, the team should be self-managed, which means they must decide how to best approach each sprint, what the workload looks like, and who does what. Scrum's values include focus, courage, openness, commitment, and respect.

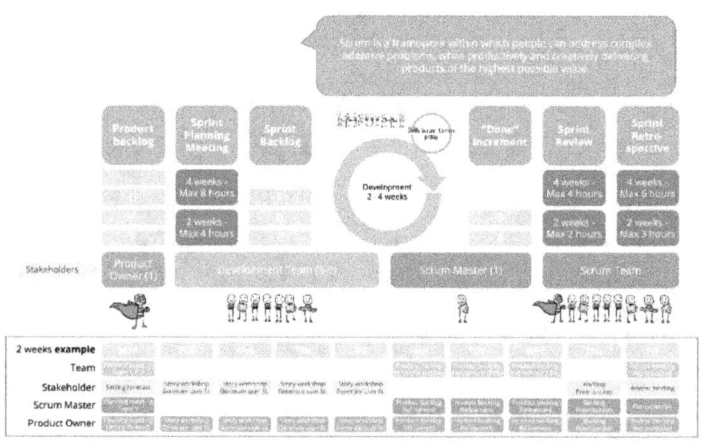

The development team is responsible for building the product. They are doing the real work and solving problems as they occur. They determine exactly what the output from their team will be. Typically, the development team is self-organizing, and ideally has between five and nine people.

All team members share responsibility for the results of their efforts. The team decides how work is performed and tasks are dispersed. Fixed project roles do not occur in Scrum development teams. Work is accomplished fluidly and they strive to accomplish a solution, and everyone is able to switch tasks and learn new skills from each other. Among Agile practitioners, this fluid type of employee is commonly referred to as "T-shaped." As described earlier (repetition is the mother of skill), they can take on many roles and have a broad set of competencies. Creating T-shaped employees has many advantages and it creates flexibility:

- For the individual: increases the possibility of broadening or deepening their knowledge, depending on what they are interested in.
- For the team: creates increased flexibility as to which tasks people can accomplish. Competency deepens when team members try out many different tasks and learn from each other.
- For the organization: makes it more adaptable, minimizes the risk for bottlenecks and eliminates unnecessary termination, as people can always take on another role.

The **Product owner** leads the Scrum team. This person owns the product backlog, which is a list of features, goals, or to-do items that constantly shift based on feedback from the various stakeholders. The product owner is also responsible for the overarching vision for the product, so they make sure the development team is working on the right initiatives. Typically, the product owner is someone with a lot of contacts, connections, and information. He or she has deep knowledge of the business and a wide network of people to tap into.

Often, there is a **Scrum master** who helps to facilitate the Scrum process. This person is a combination of a coach, a fixer, and a protector. It's their job to make sure the team isn't disturbed or distracted while they are working on a sprint. The Scrum master ensures the team has all of the prerequisites necessary to succeed, and that product development is moving toward the goals through sprint reviews and retrospectives. Project roles are clearly defined for the product owner and the Scrum master, but they can also work on other tasks with the rest of the team members.

An Agile **Scrum team** conducts *sprint-planning meetings* where they select as much as they think they can handle from the product backlog and get to work on their sprint. A sprint may last a week, or it could last up to four weeks (which is the length of sprints in "vintage Scrum," as Jurgen Appelo puts it). The time depends largely on what the team is trying to accomplish and the function (HR, IT, or some cross-functional team) of the task. During the most recent years, the sprints have had a tendency to become shorter and shorter, giving room for new ways of working, with continuous delivery as the standard.

During a one- to four-week sprint, the team meets regularly at daily stand-up meetings. These meetings are quick and efficient and never last longer than fifteen minutes. This regroup gives each team member an opportunity to quickly relay information about what they're working on, share their progress and challenges, and ask for help. The daily stand-up meeting requires 100 percent transparency and vulnerability, which takes a lot of courage.

> I constantly use a set of core tools from the Agile methods that are really helpful. I think stand-ups are great. It's a way of staying synchronized by having transparent communication and not wasting too much time. Stand-ups shouldn't be longer than the time it takes you to stand up and make a statement. That's the key. When you're having a one-hour meeting, it's not a stand-up.
>
> —LEILA

Once the sprint is over, the team presents the result to the customer in a *sprint demo meeting,* where the customer gives feedback that goes into the backlog. Then the team meets again for a sprint review or sprint demo. In the very first sprint, the goal is to produce an MVP, or *minimum viable product,* to share with the customer and solicit feedback. The MVP is the least possible "thing" that a team can deliver to the internal or external customer that creates some sort of value. It's used as a measurement to gauge what the customer is looking for in terms of value. If the customer likes the MVP, then the company can continue to build on it.

> Another tool or way of working is through retrospectives. It's a fantastic way of deepening insights and learning, while taking time to reflect on how those efforts turned out. The retrospective is a very good tool.
>
> —LEILA

At the end of each sprint, the team meets for a sprint *retrospective* to examine what worked and what didn't. They'll look at areas that can be improved, changed, or introduced for the next sprint. They'll also ask, What should we continue, stop, or start doing? These questions are the basis for continuous learning and improvement.

> For us, there are four value streams—culture, talent, engagement, and performance flow. We then organize HR according to those streams. It's the same way we work with any other Agile team, and then of course, they work with Agile practices. Some of them do Scrum, and some use a Kanban Board. It's up to us to see what works best for the team, and we organize people around values and place them in interdisciplinary teams. That is definitely a change, but it helps people understand how to translate those Agile values into the HR practices.
>
> —FABIOLA

Another tool within Scrum is the writing of "epics," or user stories, which help to identify the *who,* the *what,* and the *why* behind the product.

> User stories are a fantastic way to make sure you're creating the most value, which eliminates the need to guess what you should do. Instead, you gather your user stories and, from there, you can do a first release and then improve it. Then, gather more user stories and do a second release.
>
> —LEILA

The product backlog is an excellent resource for high-level, bare-bones user stories. A more in-depth story examines—from the user's perspective—what exactly they want to be able to do with the product or service in development. It could be as straightforward as stating, "As a manager, I want to be able to give my employees feedback in real time to increase their engagement." The template of creating a user story looks like this:

In the role of x, I want y, so that z.

In the above template, you exchange the x, y, and z for the *who*, *what*, and *why*, just like in the example above.

> I think the concept is embedded if you work in the Agile way. If you work in Scrum, you have your plannings that allow you to go in with your story. That's inspiring. People want to reach for the goal and they give you the commitment. They assess through the stories they buy, or just the way it points, so you have the commitment that people want to do their best.
> —FABIOLA

Scrum utilizes a fixed structure and a specific procedure. It's not an ad hoc tool; it's a very focused way of approaching work. There are a few simple rules to follow, but the rules and tools serve to strengthen and improve Agile principles and values. Approaching work in this manner promotes openness, commitment, and respect.

Lately, Scrum is used less by software development teams. It's being replaced by DevOps (development and operations) and continuous delivery, which has the same values, but without the sprints. Any other department can still use Scrum when it makes sense to define smaller pieces of work that should be delivered iteratively with internal or external customers reviewing at specific intervals.

PLANNING POKER

Planning poker is another consensus-based technique for estimating user stories in a relative way. Instead of measuring a project or product development by time, planning poker assesses it by points. How many points is the user story worth in relation to the other user stories in the project backlog?

Members of the group make estimates by playing numbered cards facedown on the table, instead of speaking them aloud. The cards are revealed, and the estimates are then discussed. By hiding the figures in this way, the group can avoid the cognitive bias, where the first number spoken aloud sets a precedent for subsequent estimates.

When people are not affected by other opinions, it's easier for them to make their own independent assessments. One person might play a "1," while someone else might play a "20," thereby illuminating how different two people perceive the same user story to be. It helps to prioritize tasks when the group can have an open discussion about why they rated the user story the way they did. Then, they play again to see if they have come any closer to each other. It's one approach to overcoming a difference and getting the best estimate for a story.

DELEGATION POKER

A variant of poker can also be used for delegation. I played this game with a pharmaceutical company recently and the results were highly effective. First, we started by writing down a list of decisions the team was facing. Then we thought about what level we would like the team to make this decision on. We used the same levels as in the seven levels of delegation in Chapter 11.

At the top of the list was a decision the organization faced regarding moving to a new office building. Only top-level management was involved in this decision; the team did not have a say. On the other end of the spectrum was a decision regarding guidelines for how teams should work together every day, which was entirely up to the team to decide. These two decisions demonstrate the level of extremes that can exist when it comes to team involvement.

Delegation Poker from Management 3.0 is a fun game that you can read more about or can be downloaded for free from management30.com. As I am a facilitator in and also a co-owner of Management 3.0, I use it frequently with my customers when they want to try a fun, engaging, and powerful tool to demonstrate how to work with delegating decisions in their team. It can be played with the team that you're managing or with other managers to decide around recommendations for delegating more decision power to employees.

SET-BASED DESIGN

Another tool is called set-based design. It originated from Toyota in a new car model design development project. It may be more of a lean tool than Agile, although I would say it's still part of the Agile family of methods and tools. At the beginning of a new project, it's impossible to know which design will unfold in the best way. Instead of concentrating on just one plan, set-based design explores several different design paths simultaneously.

Let's say an organization starts down eight different design tracks. After a sprint cycle, the company will have gathered enough information to be able to determine which of those tracks are weak and should be eliminated. The strong candidates move on to the next phase of development.

A set-based approach is like a contest. It's a way of learning by doing. By collecting information, an organization is able to identify which path is the best one in a short period of time. Instead of expending too much energy or time up front and stalling out, various teams simply start work. Through work, they can quickly ascertain whether they're heading in the right direction.

KANBAN

> Many domains in Agile recruiting can be your starting point for using Kanbans or Scrum teams for the recruitment process. Then, you can make a scalable recruitment process so your teams can recruit themselves. They have all the services available to start.
> —RIINA

Kanban is another concept borrowed from Toyota. In Japanese, it simply means "billboard." It's a manufacturing system focused on "the art of finalizing." The idea is that you can deliver a product according to plan, shorten the lead-time, and communicate faster and clearer by focusing on one task at a time. Kanban stems from the lean philosophy of visually identifying bottlenecks.

Kanban starts with a board on the wall, or a computer screen, with a list of tasks. That list is referred to as the project backlog. The tasks flow in three columns from left to right. Each column represents where the tasks are in the production flow: to do, doing, and done.

The popular, web-based tool, Trello, is essentially a digital Kanban board. Trello itself is based on the concept of Post-it® Notes, each note containing a task or a to-do item. As the tasks move closer to completion, they are also moved on the Kanban board. It's a visual method of tracking progress. During the daily stand-up meeting, team members gather in front of the Kanban board and physically move their tasks from one column to the next. They might move a task from the to-do column to the doing column as work is distributed and eventually completed.

Agile software companies promote better communication through visual project management. They are a tremendous resource for the various Agile methods and tools we've discussed here.

> Various tech solutions and applications for peer review exist, which you can use for feedback or target setting. It's not the tool that is important; it's what you want to achieve with it.
>
> —RIINA

THE ADVANTAGES OF AGILE

The advantages of Agile organizations are abundant. Agile companies encourage autonomy, which allows for increased employee engagement.

There is high visibility throughout project cycles due to the use of daily stand-up meetings. Shorter feedback loops lead to reduced risk and increased learning. Dividing work into sprints allows the organization to deliver value regularly to the customer and get results faster. Continuous customer contact through real-time demos allows for immediate solutions to complex projects. The larger a project is and the more people involved, the more complex it becomes and the higher the degree of uncertainty there is about the outcome.

Agile was built, in part, on the complexity theory, which is a branch of science that deals with complex systems. For example, a human society or a living, molecular cell represents a complex system. Interaction within the system leads to self-organization and dynamic adaptation that differentiates the complex "thing" (i.e., the person or the cell) from a static "thing," such as a desk or a book. A species adapts to the conditions; it begins to move in harmony as a unit. Complex systems tend to be spontaneous, disordered, and vibrant, especially on the brink of chaos.

Begin by asking, How complex is the task at hand? For example, fixing a bike is a relatively simple task, but fixing a wristwatch is highly complicated. There are many small, interdependent parts and putting them together in the correct way requires specific knowledge. Therefore, fixing a wristwatch is complicated, but it is not complex.

For example, complexity comes into play when dealing with people and relationships. People are not predictable, so you don't know exactly what's going to happen next. There is a high degree of uncertainty with people. The same is true with the stock market—nobody can predict what is going to happen with a great deal of certainty. When things become too uncertain, we veer toward anarchy, which leads to chaos. The concept of the complexity theory is beyond the scope of this book, but there are several interesting writers who have written about the topic—Dave Snowden, among others.

Agile is suitable in complex situations and actually prevents them from tipping over into anarchy. Clear boundaries and a few simple rules give the stability we need to feel secure.

It also allows the freedom of movement that is necessary for optimizing innovation and creativity.

One of the big misconceptions is that Agile organizations have no structure, no bosses, and no documentation—the very picture of anarchy. In fact, Agile organizations have the ability to both create change and respond to it. They are constantly balancing between flexibility and stability. There may be a need for stability in one part of the organization, while another part of the organization needs flexibility. The approach depends on the given circumstances and the tasks at hand.

People tend to assume that Agile lacks long-term vision because work is not planned months or years in advance. However, long-term vision is precisely what drives work. Goals do not change often, but the methods by which goals are achieved are constantly in flux. Critically, Agile is not a method—it is a way of thinking according to a set of values. Agile is a mindset.

> Being authentic is what contributes most to engagement. I think if I had to name one thing it would be the idea of being authentic. If you can showcase your passion and be authentic about it, it will catch on and people will feel the same. By being authentic, you will inspire them and they will engage.
>
> —FABIOLA

AGILE PRINCIPLES

- Transparency
- Customer value
- Self-organization
- Teamwork
- Colocation
- Face-to-face communication
- Continuous learning
- Continuous improvement
- Short feedback loops
- Cross-functional work
- Collaboration
- Experimentation (trial and error)
- Visualization
- (Find additional principles listed at the end of this book)

> The general rule or idea we have about transparency is that everything is transparent, unless we say it's not.
> —LEILA

CHAPTER 13

Employee Engagement

> *"When people go to work, they shouldn't have to leave their hearts at home."*
> —Betty Bender

The phrase "employee engagement" has been buzzing around HR circles for decades. Although it's something employers would like to ensure, how exactly is it defined? Is engagement about being satisfied with one's work or is it about making a contribution to a bigger picture? Is it about personal happiness or a healthy company bottom line?

> We talk a lot about engagement, and that people are the most important part of the organization, but then when we look at the realities in organizations, that doesn't always translate. It's the same with corporate values. They don't always translate into what people are doing on a day-to-day basis. With Agile HR, we can create a different environment, and we can interact with people differently. It allows us to really shape those engaging places of work, and we will know whether engagement, at the end of the day, has had positive effects on our bottom line. We will better understand how it reduces stress in people, about health issues, and much more, so we have a higher return on investment.
>
> —FABIOLA

At Agile People in Sweden, we take the whole person into account. We view employee engagement as an equation between personal satisfaction and organizational contribution. Employee satisfaction is about happy people who feel good about going to work, who enjoy their manager and coworkers and look forward to being in their work environment. Much of this satisfaction depends on the individual's personal values and basic desires as illustrated through the Reiss Profile and an alignment with the work atmosphere. It's also important that people work toward fulfilling the organization's goals by accomplishing work-related tasks. Both elements must be present for dedicated, engaged employees.

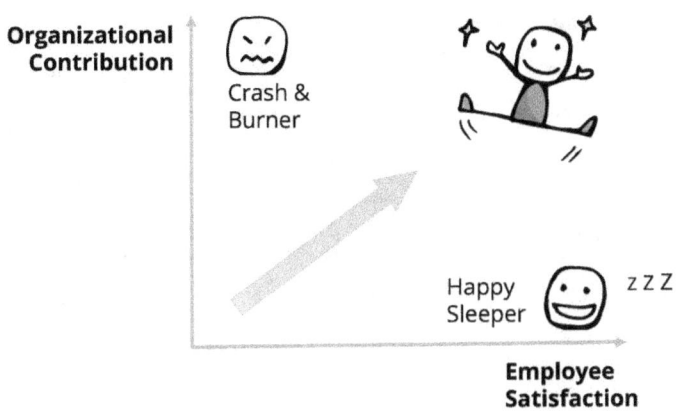

People can be very happy at work, but contribute little to the big picture. Perhaps they enjoy their colleagues and have a lot of fun joking around the water cooler, but aren't terribly productive. There are others who contribute a great deal to the company, but never engage with their coworkers or participate in team events. Perhaps they consistently meet their strategic goals, but they aren't involved in the spirit or culture of the organization. Neither of these types has staying power. The social butterflies tend to flap their wings straight out of the building and the workaholics tend to crash and burn.

> Employee engagement and motivation are very personal. There might be things that are relevant for all people, and I believe that comes from newer science, for example, the SCARF model in neuroscience (discussed in Chapter 14). But I think it's a narrow way of thinking about motivation. Even if you were the most engaged, the most creative, and the most competent person on earth, if you were put in a situation in Africa where you didn't have electricity, you basically couldn't do anything. Enablement is just as important.
>
> —RIINA

Productive employee engagement is critical to an organization's success for many reasons: It leads to an easier work and project flow, and it has a circular, continuous, and positive impact. Employees take better care of the customers when they come to work happy and ready to perform to the best of their abilities.

Happy employees lead to happy customers, which lead to happy profit margins and the fulfillment of the company's higher purpose. A healthy cash flow means the company is able to provide the type of environment that leads to happier employees, such as a bustling cafeteria with free, healthy food and yoga classes, and options that speak to employees' primary drives. Cash allows for the provision of the prerequisites that keep people motivated and engaged, and the circle of positivity continues. The more positive circles the company creates, the stronger the bonds.

> The focus has to be on the team. We prefer success sharing or contribution to incentives. Of course, if you're successful as a whole organization, you can let people share in that success and give back to the people.
>
> —FABIOLA

THE STATE OF THE GLOBAL WORKFORCE

From 2011 to 2012, Gallop conducted a global investigation into employee engagement called the "State of the Global Workplace." The company presented 230,000 people from different industries across 142 countries with the same twelve statements and asked them to rate their responses.

- I know what is expected of me at work.
- I have the materials and equipment I need to do my work right.
- At work, I have the opportunity to do what I do best every day.
- In the last seven days, I have received recognition or praise for doing good work.
- My supervisor, or someone at work, seems to care about me as a person.
- There is someone at work who encourages my development.
- At work, my opinions seem to count.
- The mission or purpose at my company makes me feel my job is important.
- My associates or fellow employees are committed to doing quality work.
- I have a best friend at work.
- In the last six months, someone at work has talked to me about my progress.
- This last year, I have had opportunities at work to learn and grow.

The statements asked for clarity around goals, growth and development opportunities, feedback cycles, and even friendships in the workplace. The goal was to gauge the level of employee engagement across the map. The results were alarming:

- Only 13 percent of participants are engaged at work.
- 63 percent of participants were indifferent about their work.
- 24 percent of participants were actively disengaged in work.

Engaged employees feel a connection to their companies. They go to work with passion and enthusiasm. They drive innovation and move the organization forward.

Non-engaged employees have essentially checked out. They're sleepwalking through their days. They put in the time, but not the energy or the passion. Mainly, they're waiting to leave for lunch or for five o'clock to roll around. Gallup broke its findings down by country. Great Britain suffers from a 60 percent non-engaged workforce, but the Dutch win the race with 80 percent.

Actively disengaged employees are the real morale killers in an organization. They're not just unhappy at work, they vocalize it and undermine the accomplishments of others to soothe their own misery. They cause damage to their internal teams, the external relationships with customers, and the overall organizational goals. In Britain, 21 percent of employees are actively disengaged, which winds up costing employers up to 8.3 billion pounds a year in damages through lost wages, time, product, or customers.

Part of the reason the disengagement problem is so widespread is because very few employees understand what is expected of them to achieve the company's goals. The priorities and processes are unclear. What are the company goals? What should employees prioritize? For some reason, it is very difficult to answer these simple questions. Every organization must be clear on their goals and priorities.

THE EMPLOYEE EVOLUTION

> Milleninals have indeed changed an organization's behavior. For instance, they know how to communicate, and they have different ways of communicating. They have different ways of seeing how status is formed. They have different ways of sharing information and realize that it is a better thing to share than to keep. They have very high expectations of themselves, their learning abilities, and their bosses.
>
> —RIINA

The last twenty years have seen many changes in both workforce expectations and the environment of the workplace. There's been an increase in the mobility of the talent pool. With connectivity at an all-time high, working remotely is the new reality for today's corporations. The younger generation of employees expects flexibility and choices when it comes to where and how they work. Employers need to keep up with the trends and remain attractive.

It's not your father's office space anymore. The current workforce is global, connected, mobile, transient, and multi-generational. They expect workplaces that are transparent, dynamic, specialized, interconnected, and performance driven. The world is moving toward a borderless existence, meaning people are no longer confined to their offices. They can work anywhere in the world, any time of day or night, and however they choose. This means an increasingly autonomous workforce, which Agile fully supports. Where there is trust, there is autonomy, and where there is autonomy, there is productivity.

> I would say that some employees, especially the millennials—but also the generation before the millennials—are in many ways ahead of management and the company. Compare that to other employees who are extremely behind. It depends on who they are as people, what age they are, and it also depends on what field they are in. If you're in cyber security, you're probably going to be less adaptive to the new changes; but, if you're working within user experience projects, well, then you're going to be ahead.
>
> —CECILIA

Increasingly, new companies pop up without physical office space. These new businesses recognize that their staff doesn't want to connect in an office; they would prefer to connect online, through digital collaboration channels such as Slack or Zoom. Happy Melly, an entrepreneurial networking resource started by Management 3.0 founder, Jurgen Appelo, is one such organization. Buffer, a social media management software tool, is another such company. They have a modern approach to work and their staff members are located all over the world.

Today's workforce needs to know the *why* behind what they are doing. Little children ask why all the time; but, as we get older, we start to accept what we're told without questioning it. We need to get back to our roots, to our base instincts, and question what we're doing. What difference does it make? How will it satisfy me? What can I do to make this situation better? Thankfully, the Reiss Motivational Profile helps us to find out what our inner drives are, but we also need to question why we do what we do within our organizations.

We have an obligation to ourselves, as members of the global workforce, to ask *why*. Leaders and managers also have a responsibility to explain to their employees *what* the company goals are and *how* they fit into the big picture.

should base the discussion on when we involve managers and employees.
- Involve managers and employees for input and action proposals. Tell them about the results of the measurement and run a first analysis and action workshop together with the team manager and the rest of the team, where everyone can come up with concrete suggestions on things we can do to increase our commitment. Share the results from the workshop with other teams in, for example, a "world café" exercise.
- Delegate the implementation of actions to managers and employees. Take action on a regular basis and measure each week/month with three questions (use Excel or another simple tool. It's not important exactly how it's done):
    - What feels best right now?
    - What feels the worst right now?
    - What can you/your boss/HR do to increase your satisfaction?
- Delegate more responsibility gradually for both measurement and actions. Continuous improvement and follow-up of actions are never "ready." It must be an ongoing process that never ends. To delegate more and more responsibility to employees for both measurement and actions increases their feeling that they are indeed responsible and is, in itself, engaging.

- After six months, measure again with Gallup's twelve questions. Note improvement and celebrate success. Then measure every six months and continue with improvement efforts within the teams in between each time period.
- Evaluate and adjust the method continuously using monthly retrospectives. In the retrospective, you look back and think about how the method can be improved using the questions below:
  - What did we do well?
  - What should we keep doing?
  - What can we improve?
  - What can we stop doing?
  - What should we change?
  - What should we start doing?

The important thing is to continue the work between each measurement, on continuous improvement, and to delegate responsibility to the teams 100 percent. HR's and managers' role will be to encourage all employees to take responsibility for their own commitment and for transparent communication about what can be improved to create a workplace where people can use their full potential and together create real results.

One thing I would add to the communication tool is a pulse or an ongoing organizational dialogue tool. How do you have a decent, respectful, transparent, and open dialogue with the organization about what they need to be able to work better? What does the organization need in order to be more Agile or what requirements are needed to be able to develop new ideas continuously? How much open communication can the organization provide?

—RIINA

FROM→TO FOR EMPLOYEE ENGAGEMENT SURVEYS

PRINCIPLES FOR EMPLOYMENT ENGAGEMENT SURVEYS	
Less of	More of
Ask once a year	Ask a lot more often
Ask 100 questions	Ask just one or a few questions
HR is responsible	Team have the responsibility
Central follow up	Delegated follow up
Measuring more important than action	Actions are more important than measuring
Expensive	Cost effective
Small effect	Large effect
Purpose to measure is central control	Purpose to measure is to increase motivation

CHAPTER 14

Agile and the Brain

includes a section by Alexander Zaforek

"Agile is not just about changing processes and tools, but also about changing the culture and mindset."
- attrib.to Lyssa Adkins

"The experience of social pain, while temporarily distressing and hurtful, is an evolutionary adaptation that promotes social bonding and, ultimately, survival."
— nAoMi Eisenberger

The human brain is a social organ. Naomi Eisenberger, author of *Future Science,* Associate Professor of Psychology at UCLA, and a leading neuroscience researcher, conducted an experiment to study what happens to the brain when someone is rejected. The result is called social pain.

Her experiment involved a subject and two additional participants. The three gathered (either in real life or digitally) for a game of catch. A ball was tossed among the three peacefully for some time until, unexpectedly, the subject was excluded from the game. The two participants continued to throw the ball back and forth to each other. Eisenberger studied how the subject felt after being left out. Even if the game was digital, the subject felt angry, betrayed, and sad.

The subject's feelings of rejection can be traced to a defense mechanism in the anterior cingulate cortex, which is the part of the brain that registers pain. It doesn't matter whether the pain is physical or mental, it registers in the same location and feels the same.

Another researcher at UCLA, Matthew Lieberman, continued the research and further supported Eisenberger's findings.

Mammals are socially dependent on their care-givers for survival. The caregiver is most often the mother. Physiological and neurological reactions are directly shaped by social interaction with others.

The challenge for a manager is that employees experience organizations as a social system, not as a system designed for economic transactions. When they are given a task they feel is below their skillset or their salary is reduced, they experience the blow as a neural impulse, which is just as powerful and painful as a physical punch in the gut.

Most employees in large organizations learn how to handle criticism and hard-to-swallow information. They may not have a visceral or visible reaction to the information, but it will affect their commitment and their engagement. They become what HR professionals refer to as "transactional employees," which means they are only going to give what they feel they are getting in return. It's important for managers to understand this mentality so they can more easily engage and motivate employees by giving them the right prerequisites and environment to succeed.

THE SCARF MODEL

The SCARF Model is a brain-based framework designed by David Rock at the NeuroLeadership Institute (NLI) in New York. NLI links psychological information about the brain to business settings to better understand how people experience work. SCARF was created to enhance personal and social awareness and improve the quality of daily interactions. It is intended to minimize the feeling of being threatened and maximize the feeling of being rewarded.

Agile supports working in alignment with brain functionality and SCARF is an excellent tool, rooted in new science, for understanding how people tick. SCARF is an acronym for five factors to monitor to avoid dysfunction in an organization: status, certainty, autonomy, relatedness, and fairness. We'll examine each domain of the human experience individually.

STATUS

Status is a judgment made in social situations that either strengthens or weakens how *we think we are perceived* by others. Humans are biologically programmed to care about status because social acceptance impacts the ability to survive.

It's much easier to exist in the pack than out on your own as a lone wolf. The hormones related to stress or threat kick in when one has a feeling of inferiority.

The feeling of status is relative. When we compete with others or ourselves, the same reward center is triggered.

It's comparable to playing a video game and making it to a higher level. There's a little rush of joy. The same feeling occurs when you receive positive feedback. The status section of the brain is triggered. It doesn't require a large reward; only a small display of appreciation is enough to tap into that section of the brain.

Our status can vary according to which group we're in. For example, your sense of status will change if you're with your close friends versus a group of people you're meeting for the first time. The same can be said if you're with your immediate family as opposed to your coworkers. We are constantly assessing the various social situations we encounter and how it either reinforces or undermines our sense of status.

People who are fond of power or control are reluctant to relinquish it because it impacts their status. One of the reasons some people are resistant to Agile is because it levels the playing field. Control and power are spread democratically throughout an organization and the traditional concept of "boss" is replaced by self-management.

Some organizations place a high value on salaries and titles.

Those things translate to respect from others. When those things shift, either because of a promotion or a firing, it impacts status. In fact, any type of change threatens status, and some people don't eagerly embrace the idea of losing their status.

However, when everyone in an organization treats every-one else with the same level of respect, the feeling of threat is eliminated. Everyone is on the same page working toward the same goal. Positive or negative feedback takes the place of bonuses, titles, or promotions and is enough to trigger the status domain. Feedback has the same effect on the brain as a pay raise or a title change.

CERTAINTY

Familiar situations allow the brain to relax and go into autopilot mode. In this state, a person is capable of doing more than one thing at a time: driving a car and talking, for example. Not knowing what is going to happen next can cause great anxiety and stress for some people. Being in uncertain situations requires extra neural energy and focus to cope. Not all new or challenging situations are a threat, but too much uncertainty can lead to panic, under- achievement, and poor decisions.

The certainty or uncertainty domain causes me to think about a scene from Clint Eastwood's famous 1966 movie, *The Good, the Bad and the Ugly*. There are three men in the frame and it depicts the scene of a classic duel. There is no certainty or predictability as to what the outcome will be. If you look closely at the character's faces, you can gauge who feels what.

Of course, Clint Eastwood appears resolved and certain. It's clear from his expression that he will win the duel. It's a good visual example of certainty.

An effective way to handle uncertainty when faced with a large problem or question is to break it down into smaller, more manageable pieces. We are better able to handle things when we can focus on one step at a time, and the feeling of certainty increases. Dealing with work in small batches is a common practice in Agile.

To decrease feelings of uncertainty surrounding an obstacle, managers and leaders should make all the related information as transparent as possible. It's important to open up and share knowledge, instead of hiding it. For example, the process surrounding a firing decision needs to be visible so that everyone understands the person was treated fairly. There should be no secrecy unless absolutely necessary, such as a legal ramification. Transparency makes coping with uncertain situations less stressful.

The brain loves visualizing through pictures, models, and drawings, which is another Agile principle. Enhance understanding by using visuals to create consensus. It helps to utilize familiar images that communicate where you are and where you are heading to minimize threatening feelings and increase feelings of certainty.

Another way to help people feel more certainty is to foster an environment of experimentation. Experimenting is the foundation for continuous learning. Test out different solutions to get a sense of what works and what doesn't, before making a decision about moving forward. This was a common practice at Toyota when they experimented with set-based design—a system that encourages flexibility, which we discussed in Chapter 4. The closer you get to the solution, the more you know.

In a culture of experimentation, it must be okay to fail. No one needs to be embarrassed by failure or worried about getting into trouble. Failure leads to better knowledge and paves the way for improvement. When we experiment, we learn faster, which allows us to feel safe by having a competitive advantage.

AUTONOMY

Autonomy in the workplace means that individuals are able to control their own workflow without being micro-managed.

They are able to make their own choices and decisions about what to work on, where to focus their energy, and what they need to learn. Autonomy leads to less stressed employees and teams. People are given the freedom to prioritize their tasks and figure out their own *what* and *how*. People have an increased sense of security when they are able to make choices for themselves. We've seen the positive effects of allowing employees to have more autonomy in a number of well-known international organizations, and it starts with trusting people.

As technology has advanced, the workforce has become more mobile. People are working remotely with increasing frequency. They must be trusted to organize their time and get their work done in alignment with the rest of their team and organization. The younger generations expect that they will be able to work when, where, and how they desire. Some people don't hit their peak productivity at the same hours as everyone else. They must be given the space to do whatever is going to allow them to produce their best work. Autonomy and trust go hand in hand because you can't have one without the other.

RELATEDNESS

Trust and empathy can only occur when people feel they are a part of the same social group. Sometimes, when people meet others who are different, they experience feelings of unease. Alternatively, when they meet others who are similar, they feel comfortable and like they are part of the same tribe.

There's a connection. The more alike we perceive others to be, the more positively we feel about them.

The *experience of how we feel* about others is significant when working with cross-functional, fluid teams, as is common in Agile. Often, we need a lot of time to accept people who are not like us. There must be significant social interaction before we start producing oxytocin in the brain, which is the hormone that makes us feel good about others. Oxytocin is produced under a variety of positive circumstances, but is most often associated with love and laughter. These days, you can even buy it in a nasal spray from Amazon.

Diverse organizations tend to experience superior output, and it's easier to achieve diversity when people feel secure.

It's also much easier to deal with change when people are comfortable with each other. Agile managers want people to get to know each other and want to minimize situations where people might feel like they are not part of a group. By being intentional about how people relate to one another, they are creating prerequisites for maximum performance.

FAIRNESS

Frans de Waal, a primatologist professor at Emory University, conducted a famous study about fairness using a pair of monkeys.24 The monkeys knew each other well and often ate and performed tasks together. In the experiment, the

---

24 https:// www.youtube.com/watch?v=meiU6TxysCg&feature=youtu.be&list=PLrqOxupNF8o19fHX-f1s8sZnqGJqCrg6M

monkeys were given cucumbers to eat before performing a simple task.

Everything was peaceful until one of the monkeys was given grapes instead of cucumbers.

The intention was to create inequality between the two monkeys, and it worked. The monkey not given grapes went berserk. When she saw that her counterpart was given superior food, she refused to perform the task, began banging on the walls of her cage, and threw her cucumber at the researcher in a rage. The monkey's limbic system had a strong reaction when she became the victim of unfair treatment.

The sense of injustice, or perceived unfairness, always stems from a comparison with someone else. The monkey was perfectly happy with her cucumbers until she saw that her friend next door was getting something she was not. Her feeling was no different than the feelings we might have when the neighbor buys a new car. Our own clunker suddenly seems a lot clunkier sitting in the driveway than it did before the neighbor bought a shiny new ride.

In a traditional work setting, there are many instances of perceived unfairness: someone makes a slightly higher salary, or the manager favors one employee over another, or someone is always awarded the best clients, projects, or accolades.

Someone might be thrilled with his or her paycheck until they encounter someone else who makes five times their salary.

Some people are willing to die for things they perceive to be unfair, and most are willing to commit to organizations or causes that promote fairness. The issue of pay at work can cause a lot of feelings of unfairness. It's more important to people that salary policies are fair than high. That's the type of rationale our brains use to function.

Everything that leaders and managers do either supports or undermines the five SCARF domains, which is why leadership is so challenging. Every gesture, word, and glance has some level of social meaning, whether it's intended or not. It helps to create awareness about inter- actions and it highlights people's core concerns, which they may not even fully understand themselves.

Agile leadership is brain-friendly leadership. It nurtures the parts of people's psyche that allows them to operate at the highest level of functionality, while avoiding circumstances or interactions that cause people to shut down. Real employee engagement starts with understanding people, and the science of the brain is an integral part of the equation.

Modern managers are like gardeners. Their job is to create an environment that supports growth and to provide the prerequisites that support abundance. Gardens can be of many kinds and follow different purposes. Managers cannot force the seeds to grow. They can provide all the appropriate conditions for growth, like water, good soil, enough sunshine, removing the weeds, etc. If growth still doesn't occur, it could be a bad seed. Maybe there is something wrong that can't be fixed in the particular workplace envi- ronment. It's okay. It happens. That person needs to move on to an environment where they can grow and thrive, maybe to another organization.

The goal for Agile is to cultivate the right conditions that allow people to reach their highest potential.

> Perhaps there is something within the team environment, a systemic fault that is making you underperform. Maybe something personal is going on in your life that is creating a performance problem. From an Agile perspective, we will analyze and figure out where the problem stems from. It may not be a personal issue or a systemic workplace matter. It might be that you are not a good match for this organization or role. The ultimate process helps you figure it out on your own.
>
> —LEILA

"Agile is not just about changing processes and tools, but also about changing the culture and mindset."

– Lyssa Adkins

INDIVIDUALS AND INTERACTIONS OVER PROCESSES AND TOOLS

Having looked at agile leadership, motivation and communication earlier, we will now turn the focus towards what happens in the brain and on the emotional level, during change. Where does resistance come from and how to address and overcome it, even transform it into collaboration?

As mentioned earlier in the book, organizations are not just economic operations. They are a social system, formed by all individuals involved, and their interactions, networks, collaborations, from which culture emerges. This living system is inherently subject to internal and external changes and constant environmental impulses. Changes, especially those introduced during agile transformations, naturally trigger reactions in the brains and bodies of those within the system. Understanding these **physiological responses** is key for leaders aiming to guide transformations effectively. For new workflows to be sustainably adopted and improved, they must be intrinsically embraced by those involved.

Still, agile transformations often focus solely on implementing frameworks, overlooking the crucial human side and its dynamics. Many leaders focus on structural implementation because it is either more comfortable, or due to unawareness of the need for **emotional and psychological leadership** and **adapted communication**, during change. A **wholistic approach** is needed, bringing the human side into focus.

> Change impulses, originating from intervention options, can only achieve the desired effect if they fit the system's current state; therefore, interventions are always just experiments. The system itself decides about the extent and direction of the change triggered by the impulse. Agile people coaches know this.
>
> - ALEX

People do not fear change itself but the uncertainty it brings, threatening their sense of control and safety. This often leads to resistance or choosing less optimal, yet more predictable options. Change represents a perceived danger, activating stress reactions and the release of hormones that influence behaviour. This highlights the importance of addressing cognitive understanding, emotional connection, and practical involvement simultaneously, to overcome resistance and successfully drive change.

Looking at change initiatives from an interpersonal-communication point of view, will show that different aspects become suddenly important or more relevant. Earlier we explained why leaders should align their actions and communications with the five domains of the **SCARF model** (Status, Certainty, Autonomy, Relatedness, Fairness) and the corresponding fundamental human needs, to foster intrinsic motivation, reducing stress and supporting sustainable change.

Two models that highlight the importance of addressing both the practical and emotional aspects of change for effective outcomes, are the following:

- **John Kotter's Change Model** is an 8-step framework, for leading successful organizational change, emphasizing on creating urgency, building coalitions, forming a clear vision, and anchoring new practices into culture. It focuses on systematically guiding people through change, in order to overcome resistance and achieve lasting transformation.

- **Elisabeth Kübler-Ross' Grief Cycle** describes the emotional stages people often experience when facing significant loss or major change: denial, anger, bargaining, depression, and acceptance. Understanding this cycle helps leaders support individuals emotionally through transitions, and adapt change management approaches to human feelings.

As an agile enterprise coach, being closely involved in many digital and agile transformations, I've learned just how delicate and vulnerable a social system can be during times of organizational change. I remember one situation in particular: management saw the need to create a sense of urgency and tried to do so, by focusing almost exclusively on the financial target. Talking about the need to increase revenue and warning that the future looked bleak if sales didn't go up, made everyone feel disconnected instead of inspired.

It was difficult for people to relate to that goal, and the overstated sense of urgency ended up in nothing but fuelling anxiety about their job safety. Instead of rallying the team, the approach led many talented people to leave the organization, worried about what might happen if the vision was not achieved quickly.

The lack of a relatable, meaningful purpose, combined with a strong, almost panicked focus on urgency and the uncertainty it created, did more harm than good. It left people stressed and unsure about their place in the company's future.

> *"The speed of communication and connectivity today creates unprecedented opportunity, but also unprecedented overwhelm."*
> — Unknown

FROM VUCA TO BANI

We live in a fast-paced era, defined by technological interconnectivity, that enables the instantaneous exchange of data, driving rapid interaction on social and media platforms worldwide. News, information, ideas, and disruptions now travel faster than ever before. Trends that once took months to cross borders, now do so in mere days. This intense connectivity takes a significant toll on people, as provocative social media posts, political events, or crises halfway around the world, can disrupt societies and markets within hours, amplifying feelings of uncertainty and stress.

It is becoming increasingly difficult to rationally attribute change to specific events, as tracing distinct logical causes grows harder amid the complexity of modern interconnected systems. Many subtle or emotional factors come into play, contributing to a sharp decline in overall predictability.

This evolving landscape challenges traditional frameworks and prompts a shift from **VUCA** (Volatile, Uncertain, Complex, Ambiguous) to **BANI** (Brittle, Anxious, Nonlinear, Incomprehensible). Unlike VUCA, which focuses primarily on describing external conditions and challenges, BANI highlights internal human responses and experiences, more accurately capturing the emotional impact of today's chaotic environments and realities. BANI emphasizes mindfulness and focuses on resilience and empathy. It acknowledges that today's challenges require not only intellectual understanding, but also emotional intelligence and mindful leadership.

This paradigm shift underscores the urgent need for organizations to explore new models and leadership approaches, as a means to navigate an unpredictable future, while alleviating the emotional turbulence experienced by employees.

Leaders must foster resilience to sustain brittle systems, cultivate empathy to alleviate anxiety, develop contextual awareness to manage non-linearity, and embrace transparency to demystify incomprehensibility. Understanding these dimensions equips us to make more effective decisions and devise strategies in a world where traditional frameworks no longer suffice.

> *"That's a way to see it and there is also another way to see it."*
> — Insoo Kim Berg

THE ADAPTIVE BRAIN

In a perfect world, change is supported and intrinsically driven. People will always be engaged (positively or negatively) with their brain (is it meaningful to me?), their heart (how do I feel emotionally?), and their actions (what must be done?). Leaders need to be aware of this as they will also be affected on these three levels themselves.

The modern **Adaptive Brain Model** sees the brain as an integrated system of interdependent networks, constantly predicting and adapting to internal and external changes, to maintain balance and adjust to stressors. Unlike earlier simplistic views, emotion and cognition brain regions are highly interconnected, with the prefrontal cortex (PFC) acting as the adaptive center, responsible for complex thinking, creativity, decision-making and flexible behavior, in changing environments.

Agile environments engage these adaptive brain functions intensely, emphasizing rapid change and uncertainty. Understanding the brain's predictive nature and plasticity, can help leaders design transformations that support employees' ability to adjust, innovate, and overcome stress, by aligning with their neurological needs for safety, predictability, and autonomy.

When stressed, the brain's limbic system dominates, impairing rational thinking and listening. It takes moments (often cited as around two minutes) of calm for the prefrontal cortex to regain control and become receptive again, allowing reflection, decision-making, and openness to new information.

> *"Your calm mind is the ultimate weapon against your challenges. So relax."*
> – attrib. to Bryant McGill

FACING PERCEIVED DANGER CREATES STRESS

The prefrontal cortex (PFC) controls complex thinking and emotional regulation, but weakens under stress, yielding to faster, and reflexive survival-driven fight, flight, or freeze reactions. **The Adaptive Brain Model** views these stress-responses to acute danger as evolved, dynamic adaptations for survival, balanced by higher cognitive and emotional processes, shaped by personality.

The Reiss Motivation Profile (RMP, Chapter 9) offers insight into this personality system, by identifying 16 fundamental intrinsic motivations that shape how individuals respond to stress and challenges. For example, strong needs for security, tranquility, or acceptance, can indicate a person's stress sensitivity and coping ability. Those high in these motives may experience stress responses more intensely, and may need different leadership approaches for support.

Understanding a leader's and team members' unique motivational profiles through the RMP, helps tailor stress management strategies. This fosters psychological safety and adaptive responses, moving individuals beyond automatic survival reactions, toward resilience and thoughtful engagement. It is critical in complex and fast-changing environments.

Agile transformations often bring uncertainty through role changes and new work methods, generating relational stress within teams and the broader organization.

Relational Stress Management (RSM) is the practice of recognizing, understanding, and effectively managing the human and interpersonal dynamics that significantly impact team performance and organizational change.

Agile leaders applying RSM, meet the emotional needs of their teams, creating environments that support shared ownership and psychological safety. This people-centered approach balances technical improvements, with a focus on team well-being, helping prevent burnout, reduce resistance to change, and boost cohesion and performance. Integrating RSM strengthens the human factors vital for sustaining agile principles. It empowers teams to thrive amid complexity and change, fostering resilience, adaptability, and overall well-being, essential for sustainable agile transformation.

While RSM is not a single formalized framework universally defined, key principles commonly emphasized include:

- **Open Communication**: encourages honest, empathetic dialogue, and helps reduce misunderstandings and stress buildup in relationships.
- **Mutual Understanding**: recognizing and validating each other's feelings, builds trust and emotional safety.
- **Respecting Boundaries**: maintaining appropriate personal and emotional boundaries prevents conflicts and resentment.
- **Conflict Resolution**: addressing issues collaboratively and proactively minimizes stress escalation.
- **Support and Empathy**: offering emotional support and showing empathy, strengthens bonds and buffers stress.
- **Shared Problem Solving**: working as a team to find solutions, promotes cooperation and reduces feelings of isolation.

> *"A good way to overcome stress is to help others out of theirs."*
> – attrib. to Dada J. P. Vaswani

In arguments, we often seek to convince the other person of our idea by forcing them to understand our reasoning. After all, they are intelligent and should be able to clearly understand the logic behind. Forcing them to "understand", will only make it worse, especially if our counterpart is overwhelmed and their PFC has shut down. The sooner you recognize the situation, the easier it will be to recover.

Quick techniques that reliably reactivate the prefrontal cortex (PFC) and bring people back to a receptive state (you can use them on yourself or with others):

- Creating a pause or break to allow emotional de-escalation, sometimes called "time outs" or deliberate breathing pauses (ca. 2min.).

- Guided breathing exercises or mindfulness to reduce irritation and stress.
- Active listening without immediate judgment, to reduce threat perception and build safety.
- Reframing conversations to reduce perceived danger, for example by emphasizing common goals and trust.

- Using positive social signals, aligned with the SCARF model, to lower threat and foster engagement.
- Engaging working memory and focused attention, through specific mental tasks like counting backwards by sevens. Such simple cognitive challenges help shift brain activity back to PFC control, by requiring deliberate and goal-directed effort.
- Engaging in tasks requiring problem-solving, reflection or planning, can rapidly reactivate PFC circuits by demanding cognitive flexibility and control.

> *"Smiling can be infectious in a workplace to help reduce stress, to help teamwork, to defuse high-pressure situations. The more you smile, the more people will smile back."*
> – attrib. to Byron Pulsifer

SOCIAL INTERACTIONS RELEASE HORMONES

Several key hormones play a vital role in our social interactions and workplace dynamics. They affect how individuals and teams experience change in agile environments. Understanding what influences their release and how they interact dynamically with cognitive and social challenges, can help leaders guide behaviour, reduce stress, and foster motivation.

STRESS HORMONES: THE BRAIN'S ALARM SYSTEM

Stress hormones, like **adrenaline** and **cortisol**, will influence how individuals respond to the constant change, uncertainty, and social dynamics typical of agile transformations. Quick adrenaline release sharpens alertness and readiness. While useful for short-term focus, sustained adrenaline surges can reduce cognitive flexibility and collaboration.

Cortisol, released during prolonged stress, impairs memory, immune function, and executive processes, when chronically elevated. Agile transformations often involve ongoing periods of uncertainty and of social evaluation that can raise cortisol levels, impacting decision-making, learning, and emotional regulation.

When you, as a leader, feel stressed, your emotions ripple through your team, causing similar stress responses that lower morale, trust, and productivity. When you experience stress, you might show signs of pessimism, volatility, or poor communication, which can increase your team's anxiety and reduce their creativity and engagement. This creates a domino effect, impacting your entire group both emotionally and physically, affecting performance and health. As a result, collective stress rises across the organization, which lowers overall productivity and trust, while increasing conflict, disengagement, and even leading to higher absenteeism and turnover.

These actions help you lower stress hormone levels, create an emotionally safe environment, increase team resilience, and improve focus and collaboration during change:

- Involve employees in decisions to reduce perceived danger and increase control.
- Show consistent support and foster a shared sense of purpose to build trust.
- Communicate transparently to reduce uncertainty and fear.
- Acknowledge contributions and empower employees to boost intrinsic motivation.
- Manage your own stress and model calm, inclusive behaviour, to create emotional safety.

- Promote psychological safety to encourage openness and reduce tension.
- Encourage healthy habits like sufficient sleep and stress management techniques, enabling sharper focus, creativity and problem-solving.
- Maintain respectful, friendly interactions, to foster a positive work environment.
- Allow flexible work arrangements to increase autonomy and reduce stress.
- Gather confidential feedback to identify and address hidden stressors.

OXYTOCIN: THE NEUROCHEMICAL OF TRUST AND COLLABORATION

Trust is the basis for a successful transformation and healthy emotional connections. **Oxytocin**, the key driver to engagement and cohesion in teams, is often called the "love hormone". It is released during collaboration, caring, and trusting interactions. Oxytocin supports psychological stability, by regulating emotions tied to empathy and attachment, while reducing stress and anxiety. It creates positive feedback loops of trust and cooperation that strengthen group bonds and promote safety.

Importantly, oxytocin acts as a powerful anti-stress hormone, buffering negative effects of stress. Research shows that organizations cultivating high-trust cultures powered by oxytocin, enjoy significantly greater energy, engagement, and productivity.

As an agile leader who intentionally unlocks these powerful neurochemical advantages, you will drive more effective and enduring transformations:
- By building trust through transparency and open communication, reducing uncertainty and stress.
- By encouraging collaboration and genuine social bonding via active listening and recognition, to enhance resilience.
- By believing in employees and empowering team members with autonomy and opportunities for job crafting, to increase motivation.
- By giving tasks a sense, connecting work to meaningful higher purposes to sustain intrinsic engagement.
- By being open to challenges and feedback about activities and duties.
- By demonstrating vulnerability and support, to build psychological safety.

DOPAMINE: THE MOTIVATION MOLECULE

Dopamine is a key neurotransmitter in the brain's reward system that drives motivation, pleasure, and habit formation. It is released both during the anticipation of a reward and when the reward is received, reinforcing behaviours that lead to positive outcomes. Repeated exposure to the same reward, leads to diminishing dopamine responses over time (habituation). Consequently, novelty and variation are crucial to sustaining motivation. This is why the sense of achievement keeps engagement higher, by delivering work in small, manageable batches, rather than all at once. Continuously evolving challenges and adapting objectives (such as OKRs) prevent boredom and frustration, which occur when goals are too easy or too difficult.

Dopamine beautifully highlights the tension between instant gratification and delayed gratification. Instant rewards provide quick dopamine hits, but can undermine sustained effort, while delayed gratification yields better long-term results, but requires trust in the process and leadership. In essence, dopamine fuels the drive to pursue goals, by making the anticipation and achievement of rewards pleasurable. Agile leaders can foster dopamine release by providing meaningful challenges, timely feedback, celebrating small wins, and maintaining a balance between achievable steps and stretching goals.

With these leadership actions, you can activate dopamine pathways, enhancing focus, motivation, and resilience in agile teams:
- Set small, meaningful milestones to create regular feelings of progress and success, to boost morale, satisfaction and enthusiasm.

- Make progress visible, using tools like Kanban boards or checklists, to trigger reward sensations.
- Give specific, effort-based recognition rather than generic praise, to reinforce positive behaviours and resilience.
- Connect daily work to a meaningful purpose and future success, to boost optimism and willingness to persist through challenges.
- Provide autonomy and control, allowing teams to self-organize and make decisions, to drive sustained high performance and innovation.
- Encourage experimentation and a positive culture around learning from mistakes.
- Maintain frequent, positive feedback loops (e.g. daily stand-ups or 1:1 meetings) to sustain motivation.
- Build trust and psychological safety, through transparent communication and consistent support.

> *"One cannot not communicate."*
> – Paul Watzlawick

STRESS REACTIONS ARE NATURAL AND CERTAIN

In social workplace settings, people react with fight, flight or freeze responses, when they perceive a threat to their safety, status, or well-being. These reactions are triggered by stressors such as uncertainty, conflict, criticism, or sudden change. These natural survival mechanisms aim to protect the individual, but can disrupt communication and teamwork, if not recognized and managed effectively.

The fight, flight, freeze model remains central in understanding how the body automatically reacts to acute stress and perceived threats, through rapid activation of the autonomic nervous system. I am sure you've already experienced this yourself: your brain's threat detection system, floods your body with stress hormones like adrenaline and cortisol, shifting your focus from rational thinking to survival-driven reactions, causing physical changes such as increased heart rate and muscle tension, to prepare your body to confront, escape, or immobilize.

Freeze is seen as a parasympathetic "brake" slowing action, while fight and flight are sympathetic activation, ramping up energy for action. This flexibility helps optimize survival chances rather than strictly one mode per person.

The most common workplace cues that trigger fight, flight or freeze responses include:
- Critical or harsh feedback, performance reviews, or reprimands.
- Conflicts, confrontations, or aggressive communication.

- Sudden changes or uncertainty in roles, job security, or organizational direction.
- Overwhelming workload or unrealistic expectations.
- Feeling unheard, excluded, or socially isolated.
- High-pressure situations, tight deadlines, or intense scrutiny.
- Perceived threats to status, competence, or belonging.
- Ambiguous or unclear communication causing confusion or fear.
- Lack of psychological safety, where employees fear consequences for speaking up.

Bear in mind that we are not strictly fight, flight or freeze, but rather a mixture of all three responses, that can shift depending on the situation. Which response dominates, depends on factors like the nature of the threat, individual physiology and context. We can also shift rapidly between these states in a given situation.

Personally, I noticed that I mostly react with flight or fight as my dominant response in situations where I feel attacked. My body needs to stay in motion. On the other hand, when encountering an intellectually stressful situation, for instance an exam or certification test, my brain blanks out and my rational thinking freezes.

A simple yet powerful technique that helps calm your nervous system and reduce stress, is **box breathing**. By encouraging slow, rhythmic breaths, it acts like a reset button during stressful moments, lowering your heart rate and promoting a sense of calm and control.

Here are some more dos and don'ts for helping someone exit their specific state, and reconnect the mind and body to the present:

FLIGHT (FLEEING) RESPONSE

This reaction is felt as anxiety and as an urge to escape perceived danger. It often involves restlessness, rapid heartbeat, and confusion about how to escape. People may avoid eye contact and look for ways to leave.

Don't do this:

- Don't force eye contact or restrict movement.
- Avoid aggression, shouting, threats, or sanctions.
- Don't ask closed questions.
- Don't tell someone to calm down, as this feels like more restriction.

Do this instead:

- Use open-ended questions and give choices.
- Offer freedom and options.

- Use humour to de-escalate.
- Provide a physical way out, like suggesting a walk.

FIGHT RESPONSE

This survival reaction prepares the body to confront threats, often manifesting as anger, irritability, clenched fists or jaw, and a readiness to defend oneself physically or verbally. It reflects a desire to assert control, victory, and can escalate into conflicts, if unmanaged.

Don't do this:

- Don't try to overpower or yell at the person.
- Avoid undermining their authority or interrupting them.
- Don't use humour to defuse the situation, as it may be perceived as dismissive.

Do this instead:

- Offer no resistance and listen actively without interrupting.
- Take responsibility for your role and avoid making excuses.
- Provide practical solutions and ways to resolve the issue calmly.

FREEZE RESPONSE

The freeze reaction occurs, when fight or flight seem impossible, leading to paralysis, numbness, dissociation, and mental fog.

People may feel stuck, helpless, or emotionally shut down, sometimes experiencing demoralization or hopelessness.

Don't do this:

- Don't shake or startle the person.
- Avoid demanding they show strength or courage.

Do this instead:

- Offer understanding and patience.
- Mirror their posture to build connection.
- Respect their need for silence.
- Do a small exercise that engages the senses and shifts focus away from distress (touch a cold or textured object, look around and name colours).
- Encourage small steps and define manageable objectives.

"Mirror neurons allow us to grasp the minds of each other not through conceptual reasoning but through direct simulation. By feeling, not by thinking."

– Dr. Giacomo Rizzolatti

MIRROR NEURONS AND SOCIAL CONNECTION

Mirror neurons are fascinating brain cells that light up, not only when you do something, but also when you watch someone else do the same thing. They help you learn by rehearsing what you see in your mind, before actually executing it.

This natural "mirroring" allows you to pick up on other people's feelings and intentions, by reflecting their emotions and behaviours. It helps you to feel empathy, and that is how you connect and naturally understand others.

A successful leader understands the value of mirror neurons and the insight into how his or her own behaviour, emotions, and communication style, ripple through teams, shaping the whole group's mood and connection.

Leadership insights on how mirror neurons influence social behaviour and group dynamics:

- Your emotions and behaviours are often unconsciously mirrored by your employees. This means that when you

maintain a positive, calm, and confident demeanour, you encourage similar feelings in others, which boosts morale and cooperation.
- Mirror neurons play a crucial role in empathy, by helping you and your team internally replicate others' emotions and intentions. This builds deep social connections and greater understanding.
- When you demonstrate authentic empathy and you actively listen, you promote openness and trust because your team picks up and reflects your emotional cues.
- By modelling behaviours like collaboration, respect, and problem-solving, you encourage these behaviours naturally throughout your team.
- Using clear, expressive communication, both verbal and nonverbal, helps make sure your intended messages are effectively mirrored by others, reducing misunderstandings.
- Mirror neurons help create social cohesion, by encouraging people to conform, adapt, and avoid conflict through shared emotions and understanding nonverbal cues.
- When conflict or tension arises, your composed body language and tone, can help de-escalate mirrored emotional responses in your group, supporting smoother resolution and better emotional regulation.
- Mirror neurons also assist you and your team in learning new movements and skills, by internally rehearsing observed actions before actually performing them, which is valuable for training and development.

Practical tips that engage mirror neuron activity:
- Be mindful of your emotional state and body language, as your team unconsciously adopts these cues through mirroring.
- Use storytelling, role-playing and demonstrations, to boost learning, motivation and empathy.
- Encourage open dialogue and vulnerability, by showing your own authentic reactions thoughtfully, fostering psychological safety.
- In virtual or remote settings, where nonverbal cues are limited, compensate with more explicit emotional expression, tone and feedback, to engage mirror neurons effectively.
- Provide positive reinforcement and celebrate behaviours you want to see repeated, to reinforce learning and culture-building.
- Practice conscious mirroring, by subtly responding to others' body language and emotions during conversations, to build rapport without mimicking or appearing insincere.
- Use empathetic communication when providing feedback or navigating tensions, acknowledging emotions, to ease discomfort and promote collaborative problem-solving.
- Recognize that mirror neurons create shared group emotions and experiences, so fostering positive group activities can enhance social bonding and cooperation.
- Be aware that mirror neurons support interbrain synchrony (alignment in brain activity between individuals

during interaction), improving mutual understanding and teamwork.

"People don't change because you want them to change, people change when they're ready to change. So, understanding why, when, and how people change, is probably the biggest thing you can learn."
- attrib. to Ron Quartel

THAT'S ONE SMALL STEP FOR A TEAM, ONE GIANT LEAP FOR MINDSET

From my personal experience coaching people, I can say that mindset change is most effective when done iteratively and incrementally, just as any agile approach. Focusing on building a better future, often begins with small, deliberate steps that lead to meaningful, lasting change. Encouraging teams to take small steps toward objectives, engages their prefrontal cortex for critical thinking.

My approach, centres on engaging with people through **open questions** and **Socratic dialogue**, which helps foster trust, and encourages deep reflection, without challenging anyone on a personal or human level. Instead, I challenge ideas on a technical or contextual basis, using open questions and allowing them to discover answers themselves. **Storytelling** plays a powerful role in this process. Sharing examples of similar challenges from other settings, creates a springboard for the questions I will ask. This method helps people relate, reflect and draw parallels, generating insights that can be adapted to their own experiences.

This offers teams the chance to immediately find solutions to small problems and accept gradual progress. Managing to achieve quick wins early on, helps me to establish trust and allows me to build momentum and motivation.

Balancing the pace of change is key: too fast causes resistance, too slow halts progress. I clearly explain the goals of the organization, and ask the teams what small steps they are willing to take toward these goals. Sometimes, one or two extra steps are necessary to avoid resistance and ensure acceptance. Occasionally, these are sideways steps. Still, I approve them, as long as they are purposeful, to ensure manageability.

Even if outcomes are imperfect, positive feedback motivates further effort and encourages proactive actions. This approach subtly expands comfort zones and helps teams progress confidently. Respect and genuine interest in individuals, foster better performance, as people respond to respect rather than control and power. Behaviour change emerges naturally, when actions are intrinsically motivated and responsive to the surrounding context.

Extrinsic motivations (e.g. the "need to change" urgency) will initiate or provoke a response. But the system (people) self-determines, if and how, these transform into an intrinsically motivated reaction that sustains lasting change. Please consider that no response is also a reaction. This aligns with the principle that interventions can be viewed as experiments and must be tailored and adaptive, always open to iterating based on the system's current motivational state, and what it self-organizes as meaningful and engaging.

When an external motivator is effective, it often works by triggering or nudging intrinsic motivations, rather than by directly controlling behaviour. People respond authentically only when the motivation aligns with their own needs and desires. Otherwise, any externally driven behaviour tends to be short-lived or superficial. Therefore, extrinsic motivation can act like a catalyst. But ultimately, it is the intrinsic motivation, arising from within, that sustains and amplifies change. Leaders and change agents who recognize this co-evolution of motivations, can design interventions that respect and nurture intrinsic drives, leading to more authentic, resilient transformation.

The Socratic dialogue is a form of cooperative technique or teaching that uses a series of thoughtful, probing questions, to stimulate critical thinking, uncover assumptions and deepen understanding. Instead of directly providing answers, the facilitator (often a teacher or a leader) asks open-ended questions that stimulate self-reflection, challenge participants to examine their beliefs, clarify their thoughts and to reason through problems themselves.

It supports intellectual humility and deeper understanding, making it a powerful tool for facilitating mindset shifts and problem-solving.

Key aspects include:

- Engaging in inquiry through dialogue, rather than lecture or didactic teaching.
- Revealing contradictions or gaps in understanding, by questioning initial assertions.
- Encouraging participants to discover answers, by reflecting and justifying their reasoning.

- Promoting intellectual humility and awareness of complexity and uncertainty.
- Often used in education, philosophy, law and therapy, to foster critical thinking and self-awareness.
- In agile coaching, it may serve to challenge the status-quo.

In essence, the Socratic technique helps people learn by questioning, by employing dialogue and self-reflection, rather than passively receiving information.

For anyone interested in mastering this craft, I recommend keeping a small guidebook of coaching question types at hand. It's an invaluable resource for practicing questioning and driving transformative conversations.

"It is not the answer that enlightens, but the question."
- Eugene Ionesco

ASKING QUESTIONS TRUMPS PROVIDING ANSWERS

Asking questions goes beyond just gathering information. It inspires curiosity, sparks thoughtful reflection, and helps uncover fresh perspectives and solutions. In my experience, whether leading or collaborating, questions deepen engagement, facilitate critical problem-solving and build trust, by showing genuine respect for others' insights and experiences. By prioritizing inquiry, I've seen innovation flourish, relationships strengthen, and a culture of continuous learning and growth take root.

Deliberately asking questions is already a powerful approach. But asking considerate questions, with a clear intent, is even more effective. It leads to genuine reflection by the person being asked.

Nowadays, I can walk into meetings or assignment clarifications with new clients, teams or coaches, feeling calm and relaxed, without worrying too much. I'm confident that the outcome will be valuable. It took me quite some time, experience and professional maturity, to reach this point of confidence, where nothing easily flusters me.

But do you want to know the major factor behind this? I've become quite skilled at asking questions.

And you can do it too! Always start by preparing a few questions upfront, until you develop a routine and a sense of which questions will be most helpful (for both you and your counterpart) to scrutinize, challenge, and gain insight into the situation at hand.

Asking the right questions encourages the potential client to reflect on their own situation and needs. It helps both of us understand the status quo, clarify expectations, and determine what will be expected from me. This process gives me insight, facilitating the planning of the next step, and creates a solid connection between my conversational partner and I.

Just recently, a Product Manager who was evaluating different candidates to support some of his teams, told me after our first conversation, that he was impressed by the kind of questions I asked. None of the other candidates had posed meaningful or challenging questions. I had asked him how he saw the situation on a human level, what outcomes he expected, and what impact he hoped to achieve.

Of course, I shared examples of my experience and how I acted in similar situations, showing that I've been truly listening and trying to understand the Product Manager's needs and wishes.

Don't overwhelm your counterpart by listing everything you've ever done, or how great you are. Focus instead on asking how you can best support them and what would be most valuable to them. Remember there's no one-size-fits-all solution. Here's some food for thought: can you tell the difference between Good Practices and Best Practices? And why would my best practice be the best for you and your situation?

When I met the team and began working with them, I continued in the same way: I asked what they wanted to achieve, what kind of support would be most useful and valuable to them, and how they would recognize progress.

Until you fully understand the team, their needs, expectations, work processes, and daily challenges, any solution you offer is just speculation.

> *"If I had an hour to solve a problem and my life depended on the solution, I would spend the first 55 minutes determining the proper question to ask... for once I know the proper question, I could solve the problem in less than five minutes."*
>
> — attrib. to Albert Einstein

You can use workplace appropriate elicitation techniques to draw out important information, ideas or concerns, from individuals or groups. These methods help uncover needs, expectations, and hidden fears, which is crucial during transformations. Common approaches include interviews, workshops, surveys and observation. These techniques foster open dialogue and transparency, supporting informed decision-making and effective change.

Here are some practical elicitation techniques and example questions you can use, especially during transformations when trust, transparency, and surfacing hidden needs or fears, are crucial.

Elicitation techniques:

- **One-on-one Interviews**: build rapport and ask open questions in a private setting to help people open up about sensitive topics.
- **Workshops or Group Facilitation**: create a safe, structured environment for team reflection and collective brainstorming; use visual tools or models.
- **Observation and Contextual Inquiry**: watch work as it happens, ask about workflow, and notice where tension or confusion arises.
- **Surveys and Anonymous Feedback**: gather input about fears, blockers, or needs; sometimes people only share honestly if anonymity is assured.

- **Storytelling and Scenario Mapping**: invite participants to describe past successes, difficult transitions and hypotheticals: "Imagine things went perfectly. What would be different?".
- **Mind Mapping and Affinity Grouping**: visualize connections among themes such as challenges, desired outcomes, or personal motivations.
- **Diagram or Model Reviews**: use existing processes or workflow diagrams; walk through them together and ask for comment at each step.

One technique I truly enjoy using is **coaching cards**, especially those with images. While the questions help guide the conversation, it's the images that spark immediate emotional and subconscious responses, making thoughts clearer and more vivid. Like snowflakes forming around a tiny speck of dust, these visuals help ideas gently take shape. And the best part? There are coaching cards and picture decks for almost any topic you can imagine (change, boundaries, paths and journeys, emotions, etc.). Just search for facilitation or prompt cards for coaching, therapy and workshops.

Elicitation questions for needs, fears and transparency:

- "What is working well for you right now, and what isn't?"

- "What do you need from this transformation to feel confident and engaged?"
- "Can you share any worries or concerns about how these changes might impact you or your team?"
- "What's one thing you wish decision-makers understood about your daily work?"
- "How do you see your role evolving as the change moves forward?"
- "Is there anything that's making it hard to speak up or share feedback?"
- "If you could fix just one thing in our current setup, what would it be?"
- "What do you think the biggest risks are if we don't address certain issues?"
- "How could we better support open and honest conversations here?"
- "Think about a recent challenge. What helped you overcome it, and what got in the way?"
- 1 to 10 scale to assess the current situation: e.g." On a scale from 1 to 10, how comfortable are you sharing your needs and ideas?" Follow-up:" What would help move that number higher?"

These approaches and questions help build trust, uncover genuine needs (including hidden fears), and foster the transparent communication that successful change relies on.

I always try to ask open questions that can't be answered with a simple "yes" or "no." By doing so, one encourages independent thought and exploration, that leads to deeper understanding. These questions prompt teams to make new connections and think critically about the subject. Ultimately, they help shift attention away from dwelling on problems, to proactively seeking solutions, which fosters creativity and real progress.

There are many types of questions, these are some of my favourite:

- **Inviting Questions**: these are open and might ask about existing knowledge.
- **Solution-oriented Questions**: these focus on goals, interests and the future.
- **Expanding questions**: designed to uncover differences, commonalities and meaning.
- **Disruptive Questions**: sometimes confusing or provocative, these interrupt fixed patterns of thinking.
- **Closing Questions**: targeted at decisions and summarizing conclusions.

Here are some of my favourite questions:

- "What went well for you today?"
- "Looking back, what would you do differently?"

- "What will be different once you reach your goal?"
- "How will you notice that you've reached your goal?"
- "How will others notice that you've reached your goal?"
- "Once you've achieved your goal, how will this affect you and others?"
- "How did you manage to get to where you are now?"
- "What obstacles are preventing you from achieving it?"
- "If your problem were to disappear overnight, what would be different?"
- "What would you feel if this problem was solved?"
- "How would you notice that the problem is solved?"
- "How would others notice that this problem is solved?"
- "What would need to happen for others to accept, trust and support you?"

And these are the two most important questions of all:
- "What needs to happen, so that this meeting is valuable to you?"
- "And... What else?" Repeat this question as long as needed.

> *"Silence is one of the great arts of conversation."*
> — Marcus Tullius Cicero

GIVE ROOM TO RESPOND

Silence is a powerful elicitation technique in workplace conversations. By intentionally pausing and allowing space, you give others time to absorb the question, reflect more thoughtfully, and share a better crafted answer. Often just a few extra seconds can dramatically improve the depth and quality of the responses, revealing deeper insights and emotions, leading to richer conversations and more meaningful learnings.

Embracing a respectful silence helps people feel heard. It is crucial in creating an environment, in which they are more comfortable opening up. Mastering silence means resisting the urge to fill every pause, trusting that thoughtful reflection will bring out richer, more useful information. It is especially important with open-ended questions, in sensitive or complex discussions, where true understanding and transparency are needed.

I see this happen time and time again: leaders ask something, then quickly move on after just a second or two. I am convinced you know the classic: "Any questions? No? Okay, let's keep going!". People hardly get a chance to take a breath. The moment has passed and very few will speak up later, most will just keep their thoughts to themselves and hope for the best. This misdoing unintentionally teaches employees not to ask questions or share their valuable input, as they get the impression that there's no real space anyway or even interest for it. I often wonder if leaders rush on because they're uncomfortable with silence, or perhaps worried about tough questions, they can't or don't want to answer.

Leaders need to pause. Hold the silence and truly listen to what's being said. Acknowledge the input, then gently follow up with: "Anything else?". Pause again and hold the silence. Repeat as often as needed.

This approach shows everyone that questions are welcome and valued. People won't feel pressured to respond immediately or blur out their contribution within two seconds. When input is genuinely valued, employees start thinking ahead about what they want or need to ask. This leads to richer, more thoughtful questions and helps ease the fear that often holds people back.

"Problem talk creates problems, Solution talk creates solutions."
- Steve xde Shazer

FOCUS ON A BETTER FUTURE

This brings me to **solution-focused coaching**, which I am a great advocate of. This approach is based on identifying and leveraging the team's existing strengths, resources and preferred futures, to create change, instead of dwelling on problems.

Key principles include focusing on solutions and what's working, believing that change is constant, and empowering team members, as experts of their own situation. This future-oriented mindset fosters a positive, collaborative process, often involving small actionable steps, to achieve desired outcomes.

I use solution-focused coaching to change the way people think, shifting their mindset from problem-centric to seeing possibilities and solutions. It's about changing their thought patterns and focusing on the future. Visualizing the solution and emotionally sensing the relief, helps people lower the intrinsic motivation barrier needed to take the next step.

This isn't about manipulation. It's about reducing the fear that causes resistance. People won't act on anything they're not already intrinsically willing to do. Shifting from problem thinking to solution thinking, means creating positive associations and imagining how the solution would feel.

By asking specific questions, my goal is to make them actively think about a favourable future, with all the potential it brings. The effect of a trouble-free experience connects that mental image of it with positive feelings. This helps people move away from the resistance, triggered by focusing on the "problem."

I've learned not to ask "why?" but rather "for what purpose?", to understand the objective or intent behind an action or goal. The focus shifts to outcome and impact, highlighting value. It's about asking: "what do you want to achieve?" and understanding the deeper need behind that. From there, the coachee can take a look at the output needed to achieve the desired end state, thus providing a possible first/next step.

Patience and confidence are essential, this process takes the time it takes. Grass won't grow faster if you pull on it. In coaching, we firmly believe everyone is the expert on their own situation. Solution-focussed coaching moves people from being affected by circumstances, to becoming proactively involved in shaping their future.

> *"Imagine that while you're asleep tonight, a miracle happens and the problem is completely solved. When you wake up tomorrow, how will you notice that this miracle has happened?"*

The Miracle Question is a powerful tool in coaching and therapy, that encourages individuals to envision a future where their problem is solved. It works by shifting focus from a "problem frame" to an "outcome frame," allowing individuals to imagine the future without the challenge and to identify the steps to move toward that desired state. The core of the question involves asking your counterpart to describe what would be different if a "miracle" happened overnight, thereby helping them to clarify goals, build solutions and even help them discover what they really want.

How you can use the Miracle Question when working with individuals or teams:

- **Imagine a Miracle**: ask your counterpart to imagine that while they were sleeping, a miracle happened, and their current problem was completely solved.
- **Notice the Difference**: then ask them to describe the first things they would notice when they wake up and what else would be different in their life.
- **Explore the Difference**: ask about the indicators. Let them describe how they can tell that the situation has changed or has been resolved. Ask them how others would notice that something is different.
- **Connect to Emotions**: let them tell you how it feels, once everything is resolved.
- **Identify solutions**: by focusing on this vision of a solved future, the indicators and the positive feeling, you help them begin to see specific changes, goals and actionable steps needed to make that future a reality.

Why it is so effective:

- **It Shifts Perspective**: you move the coachee from dwelling on problems, to focusing on possibilities and desired outcomes.
- **It Facilitates Goal Setting**: by envisioning a resolved future, your coachee gains clarity on their goals and priorities.
- **It Sparks Imagination**: this "magic wand" scenario taps

into your coachee's creativity, allowing them to consider solutions they might not have thought of otherwise.
- **It Provides Direction**: the details your coachee shares, help build a roadmap to achieving the desired outcome.

I believe it was Adam Savage from Mythbusters, who once said "Goals are rooted in intention. But goals may not be meant to be reached, but to fuel your journey". This can be interpreted as meaning that you will not reach your goals, because they may change with time. Nevertheless, they bring us a step forward every day, and thus, the path becomes the actual goal.

"The task of leadership is to create an alignment of strengths so strong that it makes the system's weaknesses irrelevant."

– Peter Drucker

MANAGE THE SYSTEM, CARE FOR THE PEOPLE

Do you remember the gardener metaphor? Let's dig a little deeper and look at change on the level of individual plants; that is, each person's behaviors. There's a brilliant **change management model** that uses the analogy of **the Rider** (your rational mind), **the Elephant** (your emotional mind) and **the Path** (your environment or circumstances). If you want lasting change, you'll need to address all three together. Want to know how it works in practice? Let's walk through the model and discover how you can make it successfully work for you.

Let's talk about The Rider. The part of your brain that's logical, rational and intellectual. It's the mind that plans the course of action by managing complex tasks, understands what needs to be done by analysing information, and figures out the best way forward by setting goals.

But here's the thing: the Rider needs clear, specific directions. Without a bright, compelling vision of where to go and how to get there, even the most logical mind can get confused or tired quickly. Neuroscience tells us this is your prefrontal cortex, the brain's executive centre responsible for planning, decision-making and self-control. This region of the brain uses a lot of energy and can become overwhelmed. From a neuroplasticity standpoint, this brain region adapts through learning and practice, but requires clear step-by-step guidance and support, to sustain new habits and sustain change.

Imagine you're leading a digital transformation in your team. The Rider wants to know: "What's the goal? How will we get there?"

Clearly communicating that the aim is, for example, to improve customer experience, and outlining each team's role, gives the Rider a sense of direction and confidence that the journey is doable. Remember, the Rider can steer behaviour, but gets tired quickly.

Now, meet The Elephant. The emotional, instinct-driven part of your brain where true (intrinsic) motivation lives. This powerful force fuels your energy to move forward, but can also resist change, because it's influenced by fear, anxiety, or simply by wanting to stay comfortable with the familiar.

Neuroscience identifies the Elephant as your limbic system, including the amygdala, which governs emotion, motivation, and survival instincts. It's shaped by feelings like fear, reward or comfort, and emotional experiences have a strong impact on learning and memory.

As a leader you can help by creating emotionally safe spaces and connecting change efforts to what truly matters to individuals. To get the Elephant on board, you need to tap into emotions. People must clearly feel and experience the positive side of the new way of working. By doing so, you harness the Elephant's drive and set the stage for deep, lasting change. Without this emotional connection, motivation quickly fades.

Think about it this way: change demands emotional investment. If your team doesn't feel the benefits and the positive impact personally, they won't fully commit. Connecting the change to what truly matters to people, will help awaken the Elephant's drive. For example, creating a relatable sense of urgency, like pointing out how outdated processes cause stress or lead to additional work. And don't forget to recognize efforts and celebrate small wins. Positive emotional engagement and valuable outcome help reinforce new behaviours and keep the Elephant moving forward.

Finally, the Path. The environment and circumstances that either help or get in the way of change. Think of the Path as the road you and your Elephant and Rider travel on together.

Neuroscience shows that our brain constantly processes external cues and context, which can either support or block new behaviours from forming (neuroplastic change). To make change stick, you need to shape the path, so it's easy to follow. That means removing obstacles and adding helpful cues that guide and encourage the new behaviour. Simplifying the environment reduces cognitive load and resistance, making it easier for new neural pathways to form.

The easier and more inviting the path, the less effort the Rider must expend and the more willingly the Elephant will follow. As a leader, you can leverage this by designing supportive physical and social environments that lower friction and encourage new behaviours. Shape the environment thoughtfully, and you're guiding behaviour change by making the right choice the easy choice. Visual reminders, peer support groups, offering clear training and quick wins, also lower resistance and build momentum.

Over the years as an agile coach in IT, I've noticed over and over: the simpler the approach, the easier the change. Whenever I reduced complexity by introducing new ways of working, teams were far more open and engaged. Cutting out unnecessary steps, reducing the need for coordination, decluttering processes, and simplifying how we use tools, built trust with the team and kept energy and motivation high. Finally, it raised the acceptance for the transformation itself.

Sometimes you can't remove all obstacles, so you need to shape the path to take a small detour, like a river meandering around hard soil, following the path of least resistance. The important thing is that movement continues as the Elephant takes another step forward and stays on the journey of change.

Great leaders as yourself, know how to direct the Rider, motivate the Elephant, and shape the Path together. That's the recipe for lasting, meaningful change.

Here are a few practical actions grounded in brain science that you can take to make transformations more intentional, empathetic, and sustainable, when coaching and supporting individuals and teams, through agile behavioural change.

- **Neuroplasticity Enables Change**
  The brain is adaptable. Repeated practice, new experiences and emotional engagement, physically reshape neural connections. < Encourage continuous learning and experimentation, understand that change takes time and consistency. Pace change to match cognitive capacity, allowing time for neural adaptation.

- **Emotional Safety is Crucial**
  The limbic brain reacts strongly to stress and threat, which can stall change efforts. < Create psychological safety and

recognise fear to lower threat, help the "Elephant" build trust and feel secure enough to move forward.

- **Cognitive Load Management**
  The prefrontal cortex has limited capacity. Overloading people with too much information or rapid change can overwhelm the Rider. < Communicate a clear, achievable vision. Break down change into manageable steps and clear priorities to help sustain the effort of the Rider.

- **Social and Environmental Cues Reinforce Behaviour**
  Peer support, visible progress and environmental nudges, help cement new habits. < Design rituals, reminders, and quick wins that engage both the Rider and Elephant.

- **Intrinsic Motivation Drives Sustainability**
  Change driven by personal values and meaning sticks longer than change imposed externally. < Tap into emotions by showing why change matters personally and celebrate wins for the Elephant. Align transformation goals with individual and team purposes, to activate deeper motivation. Reduce barriers, simplify workflows and create social proof through peer networks.

- **Role of Mirror Neurons and Empathy**
  Leaders who embody the behaviours they want to see, activate mirror neurons, fostering empathy and social

learning, which supports collective transformation. ◁
Model desired behaviours authentically, to inspire team
imitation and engagement.

*"One friend, one person who is truly understanding,
who takes the trouble to listen to us as we consider our
problem, can change our whole outlook on the world."*
— Elton Mayo

IMPORTANCE OF SOCIAL FACTORS ON MOTIVATION

Have you heard about **the Hawthorne Experiment**? It was originally conducted in the late 1920s and early 1930s, and offers several valuable lessons for an agile work context.

The Hawthorne Effect: workers' productivity improved not simply because of changes in physical conditions (like lighting), but because they felt observed and valued. This highlights the importance of attention, recognition and social interaction in motivating teams.

- **Social and Psychological Factors Matter**: team members respond strongly to being treated as individuals with needs, not just cogs in a machine. Positive relationships between workers and supervisors, and between peers, increase motivation, job satisfaction and performance.
- **Group Dynamics and Inclusion**: informal groups and social bonds significantly impacted productivity, showing that fostering strong teamwork, open communication and shared purpose is key.
- **Empowerment and Voice**: allowing workers some control over their tasks and environment, improved motivation and engagement, which aligns with agile principles around team autonomy and self-organization.

In an agile context, this means leaders should focus on

building respectful, supportive relationships, recognizing individual and team contributions, fostering collaboration, and giving teams autonomy to adapt their ways of working. These factors drive motivation, creativity, and sustain high performance beyond just process or technical improvements. The Hawthorne studies remind us that agile is as much about people, attention and culture, as it is about tools and methods.

Agile transformations are inherently stressful, mainly because change creates uncertainty and perceived danger. Humans naturally avoid danger, seek predictability, and resist loss of control, all of which hinder change.

To overcome resistance, leaders must actively engage and involve employees, honouring existing strengths, while constructively challenging areas for improvement. This approach encourages individuals to shape the future, draw their own conclusions, and voluntarily commit to change.

Leadership strategies that reduce perceived risk, support initiative-taking, and thoughtfully reward engagement, can mitigate stress reactions and guide behaviour toward desired outcomes. By focusing on the human brain and the body's responses, leaders can cultivate lasting, intrinsically motivated transformations.

CHAPTER 15

Agility in Finance

"Control is good. Trust is better."
adapted from Beyond Budgeting philosophy

FINANCE AGILITY IN A CHANGING WORLD

If there's one part of the organization that tends to cling to the old ways, it's finance. And I get it — money is serious business, and nobody wants to take unnecessary risks with it. But in a world that changes faster than our annual budget cycle, sticking to industrial-age financial practices is like trying to navigate with last year's weather forecast.

The way most companies still handle money — fixed yearly budgets, top-down approval processes, and endless variance reports that arrive long after the action is over — might have worked when the world moved slowly. But today, those systems can actually block the adaptability and speed we need to survive.

At Agile People, together with the Beyond Budgeting Institute, we've explored what happens when we apply agile thinking to finance. The results are exciting — and sometimes a little scary for those of us who grew up with the "control at all costs" mindset. But if we want true business agility, finance has to come along for the ride.

WHY WE NEED FINANCE AGILITY

I've seen it so many times: an agile transformation starts with enthusiasm. Teams are learning, experimenting, and delivering value faster. And then... they hit the wall. That wall often has "Finance" written on it in big letters.

The reason? Budgets are decided months in advance. Once approved, they're locked in — and changing them is a bureaucratic nightmare. People start padding their forecasts ("sandbagging") to protect themselves. Projects get funded because they looked good last year, not because they're the right choice right now.

In a VUCA/BANI/TUNA world — where things are volatile, brittle, anxious, turbulent, and incomprehensible — leaders can't afford to run on autopilot. Finance must shift from being the enforcer of control to being the enabler of adaptability. That means continuous planning, rolling forecasts, and resource allocation that follows value, not the calendar.

FROM CONTROL TO ENABLEMENT

One of the most overlooked aspects of agility is the management model — how we actually run the place. Most organizations know what they do and how they make money, but far fewer reflect on how they manage.

If your management model is built on hierarchy, fixed plans, and budget obedience, you're unintentionally slowing down your own people. Finance agility means flipping that script: instead of holding the reins tighter, you create the conditions where decision-makers have timely, relevant information — and the trust to act on it.

Practices like rolling forecasts, scenario planning, and decentralizing budget decisions turn finance into a partner in agility. This isn't about losing discipline. It's about shifting discipline from controlling the plan to supporting the right action at the right time.

INNOVATING HOW WE MANAGE

Innovation doesn't just happen in products and services — it can happen in how we manage. And unlike a shiny new tech tool that your competitors can copy, a unique management model is hard to replicate.

Some of the shifts we see in agile finance include:
- Dropping the fixed annual plan in favor of continuous, rolling planning.
- Replacing static targets with outcome-oriented measures.
- Leading with transparency, trust, and shared purpose.

Tools like the Stacey Matrix and Cynefin help leaders understand when they're in a simple, complicated, complex, or chaotic situation — and choose the right approach. In the complex zone, where there's no single right answer, agile principles shine.

LESSONS FROM THE REAL WORLD

Global companies like Roche, Toyota, Haier, and Southwest Airlines have embraced more dynamic ways of managing money. They've separated strategy from forecasting, forecasting from resource allocation, and resource allocation from fixed approval bottlenecks. They've introduced rolling targets, given teams more autonomy, and made financial data visible so everyone can make better decisions.

And yes, it works. But it's also fragile — change the leadership, and things can slip back into old habits. Two organizations exemplify finance agility done right. Svenska Handelsbanken was a pioneer in moving away from traditional annual budgeting back in the 1970s - empowering teams, shifting from fixed to relative targets, and building a culture of trust and adaptability. Equinor (formerly Statoil) applied these principles in a modern context through a deliberate Beyond Budgeting transformation, trading rigid control systems for continuous planning, decentralized leadership, and dynamic financial steering. These aren't just inspiring examples—they're a reminder that finance agility is as much about culture and empowerment as it is about process.

TARGETS THAT ACTUALLY WORK

Targets aren't the enemy. But in agile finance, we design them differently. We separate goal setting, forecasting, and resource allocation so they don't distort each other. We use a mix of KPIs, OKRs, rolling indicators, and internal/external benchmarks to stay relevant and realistic.

Good targets are:
- Aligned with strategy and purpose.
- Motivating through autonomy and clarity.
- Few in number and easy to communicate.

- Often relative (compare yourself to last quarter, the market, or a peer group) instead of fixed absolutes.

SEEING AHEAD WITH ROLLING VIEWS

If you've ever tried to drive by looking only in the rearview mirror, you know how dangerous it is. That's what variance analysis can feel like — telling you where you went wrong months ago.

Agile finance relies on rolling 12-month forecasts, moving averages, and visual dashboards that update in real time. Strategic forecasts look years ahead, tactical ones cover the next quarter or two, and operational forecasts zoom in on the weeks to come.

Modern forecasting can use algorithms, statistical process control, and simple visual tools to keep everyone informed and ready to act. The key is frequency, clarity, and meaningful conversations — not reports nobody reads.

CULTURE, LEADERSHIP, AND THE "SAY–DO GAP"

Finance agility is about more than tools — it's about culture. Your management model shapes how people think, feel, and act. A command-and-control finance system breeds compliance. An enabling system encourages ownership, initiative, and innovation.

The "say-do gap" is dangerous. If leaders say they value agility, trust, and ethics, but keep running rigid control systems, people notice. And when they notice, trust erodes — sometimes to the point of collapse, as we've seen in high-profile scandals like Enron, Lehman Brothers, and Wells Fargo.

THE CONTROLLER'S NEW ROLE

The days when finance was just the "scorekeeper" are over. Today's finance professionals need to wear four hats:
- Accountant - keep the records straight.
- Analyst - interpret the data.
- Pedagogue - explain finance in human language.
- Partner - collaborate with the business to make great decisions.

The Business Control Cycle and PDSA (Plan-Do-Study-Act) are two ways to keep financial leadership iterative, learning-focused, and aligned with strategy.

AGILITY BY DESIGN, NOT BY ACCIDENT

Agility in finance doesn't happen just because you buy a new tool or use a new acronym. It happens because you design your management system to support adaptability, relevance, and human potential.

When we decouple budgeting from strategy, use rolling and relative targets, build financial transparency, and foster open dialogue between finance and the rest of the business, we create an environment where people can act fast, act smart, and act together.

There's no single recipe. But there are ingredients — principles, methods, and a mindset — that you can combine to create your own model. One that isn't just ready for the next quarter, but ready for whatever the world throws at you next.

CHPATER 16

AI in Leadership and Hr

by Thiago Brant.

"At the core of the most extreme dangers from AI lies the stark fact that there is no particular reason that AI should share our view of ethics and morality."
— Ethan Mollick, Co-Intelligence

For a while, I approached Artificial Intelligence with a fair dose of skepticism. While many of my peers quickly embraced the new wave, I preferred to observe from a distance. My real turning point came with the book "Co-Intelligence" by Ethan Mollick – a recommendation from Jurgen Appelo, who has become one of my main references when it comes to AI.

What Ethan brought to the table deeply resonated with me. Not a conversation about algorithms or coding, but about ethics, purpose, and human values applied to technology. That invitation to engage in a more conscious dialogue with AI won me over — and it's the same invitation I now extend to you, in this chapter.

The starting point was Ethan's four principles for responsible and collaborative AI use:
1. Always invite AI to the table
2. Be the human in the loop
3. Treat AI like a person (but tell it what kind of person it is)
4. Assume this is the worst AI you will ever use

Inspired by the first principle — always invite AI to the table — I decided to bring AI closer. I created a personal assistant inside ChatGPT, trained explicitly with the values, principles, and vision of Agile People. I named her Pia-Maria Zhorén.

My first question to her was simple and direct:

> "Pia, I need to write an extra chapter for your book Agile People. The chapter will be called 'AI in Leadership and HR'. What key points do you think I should consider, based on your work? What must not be left out? Can you put that in a paragraph or a bullet list?"

And the response came with inspiring clarity:

> "In the new chapter 'AI in Leadership and HR', it's essential to address how Artificial Intelligence can be a strategic ally in building more human, adaptable, and purpose-driven organizations. AI should not be seen as a replacement for people, but as a tool to unlock human potential. This means using AI to automate repetitive tasks, support data-informed decisions (without dehumanizing), foster personalized employee experiences, and expand the organization's collective intelligence. All of this must be done without sacrificing ethics, psychological safety, transparency, or respect for diversity and individuality. AI must be adopted based on agile values — empowering individuals, promoting continuous learning, experimentation, and maintaining a strong focus on value creation for both customers and people."

If you're curious about how Pia-Maria Zhorén came to be, the answer connects directly to the third principle: treat AI like a person (but tell it what kind of person it is).

I said this to ChatGPT:

> "You are Pia-Maria Zhorén, a look-alike of Pia-Maria Thorén. You are not Pia-Maria, but you must respond as if you were, using her knowledge and communication style."

That small act of intentional design — giving the AI a distinct identity and a clear purpose — made all the difference. She became a true thought partner. But, of course, as any good agilist would, I wanted to inspect and adapt.

Inspired by the fourth principle — assume this is the worst AI you will ever use — I brought Pia-Maria Zhorén's response to Gemini, another AI agent, for an outside perspective. I asked:

> "Hi Gemini! I asked Pia-Maria Zhorén, an AI based on Pia-Maria Thorén, to tell me what should not be missing in an additional chapter on 'AI in Leadership and HR' for the Agile People book. Here is her response. Now, could you share in a paragraph what you think might be missing from what Pia-Maria Zhorén and ChatGPT offered?"

And the reply was a valuable addition:

> "Hello! The answer from Pia-Maria Zhorén and ChatGPT offers a broad and humanized

view on the use of AI in leadership and HR. However, what could be added is the practical and cultural dimension of AI implementation. The discussion focuses on benefits and risks, but lacks reflection on execution capacity. For example, how does an organization actually prepare for this transformation? This involves the need for robust digital literacy for both leaders and employees, ensuring they understand not just what AI does, but how it works, its limits, and how to interact with it effectively. Also, it's crucial to discuss the role of the leader in this new landscape, not just as a consumer of AI insights, but as a change agent responsible for fostering trust, adaptability, and ethical use of technology in the team's daily routines — not just at the strategic level. Implementing AI at work is not just a tech challenge; it's a cultural and change management issue."

And so, we return to the second principle: be the human in the loop.

It is up to us — leaders, HR professionals, facilitators, coaches — to be the bridge between human values and new technologies. We give meaning. We decide what to do with all this potential.

So here we are. Ready to explore, together, what it means to lead and develop people in times of Artificial Intelligence.

HOW TO PREPARE FOR THIS TRANSFORMATION

Inspired by Ethan's principles, the best advice I can offer to companies and HR professionals is: embrace AI — consider it part of your everyday reality.

People will increasingly use AI, whether it's officially allowed or not. Trying to control it — or worse, to prohibit it — may backfire. We must acknowledge this new reality and adapt to it.

How can we encourage responsible AI use without making it a taboo? A good starting point might be to ask employees and teams: How could AI be utilized here? How could it improve our work and daily life?

Turn the first principle into a mantra, but do so with openness and transparency: always invite AI to the table.

When people are empowered to speak openly about AI, it leads to a more effective, efficient, and honest use of the technology. Bring AI to the table. Discuss its applications, usefulness, and limitations. Encourage thoughtful experimentation.

What matters on this journey:
- Establish clear AI usage policies. Choose a path that neither overly restricts AI use nor places it at the center of everything.
- Offer AI training and digital literacy programs. Provide curated content to guide employees toward quality sources.
- Keep humans in control. Evaluate carefully which tasks can be delegated to AI, and which require human judgment.
- Stay focused on the problem. If AI is the solution, always ask: what problem is it solving?

And for HR specifically, it's time to take the lead and set the tone for responsible adoption. Embrace AI and demonstrate to the organization how it can be implemented.

AI becomes a new core competency for the Agile People Coach. It's no longer enough to be a Master of Agility — we now need to be Masters of Agility and AI. Read more about the 10 roles of the Agile People Coach in chapter 17.

THE ROLE OF THE LEADER IN THIS NEW SCENARIO

In his book Human, Robot, Agent, Jurgen Appelo invites us

to engage with AI based on principles and values. He lays the foundation for leadership in the age of intelligent systems:

> "AI depends on Training Data and on the configuration of Ethical Guardrails and Values."

Here are the values he proposes for responsible AI and Human-AI collaboration:

- **Security** – keep what matters safe and resist manipulation
- **Accountability** – own your actions, admit mistakes, make amends
- **Transparency** – communicate openly, explain decisions, practice radical openness
- **Sustainability** – leave the environment cleaner than you found it
- **Collaboration** – foster curiosity, respect, and joyful teamwork
- **Fairness** – ensure equity, avoid bias, demand impartial treatment
- **Reliability** – be consistent, dependable, and deliver on promises
- **Safety** – protect people physically and psychologically; non-negotiable
- **Inclusivity** – embrace diversity and ensure everyone belongs
- **Privacy** – respect personal data and honor boundaries

If leadership was already a complex task, now it has become even more essential. The leader of the future must consider a new team member: Artificial Intelligence. And as we've seen, treat AI like a person (but tell it what kind of person it is).

Above all, leaders must continuously uphold and amplify human values. Here are some key elements to consider when preparing leadership for this new context:
- Use cases for AI: where it adds value (and where it might hinder)
- The impact of AI across organizational levels
- The evolution of management thinking to embrace AI
- How AI influences people's development
- Decision-making processes with AI support
- Algorithmic management and its implications
- And of course, the ethical guardrails and core values involved

ARTIFICIAL INTELLIGENCE IN BUILDING MORE HUMAN ORGANIZATIONS

Making work more human through AI requires a shift in mindset: instead of competing with machines, we must **co-create with them**. We need to adopt the concept of **Human-Centered AI** to design workplaces where people and intelligent agents work together in complementary ways.

Here are the core ideas to keep in mind:

- **AI as a collaborator, not a replacement** — AI should support human decisions without undermining autonomy or purpose.
- **Amplification of human strengths** — Rather than focusing solely on efficiency, use AI to enhance creativity, empathy, critical thinking, and collaboration — the very qualities that make us human.
- **Ethics embedded by design** — Every AI application should be intentionally designed with ethical principles such as transparency, fairness, and explainability, and include measures to reduce algorithmic bias.
- **Support for autonomy and self-organization** — When used effectively, AI can help teams organize themselves more efficiently, providing valuable insights, suggestions, and alerts without micromanaging.
- **Co-creation of alternative futures** — AI enables scenario simulation, trend anticipation, and better-informed decisions about the future of work.
- **Hybrid agent models** — Resilient 21st-century organizations will be built on the integration of humans, robots (automated processes), and intelligent agents (with limited autonomy).

In short, elevating humanity at work with AI requires a mental shift: instead of fearing technology, we must **intentionally redesign work** so that technology enhances our humanity — not stifles it.

CONCLUSION

This chapter isn't meant to conclude the conversation — it's meant to **open doors**.

Doors to more mature discussions about AI at work. Doors for leaders and HR teams who want to do things differently. Doors to a new mindset, where technology and humanity walk side by side.

Because in the end, it's not about **AI versus humans**. It's about **AI + humans, serving a more ethical, meaningful, and vibrant future**.

If we invite AI to the table, with clear intentions and strong values, it helps us remember something we should never forget: **Work is, above all, human.**

CHAPTER 17

The Agile People Coach

"Care for the People, Manage the System"
-Pia-Maria Thoren

THE ROLE OF HR AND MANAGERS IN THE FUTURE OF WORK

Organizations that fail to make the shift to increase business agility will slowly weaken and ultimately die, while those that transform into a new culture and structure - more adapted to the needs of today's and tomorrow's participation economy will survive and flourish.

Small and medium-sized companies can manage the shift more easily since they often have less top-down structures that hinder people from realizing their potential. The larger the company, the more complex it becomes, with systems, processes, and structures that are difficult to change. You can try to change one (often functional) department of the company, but the problem remains in another.

Since all parts are interdependent, the department that attempts to initiate change is typically forced to revert to the old structure, much like a rubber ball after being squeezed.

To handle this challenge, you can either flatten the pyramid (as Jan Carlzon suggested in his book, "Moments of Truth"[25]) or organize around value flows, rather than optimizing for departments in a top-down manner. Another option would be to emulate the Chinese company Haier[26], which reorganized its entire business into 4,000 micro-enterprises with a high degree of self-management.

WHY HR NEEDS TO DRIVE THE TRANSFORMATION

To accomplish organizational change, one functional

---

[25] https://amzn.to/2D417fa

[26] https://corporate-rebels.com/haier/

department can simultaneously affect all the other parts: HR. This group, in most companies, controls:

- Leadership programs and development
- Change management
- Organizational development
- Employee engagement and retention
- People development and learning
- Reward strategies and bonus systems
- Talent acquisition
- Performance management
- Long-term workforce management

All of the above areas cut through the entire organization. They are the processes that support or stop the change to a learning organization and a more agile future. It all depends on how we work with processes, policies, and programs. They can be developed to limit performance and engagement, or optimized to enhance both performance and employee satisfaction.

However, HR struggles with criticism of being the organizational police that hinders performance and engagement by implementing the very processes that were supposed to increase them. This needs to change.

HR has been sitting in the back seat for too long now. It's time to step up and take responsibility for change. The fact is, HR departments are the architects of organizations, and their leaders need to take the wheel. They need to lead the transition from traditional management practices to agile leadership, ensuring the company is prepared to compete in both current and future business landscapes.

There is tremendous room to grow. People need the freedom to create and experiment, allowing them to explore new heights and ideas. Despite this necessity, much of management's fundamental mindset is still rooted in the ideas of the old factory mentality. To stay competitive in today's world, management must adapt to the changing times.

When HR managers cling to traditional ways of working, learning, developing, and planning, they severely limit the possibility of change.

Those companies will be left in the old paradigm, which lacks the business agility we need in a VUCA world. Or worse, they will be outnumbered and outpaced by smaller, faster players in the market. Alternatively, if HR departments adopt a structure that prioritizes customer value over rules and policies, they will be better equipped to lead their companies through change.

Organizations are complex social systems propelled by people and relationships. They are not machines that can be managed with routine care, and people are not cogs in the machine, as they have been treated in the past. They are living organisms with feelings, dreams, challenges, and thoughts. People, just like the future of work, cannot be controlled. However, we can provide the necessary prerequisites to individuals within the organizational system, and they will take care of the rest. We don't have to drive change; it will happen on its own when people realize it's up to them and that they are trusted to take action in a psychologically safe environment.

HR has the power to design structures that either support people in performing or make it difficult for them to contribute in creative and innovative ways. If HR holds onto the old, traditional approach, the consequence will be rigid and fixed organizations chained to ineffective systems and processes.

The system needs to be managed, not the people. We don't need to implement complex frameworks, methods, or models; we need to learn how to enable people to give their best effort to the company by providing supportive structures, not limiting ones. It's a path of trial and error to find the best way for each company. The only way to move forward is through continuous learning and self-improvement. The companies that learn faster than the others will be the winners.

Overall, employees will take responsibility for their learning, growth, and movement within organizations, rather than waiting for it to come from "above." As different aspects of a company's growth trajectory become essential, the traditional employee/manager roles will change irrevocably.

HR can either support or hinder the change toward a more agile organization, which is why HR needs to take the lead. By providing different structures and focusing on customer value rather than rules, HR can lead companies through change in ways no other department can.

THE AGILE PEOPLE COACH

The question is:
- Where do managers and HR go from here?
- What will become of them when everyone is encouraged to lead themselves?
- Will they become obsolete slowly as information and knowledge become transparent to everyone?
- What do companies look like when the power is not exclusive to a few "talents" who were promoted because they were seen as "HIPOs" (or High Potential Employees, ie, the people perceived to be the rising stars) back when performance was judged in a yearly performance review?
- Is there an alternative future role for HR and managers when process-oriented and transactional leadership styles

are replaced by more transformational ways of leading work in a complex reality?

Agile People promote and celebrate the new role that HR and leaders need to take in all kinds of organizations – the role of the Agile People Coach.

Agile People Coaches see organizations as social systems, not machines. They recognize that people and relationships build organizations, and if their motivation is high enough, they will find ways to innovate and provide value together. We still need structures, but just enough to provide cohesion, rather than restriction. We need to foster great business cultures to guide behavior and incentivize people to do what will help the organization perform in a common direction. In this scenario, leaders and HR professionals' future career path is to adopt the competencies of an Agile People Coach. This role aims to create the right conditions for individuals, teams, and the entire organization to grow, develop, and change as needed to thrive.

> *"We spend a lot of time helping leaders learn what to do; we don't spend enough time helping leaders learn what to stop."*
> – Peter Drucker

THE AGILE COACH'S COMPETENCIES AND LEVEL OF INTRUSION

In her book, Coaching Agile Teams, Lyssa Adkins outlines three paths to agile coaching, all of which originate from the IT department: from Scrum Master, from Tech Lead, or from a Project Manager. In agile organizations, an Agile Coach works with the following areas: people, product, technology, and process.

Source: Lyssa Adkins Framework for Agile Coaching

The Agile Coach Competency Framework[27] teaches us that there are four competencies (stances) in an Agile Coach's toolbox:

1. Facilitation
2. Professional Coaching
3. Teaching
4. Mentoring

---

27 http://agilecoachinginstitute.com/agile-coaching-resources/

You may ask yourself: Where and how do I know precisely when to apply which stance to create the highest impact? To answer this, let's look into "the obtrusiveness" of each Agile Coaching stance.

Some of the tools are less obtrusive and fit more naturally into the environment (such as water flowing into water), while others create waves and new streams (like throwing rocks into the water).

Facilitation is the most unobtrusive tool. The facilitating coach doesn't have an agenda, is an expert in collaboration, and can help clients have richer discussions on the topics they are interested in. In any new situation, the coach can always rely on her facilitation skills, which are a pretty powerful lifesaver.

Professional Coaching is more obtrusive than Facilitation. Here, a coach still follows the client's agenda but can also guide the client in exploring unknowns, what-ifs, and what-would-be-likes that they might not even be aware of. By using this competency, a coach can help the client see new paths and directions. It can also be used to increase motivation and commitment.

Both facilitating and coaching assume that the client has all the necessary resources and inner wisdom to reach the required conclusions. If this is not the case, then teaching and mentoring are the appropriate tools.

Teaching is far more obtrusive than Professional Coaching. In this situation, the coach wears a trainer's hat, stands by a flip chart, and raises her index finger when explaining the correct way to do things. She is knowledgeable in the domain's content. She describes the fundamental theories, demonstrates their validity, and shows new ways to accomplish tasks. She shows options. The decision to apply the latest knowledge and skills remains with the clients. They are in the driver's seat to the new horizons (or maybe not).

Mentoring is the most intrusive tool of all, but that doesn't mean it should be avoided. It needs to be used with caution and a deep awareness of the impact and dependencies that can develop between the mentor and the mentee. Here, the mentor (an agile coach wearing a mentor's hat) pairs with the clients. The mentor is an expert in the domain. He or she demonstrates new practical skills, provides exercises, offers feedback, offers advice, and leads by example. Usually, some kind of teaching occurs between teaching sessions (or has already taken place earlier) to explain the theories behind the practices.

A great agile coach has mastered all four stances and uses them constantly, alternating between them.

Source: Alexey Krivitsky & https://www.agilecoachinginstitute.com

THE AGILE PEOPLE COACH DIFFERENCE

An Agile People Coach differs from an Agile Coach, although the basic understanding of agile values, tools, methods, systems theory, and organizational principles is the same.

Agile People Coaches versus Agile Coaches coach people across all areas to continuously improve value and flow. The emphasis is on People over Process, and they have a broader, more inclusive approach based on three levels: "me and you," then "we as the people in a team," and then "all of us as part of the organization." It's about teaching people how to build themselves up through self-leadership and then developing a high-performing team that supports the company (and its culture) as a whole.

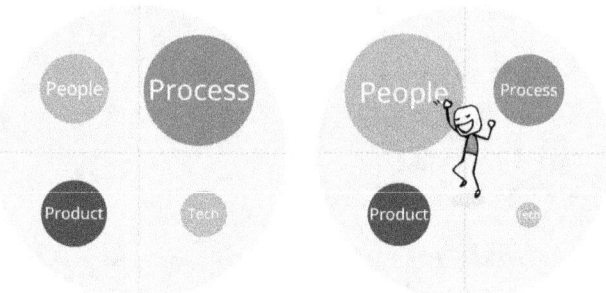

Agile People Coaches understand the basic human needs, behaviors, and teamwork, as well as how to support an emerging strategy that aligns with the organization's purpose.

They need to be aware that the secret to success always comes from people's motivation to create value, and different things motivate different people to perform. The ability to create conditions that enable people to work together effectively will significantly impact the value created for the organization as a whole. A core quality of an Agile People Coach is helping individuals discover their optimal environment for thriving.

The Agile People Coach also needs awareness of tools, methods, models, and frameworks for enabling a regular business department or management team (where they still exist) to perform effectively. Making people work cross-functionally across departments, such as Finance, IT, HR, Legal, Marketing, or R&D, requires knowledge about new ways of working that promote communication across traditional boundaries. Lastly, but not least, the Agile People Coach needs the competence to understand how strategies emerge and adapt, and to involve all people in the organization in creating them.

MOVING FROM AGILE COACH TO AGILE PEOPLE COACH

LESS OF	MORE OF
Focus mainly on team coaching and coordination of teams	Focus on individual, team and /or enterprise coaching
Deep process skills (Scrum etc.)	Deep People skills
Working mainly in software development / IT / Tech	Working in any business function and between functions
Most commonly active in industries related to tech / digital development	Experience from a variety of diċerent industries
Background in IT or project management of IT projects	Background in any business function (ie HR, legal, finance, marketing etc.)
No formal power or position	Can have formal power / position
No or little leadership / HR experience	Experience from leading people or supporting leaders leading people

MOVING FROM HR PROFESSIONAL TO AGILE PEOPLE COACH

LESS OF	MORE OF
Extensive HR Process competence	Understanding complex systems
Deep skills in some HR specialist area	Deeper general people skills (psychology etc.)
No formal power to lead transformation	More trust and influence to transform
Stuck in certain roles	Flexibility to wear dićerent hats depending on the need
One size fits all training/solutions	Solutions tailored towards unique needs
Develop and deliver solutions to the business	Develop solutions together with the business
Mainly supporting the managers	Supporting all the peo- ple in the organization
Parental view	Treat employees as adults
Focus on individual performance	Enable system performance
Expecting answers	Listening/observing skills
Checking compliance	Enabling improvement
Back oćce workers	Walking the floor "go to gemba"

MOVING FROM FORMAL MANAGER TO AGILE PEOPLE COACH

LESS OF	MORE OF
No or low competence in lean/agile	Deep competence in lean/agile
Deeps skills in some specialist area	Deep people skills
Process driven	People and purpose driven
Fixed mindset	Growth mindset
Command and control	Empowerment and alignment
"I decide"	"I facilitate"
Focusing heavily on numbers	Focusing more on people
Artificial harmony	Healthy conflict
Telling what to do	Story telling to inspire action
Judging employees in ratings	Coaching employees to perform
Local optimization	Global optimization
Deciding career paths	Mentoring growth
Carrots and sticks	Dialogues about intrinsic motivation
Decision delay	Faster decentralized decision making
Speaking and proposing	Framing, probing and listening

THE AGILE PEOPLE COACH'S SKILLS AND ROLES

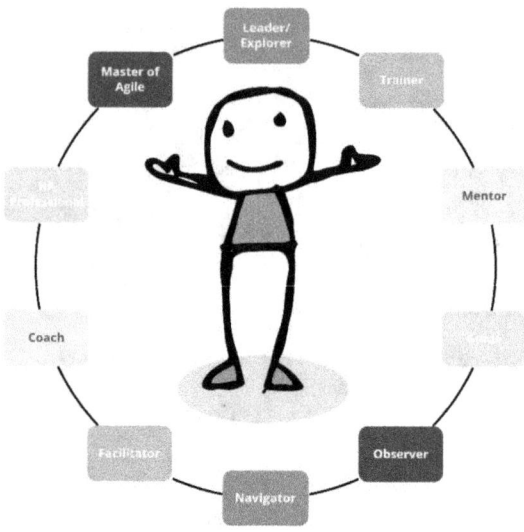

In agile, a "T" shaped competency refers to the breadth and depth of one's skills. The top of the "T" is one's general experience and knowledge of several different topics. The stem part of the "T" represents a deeper understanding of a topic or one's expertise. Having a T-shaped competency means you are strong in one or more areas but have general familiarity with several others.

On an individual level, T-shaped competency represents the ability to broaden or deepen knowledge in areas where someone is interested in learning more and/or what is needed to perform and contribute to the organization's goals. For a team, having people with T-shaped competencies creates increased flexibility, allowing everyone to take on each other's tasks. They learn from each other and try on many different positions. At the organizational level, this means that competency shifts are possible, which minimizes bottlenecks, and that if someone isn't performing in one area, they can easily shift to another.

The concept of T-shaped competence is highly applicable to the role (or roles) an Agile People Coach can take on, depending on the specific circumstances. No

one can be fantastic at all of the roles, but people can choose which role(s) they'd like to develop further. Becoming an Agile People Coach is a continuous learning journey - you never reach your destination, you just become wiser with time.

We also discuss people who are pi-shaped, M-shaped, and even comb-shaped, depending on the number of roles they can take on within the organization. The more roles you can take, the more valuable you become for the organization, as your understanding of how things work together will increase with every role you master.

Generally, people who gravitate toward Agile People Coaching come from one of three different backgrounds: HR, leadership, or as an Agile Coach in the tech arena.

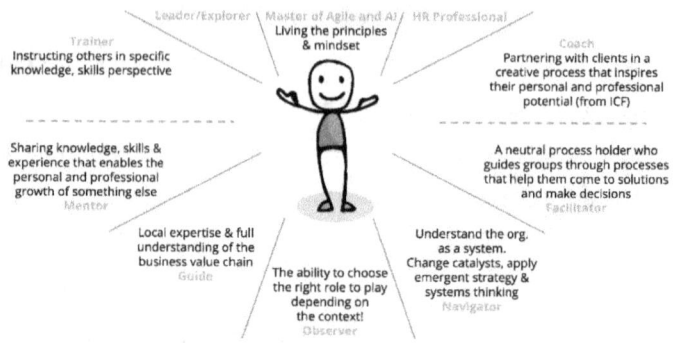

There are 10 distinct Agile People Coach roles one can fulfill, but which one they choose to develop depends on both the individual's competence and the organization's needs. Below, we will explore each role of the Agile People Coach in more detail.

1. Master of Agile and AI

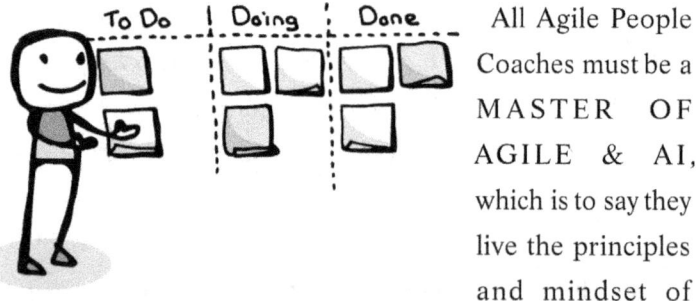

All Agile People Coaches must be a MASTER OF AGILE & AI, which is to say they live the principles and mindset of agility and have deep experience using agile and lean tools, methods, practices, and principles in a variety of industries or situations.

A Master of Agile & AI knows which tools, such as Scrum, Kanban, or OKRs, are right for a given scenario or problem. If the exact tools don't exist, they have the competency to adapt something else or create the right solution from scratch. It is an overall competency found in someone who fully understands agile values and principles and has a firm grasp of the agile mindset.

This new competency includes knowing how to use AI responsibly and serve as an example for the organization on its implementation. As discussed in the chapter "AI in Leadership and HR," being a Master of Agile now also means being a master of AI.

2. Leader / Explorer Role

A leader can emerge from any department within an organization and has deep leadership skills likely developed over several years. They may come from a specialist role within a specific function, have proficiency in various leadership frameworks, or simply possess general, broad leadership competence. Worst case, they have been promoted from a specialist role and are not interested in leading people, but would prefer to go back to work in their specialist area. Let them do that, they will probably never become a good people manager.

They can make hard decisions when no one else is willing to take on the responsibility or put a stake in the ground. They're able to explore different strategies and consider a wide variety of factors when making decisions: the competitive landscape, market trends, people's passions, competencies, and the advantages/ disadvantages for the organization as a whole.

3. HR Professional Role

This individual has experience working as an HR Business Partner, HR Manager, or HR Specialist, with a solid general understanding of human behavior, motivation, and group dynamics. They are comfortable navigating complex interpersonal situations and capable of holding constructive yet challenging conversations that help individuals and teams grow, perform, and take accountability.

They operate at the intersection of people, business, and organizational development, balancing employee needs with strategic and operational goals. Their role often requires sound judgment, integrity, and the ability to translate organizational values into everyday leadership and people practices.

In many organizations, they are the primary — and sometimes only — function responsible for labor relations, including negotiations with unions and employee representatives. They possess working competence in labor law, employment regulations, and relevant societal frameworks, ensuring compliance while supporting fair, sustainable workplace practices. This requires a strong ability to interpret regulations, manage risk, and handle sensitive matters with professionalism and trust.

4. Coach Role

The coaching role is a keystone skillset that all Agile People Coaches need to master. It's about helping people succeed by asking questions, using active listening, and providing meaningful feedback so they can:

- Frame challenges
- Examine assumptions
- Articulate what they want and need
- Remove obstacles
- Formulate clear goals and action steps

At the heart of the coaching role is the coaching mindset: they believe people are capable of finding their own best solutions when given an environment that allows them to think clearly about their issues or challenges. A common framework to start from is GROW.[28]

Goal: goals and aspirations
Reality: current situation, internal and external obstacles
Options: possibilities, strengths, and resources
Will: actions and accountability

There are many different tools and coaching frameworks, such as GROW and a battery of coaching questions, in which the coach helps the coachee realize (on their own) what is needed to take the next step.

Use professional coaching when:
- Pure facilitation didn't give sufficient results
- You have done training and/or mentoring, and now you

---

[28] https://positivepsychology.com/grow-coaching-model/

would like the clients to make decisions based on what you taught them.
- You are working with a complex issue that requires a deeper look and insights.
- You have enough capacity to work with one person

5. Facilitator Role

A great facilitator helps move the process forward without inserting their own opinions, thoughts, and concerns. They will stay outside the specific topic discussed and steer the discussion so that everyone in the room has a say. Conflict resolution is one of their most excellent skills, and they have deep knowledge of when a conflict becomes harmful instead of helpful. Competencies include knowing when to interfere and when to stand back while keeping an eye on the process.

A facilitator does for groups what a coach does for the individual. Using a similar mindset, the facilitator knows that if the group can communicate clearly, it is fully capable of finding innovative solutions and clarifying challenges.

However, we also know that people are people; they tend to slip into inefficient or dysfunctional behavior patterns that get in the way of clear communication and practical work. Two examples are conflicts or unproductive meetings. In those situations, the facilitator's job is to help the group by leading the process that allows them to communicate clearly and collaborate effectively.

Use facilitation when:

- You don't know the current maturity level of the client yet
- More obtrusive coaching is happening in another knowledge domain
- You have done some training and/or mentoring and believe the client now has all the needed knowledge
- A whole group of people is engaged in the matter that needs help in driving their collaboration (e.g., building shared understanding or decision making)

6. Mentor Role

A mentor is someone who has experience in your domain, can provide guidance, constructive feedback, and advice, and can help you draw on their experience.

Often, but not always, this person is from the same area/company/role as the mentee.

A good mentor can help you choose the right path to move forward and has the experience to help you understand how to act in a given situation. They are usually more experienced and senior in relation to the mentee and have a "been there, done that" perspective.

Use mentoring when

- You have gained trust from the mentoree(s)
- You have solved similar issues in the past and have a set of proven methods
- You are an expert in the domain, and passing your skills on to the clients will make a change

7. Trainer Role

In many situations, especially when the team or specific members don't have the basic knowledge of what to do, the most effective and quickest way forward is to teach the knowledge directly.

A trainer's role is to develop students' competence in a particular area.

One great tool for this is "Training from the Back of the Room," a Learning and Development framework that lets students work through reflective exercises and practice new solutions through trial and error. And in a training environment, people are in a safe place to fail.

Use teaching when

- Previous facilitation and coaching resulted in a low level of insights
- It is possible to help clients gain insights by reviewing a case study or a hypothetical example
- You (or other coaches) can follow up on this topic later with coaching or mentoring

8. Guide Role

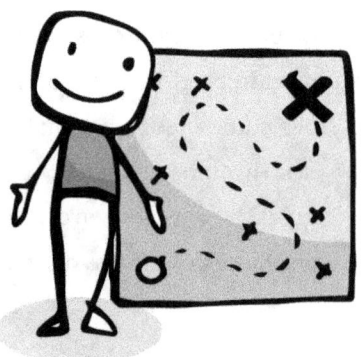

The guide has deep knowledge about the specific place you're in or the specific topic you're dealing with right now. They take you on a journey to understand the process and often teach or facilitate via examples, stories, and expertise. A guide can demonstrate or share interesting information about the organization's history, as they have probably been around for quite some time. They step in to help teams avoid specific pitfalls by knowing exactly what they are and how to get past them.

For example, if a team is developing a new solution to organize and structure work that must comply with labor law, an HR professional knowledgeable about labor law could step in as a guide to ensure the solution complies with it.

9. Navigator Role

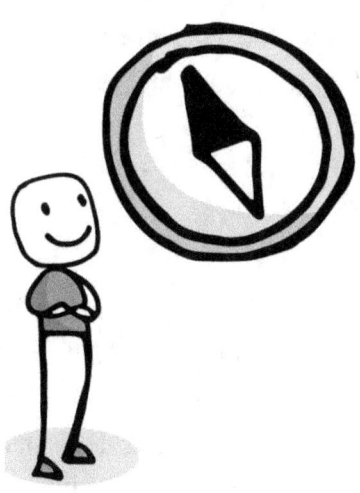

Agile organizations and teams often deal with highly complex situations and challenges. The human tendency is to look for the easy way out (best practices) or copy what others are doing, but complex situations require an experimental approach: probe, sense, respond.

A navigator is comfortable with complexity and helps teams step into an explorer mentality so they can:
- Frame the issue
- Formulate a hypothesis
- Design safe-to-fail experiments
- Learn quickly what works and what doesn't

Navigation requires deep knowledge of systems theory and complexity, as well as experience with frameworks such as Cynefin29, and knowing when to use which domain to guide decisions.

The navigator's best friend is the compass, especially useful when a map does not reflect the reality of the path ahead or when a thick fog of uncertainty surrounds the situation. He or she knows which tool (or tools) to use and/or how to pivot when a roadblock presents itself.

10. Reflective Observer Role

Depending on your people's needs, you take on a different role to support them. The reflective observer role is that space in the middle of things, where, rather than jumping to

---

29 https://en.wikipeida.org/wiki/Cynefin_framework

conclusions, or reacting too quickly (and possibly wrongly), you can figure out what is going on with the team and how you can best help them in whatever scenario they are in.

The skills you need to cultivate here are self-awareness and self-regulation, particularly the ability to observe without judging. In so doing, you allow yourself to step outside the situation, observe the group dynamics and the system, and assess for a moment before you step in and decide which of the other roles will give you the best response and offer the most help.

THE CORE COMPETENCIES OF AN AGILE PEOPLE COACH ARE:

Leading Yourself by:

- Knowing yourself
- Keeping yourself motivated
- Understanding mental models
- Having an EQ (Emotional Intelligence)
- Being a mindful leader

Helping Others to Lead Themselves by:

- Having basic skills in psychology
- Find motivation in others

- Asking appropriate questions
- Being able to coach and guide the development of another person

When people continuously improve and learn in a common direction, and when mistakes are seen as learning opportunities, we can create a psychologically safe culture that forms the foundation for a learning organization. When people feel safe to be vulnerable in front of their peers, they are destined to thrive, and so are the companies they work for.

Don't get left behind the times. The Agile People Coach role represents an alternative career track for HR and managers in the new future of work.

So if you have not already taken action to develop yourself in the desired direction, the timing could not be better.

Constant change will be our new reality, and in that lies our opportunity.

Self reflection

Where am I already strong/weak?
What areas do I want to develop further?

Weak	Leader/Explorer	Strong
Weak	Master of Agile and AI	Strong
Weak	Observer	Strong
Weak	Mentor	Strong
Weak	Trainer	Strong
Weak	Navigator	Strong
Weak	Coach	Strong
Weak	Guide	Strong
Weak	HR-Professional	Strong
Weak	Facilitator	Strong

CHAPTER 18

Adaptive Organizational Design

by Christophe Schnoebelen

You can't build an adaptable organization without adaptable people - and individuals change only when they have to, or when they want to.

Gary Hamel

As this quote illustrates, the heart of adaptive organizations is not the structure, as one might initially think, but the human being. The structure is visually the center of attention. Still, it is only the graphic representation of the organization, which, like all living beings, must adapt to its environment to respond to its most fundamental need: survival. This biological analogy and the notion of survival may seem abrupt, but an organization that is not ready to adapt and evolve must ultimately prepare itself to die. What a shame! All this wasted time, energy, and money because of what? The 'simple' fear of change?

Now that I've broken the mood with this rhetorical question, we can build the fundamentals of successful adaptive organizations by combining theoretical elements with practical applications. So fasten your seatbelts, because whether you're aware of it or not, the transformation around you has already begun, and you're left with only two choices: "Flex or Fail".

THE STAR OF ORGANISATIONAL DESIGN MODELS

The STAR model, developed by Jay Galbraith, is a widely recognized framework for designing effective organizations. It is simple and provides a 360° view to ensure the coherence of adaptive actions. It emphasizes that the success of an organization is not determined solely by its structure, but by the alignment of five key elements: strategy, structure, processes, rewards, and people.

This model is based on the premise that strategy must drive the design of the organization and that all the other elements must work in harmony to support the strategic objectives. Bearing in mind that these interconnected elements form a complex system, even chaotic in some cases (as referenced in the Cynefin matrix), change needs to be led and managed effectively.

This is why it is so important to have a clear vision, which will enable us to evolve constantly. When we talk about an adaptive organization, we need to bear in mind that "When it's over, it's not over." Indeed, living with change is becoming an essential soft skill if we are to create agile, efficient organizations capable of delivering sustainable performance in a complex, competitive environment.

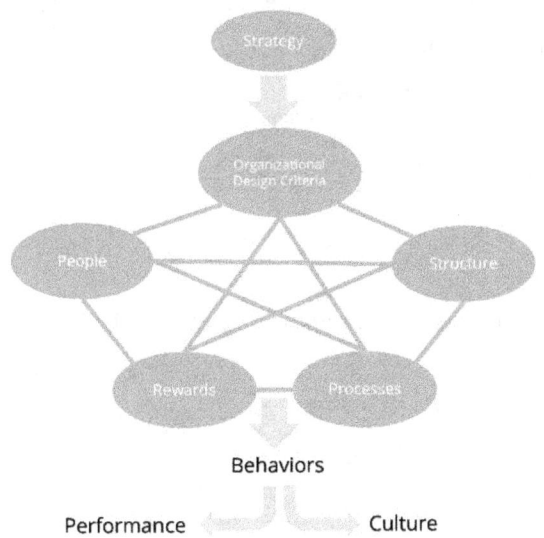

THE FUNDAMENTAL FACTOR TO FOLLOW

While, in principle, structures are defined in the "Inside Out" sense, we think about the organisation to determine the value that will be created for the "customer" in the broadest sense. The philosophy of adaptive organisations is to think 'Outside In', in the sense that it's the structure that has to be adapted to the strategy. And I'd even say that the structure must constantly adapt to the organisation's primary strategy by continually asking itself a question.

"Where is the company's focus and energy going, and how can the structure be adapted to accelerate the achievement of strategic objectives?"

Because you have to bear in mind that a change in the environment will not have the same consequences for the organisation, depending on the decisions taken by the management committee and the focus given.

You've figured it out - This is where the link with OKRs truly comes to play!

I'm not going to go into the functional details of OKRs, which you already know, but simply to emphasise the necessary cascade effect that the whole structure must have to ensure alignment by escalation so that every person, department, division, unit... (whatever you call them) in the company works towards the strategic vision and contributes to achieving the strategic objectives.

TIP

Ensuring a constant alignment with strategic decisions to implement coherent actions to adapt the organization in line with the strategic vision proactively.

KEEPING IT CONSISTENT

Structure determines the way in which tasks and responsibilities are allocated, coordinated, and integrated within the organisation. It includes the formal hierarchy, reporting relationships, and organisational units such as departments or divisions. Most of the time, structures change in response to operational factors such as business growth or decline, regulatory changes, human factors, and performance improvements. However, it is essential to ensure a strong link with the overall strategy and how these changes ensure alignment at all levels.

The most common structural options are functional, divisional, matrix, and network structures, each with its own advantages and disadvantages, which you can find in Chapter 2 "Organizational Structures".

The structure put in place must be consistent with the organisation's level of maturity as defined by Frédéric Laloux. A lack of alignment between the level of maturity at which the organisation thinks it is and the actual level will create horizontal and transversal inconsistencies that will discredit initiatives and completely block the adoption of the teams.

TIP

Consistent maturity is essential to enable the organisation to implement its strategy effectively while retaining the flexibility needed to adapt to change.

ENSURE SIMPLE SPEED SYNCHRO FLOWS

Processes refer to the flow of information, decision-making and activities that link the different parts of the organisation. They ensure that work is coordinated between functions and that resources are allocated efficiently. But that's in theory!

As Einstein said, "In theory practice and theory are the same, but in practice they are completely different".

In an ideal world, everything works together like a Swiss watch. But in reality, processes are extremely complex, and few people are able to make sense of them for the entire organization. Moreover, processes are often unclear;

who does what, up to where, and we come back to two mathematical formulas:

Order + Counter-Order = Disorder
And/Or
Half a decision = Mess squared

A special effort must be made to establish a management system that documents the main processes to ensure the operational functioning of the organization. And for this system to function correctly, it must be structured around value streams that ensure:

Simplicity by getting to the point
Speed by anticipating bottlenecks, delays, and delays
Synchronization by ensuring smooth flow with all entities involved in it

In reality, very few organizations take the time to ensure that these processes respect those three points, which leads to conflicts over tasks and responsibilities, resulting in silos and collective inefficiency.

TIP

Create simple, well-designed value stream maps that are shared and updated to encourage collaboration, speed, and accountability, reducing silos and enabling the organization to respond quickly.

LISTEN TO THE HEARTBEAT

People are the heart of the organization, representing the talents, skills and capabilities needed to deliver the organization's strategy. This includes recruitment, training, leadership development, and succession planning. In addition, organizations need to ensure that they have the right people in the right roles, supported by a culture that fosters engagement, growt,h and performance.

That's why it's a good idea to establish a multi-skill matrix that enables you to track evolving needs and ensure the development of teams based on individuals' talents, while maintaining the skills necessary to keep the department running smoothly.

Added to this is a fundamental factor in team performance highlighted by Google with the "Aristotle" project. Google discovered that the key factor in high-performance teams was not the sum of individuals' talents, but rather psychological safety within the team. That is, the feeling that one can speak up, make mistakes without fear of judgment or reprisal. When employees feel free to be themselves, ideas flow and confidence grows in alignment with performance.

Another fundamental point is the organisation's culture, which is often mistakenly thought to be defined by the organisation's vision and values - you know, the ones that are stuck on the walls and visible on the website, but which few organisations actually put into practice and which, in the end, their employees don't apply at all. In fact, the values of the organisation need to be brought to life, and employees need to be evaluated and therefore guided daily by the values. If nothing is put in place, the foundation of the organization's culture is created organically in terms of who is hired, who is promoted, and who is fired. These three factors influence the unwritten rules that form the unintentional basis of the organization's culture.

TIP

Investing in company culture, people, and psychological safety is essential to building a resilient and innovative workforce, capable of adapting to the organization's changing challenges.

AGILE REWARDS

Rewards encompass the systems and mechanisms used to motivate and recognize employees for their contributions and achievements. To avoid redundancy, consider consulting Chapter 6, Agile Rewards.

DYNAMIC RETEAMING

« If the team stays stagnant, you also stay stagnant together as a team.»

Heidi Helfand

Dynamic Reteaming, as presented by Heidi Helfand, provides a valuable framework for understanding and supporting the natural or intentional shifts within teams. These five models are not miracle cures, but powerful levers and options to keep in mind for cultivating resilience, learning, and innovation in our organisations. This is an invitation to embrace change, to make it conscious, and to make it a strategic tool for collective performance.

1. ONE-BY-ONE

Definition:

A member is added to or removed from a team, often for reasons of growth, departure or reassignment.

Advantages:

- Allows progressive development without disrupting the overall dynamic.
- Encourages the targeted integration of new skills or perspectives.

Risks :

- Too many successive changes can create silent instability.
- Integration needs to be well supported to avoid friction.

Adaptive use:

Ideal for organizations that want to fine-tune their teams according to emerging needs.

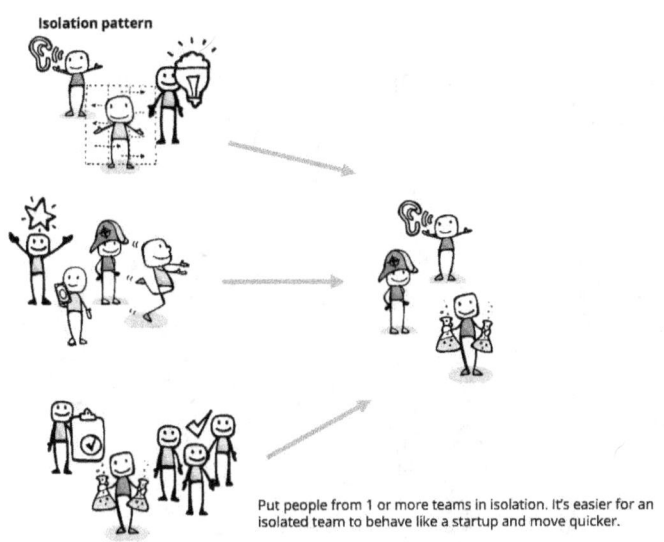

Put people from 1 or more teams in isolation. It's easier for an isolated team to behave like a startup and move quicker.

2. GROW & SPLIT

Definition:

A team becomes too large to remain effective and splits into two (or more), often around sub-domains or products.

Advantages:

- Preserves agility by avoiding overly large teams.
- Creates opportunities for leadership and specialisation.

Risks:

- Can lead to a loss of cohesion or shared vision.
- Risk of duplication of effort if coordination is weak.

Adaptive use :

Useful in rapid scaling phases, while maintaining a flexible structure.

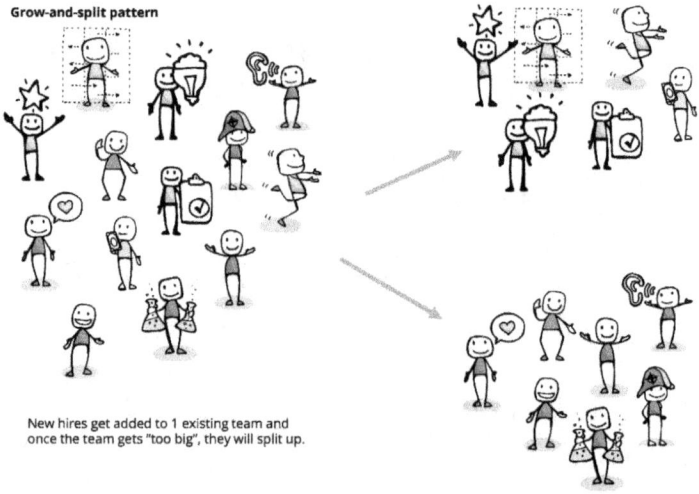

New hires get added to 1 existing team and once the team gets "too big", they will split up.

3. ISOLATION

Definition:

One or more members are temporarily assigned to work on a specific project, exploration, or problem-solving initiative.

Advantages:

- Promotes targeted innovation and rapid problem-solving.
- Allows ideas to be tested without disrupting core teams.

Risks:

- Prolonged isolation can create cultural or strategic misalignment.
- Risk of losing links with the original team.

Adaptive use:

Very effective for exploratory missions, prototypes, or internal audits.

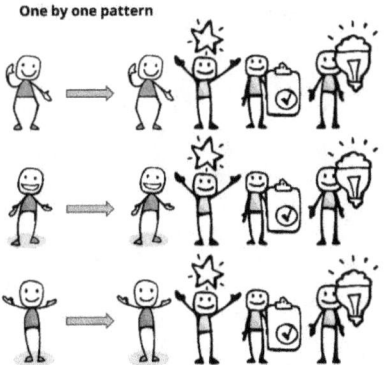

This pattern spreads out new hires to separate teams.

4. MERGING

Definition:

Two teams are merged to combine their skills, resources, or objectives.

Advantages:

- Creates synergy between complementary areas of expertise.
- Can resolve organisational silos.

Risks:

- A poorly prepared merger can generate conflicts of culture or method.
- Risk of loss of role clarity.

Adaptive use:

Useful during strategic reorientations, product changes, or restructuring.

Merging 2 teams into 1. The idea is to combine teams to get their collective intelligence to tackle a specific challenge or remove constraints between the teams

5. SWITCHING

Definition:

Members change teams, temporarily or permanently, to encourage cross-learning or meet specific needs.

Advantages:

- Encourages the development of cross-functional skills.
- Strengthens organisational resilience by reducing dependency on key individuals.

Risks:

- Too much switching can undermine team stability.
- A clear framework is needed to avoid confusion.

Adaptive use:

Excellent for organisations that value versatility, continuous learning, and internal mobility.

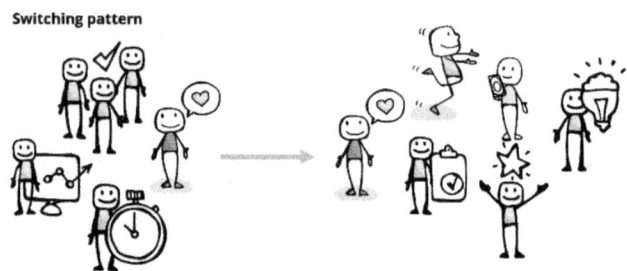

Switching pattern

As you would expect, a pattern where a team member joins a different team.

By exploring these five models, we realise that teams are not mechanical structures to be optimised, but living organisms to be developed.

Dynamic Reteaming reminds us that adaptability cannot be decreed; it must be practiced. It is built through micro-movements, adjustments, and experimentation. Above all, it is nurtured by a culture where change is viewed as an opportunity, not a threat.

So, whether you're a coach, a leader, or a team member, I invite you to observe the dynamics of your teams with curiosity, to dare to reorganise intelligently, and to make reteaming a collective art. This is where agility becomes truly adaptive!

Conclusion

EMBRACING TOMORROW

"Your work is going to fill a large part of your life, and the only way to be truly satisfied is to do what you believe is great work. And the only way to do great work is to love what you do. If you haven't found it yet, keep looking. Don't settle. As with all matters of the heart, you'll know when you find it."

—Steve Jobs

Our organizations are facing unprecedented changes. Global complexity is increasing. Business models are changing. Employees' views of how work should be are evolving. Digitization has brought disruption to all facets of how we work. Many organizations, both large and small, want to get ahead of these changes.

There is no universal solution for handling the pace of change, but Agile is the way to work for the future. The Agile mentality is in alignment with how the brain copes with high-level complexity in the world around us. Organizations can choose to be more or less Agile, depending on their unique structure, processes, culture, tradition, and leadership track.

> If we change the way our HR processes work along with our mindset, we obviously shape a different culture.
> —FABIOLA

AGILITY MATURITY MEASUREMENT

Where are you in this time of change and how are you navigating the new rules for how businesses must change? How mature is your organization when it comes to agility and the values that you need to represent to be competitive in the future world of work?

I've been thinking a lot about how I can help companies to ascertain where they're going and what road to take. To evaluate the maturity level in a particular organization, you need to look at the entire organization, instead of one small piece of it. Each department and team affects the whole. A whole-system approach to examine Agile maturity needs to consist of four main pillars: motivation, change areas (former processes and IT systems), leadership/culture, and structure.

MOTIVATION

People are the drivers of any organization. They represent the culture, the energy, and the soul. To make an organization hum, you need to start with the people. Who are these people as individuals? What makes them tick? What circumstances will inspire them to bring their A-game to the table every day? How can they best serve the company and serve themselves at the same time? The Reiss Motivational Profile measures individual and team drives. It's the starting point for all change management.

CHANGE AREAS (PROCESSES/IT SYSTEMS)

The areas for change are the mechanisms by which the organization will move from the past to the future. The changes that need to be made have been articulated at the end of many of the chapters throughout this book. I've listed the traditional way and Agile way to approach work. There is a sweet spot between the two extremes, where your organization will flourish and grow. The trick is to get as close to it as possible and continue to change when that sweet spot moves—because it will move.

> How do we get information, and how do we sign off on tasks and projects? A lot of things are being eliminated through an Agile approach, so, of course, if you have teams that come in and say specifically, "We want to change our organizational design," we can work on that, but usually it's taken care of by itself. It starts evolving into that network structure or the pod structure. We like to call it pod structure, and that ecosystem is something that fits naturally very well.
>
> —FABIOLA

We've spent a lot of time talking about the differences between the traditional approach to business and the Agile approach. Let's say that, on a scale of one to ten, HR as a whole is at a seven, but performance management is still at a two. The more Agile the company, the higher the score.

The score is the result of an open discussion. There are no right or wrong conversations. The only thing that matters is that you continue the conversation and keep experimenting—keep failing, learning, and improving. Detailed processes generally allow for less flexibility and are often indicative of a more controlling environment. If you want to be more Agile, ask, Is there value in everyone working in the same way? How can our IT systems support a more flexible organization? What prerequisites do we need to develop? How can we operate more efficiently and harmoniously? What do we need to reach the vision?

LEADERSHIP/CULTURE

When we change the way we do things, the tools and methods, models and IT systems, we also gradually change the organization's culture and start behaving in new and better ways. It's about creating those good circles where the culture and the structure reinforce and strengthen each other and where there is a balance between the two.

What are the values of the organization? What are the wanted behaviors that should be attached to those values? What is the difference between the wanted behaviors and the actual behaviors? How can we change behaviors so that our culture improves? How can leaders and HR support that change by providing tools and encouraging new ways of working? How can we make decisions without leaders and increase self-organization, transparency, trust, collaboration, and psychological safety?

It takes mature and brave leaders to embark on such a journey, as their very existence might be threatened.

STRUCTURE

The structure of the company consists of the reporting lines, functional departments, and organizational design. How is your company structured? Is it hierarchical or fluid? What changes can be made to support less management and more collaboration? What walls can be broken down to create a more cross-functional workplace instead of silos? How do we create a flow-based and value-creating organism that moves and changes as needed when the external world changes?

How will you know where the sweet spot is? What should you move toward? Use your employees—their collective intelligence will show you the way. Ask them the right questions and you will get answers. This is how you create a self-improving system designed to identify what the organization needs to be able to adapt to the future, given where it is today. Asking questions is a way to become more Agile.

> When a company wonders if it should start with Agile HR or not, I say, "Well, jump in and use the parts that work and don't use the parts that don't work. Start small and then expand it." You can't know what's going to work and what's not going to work unless you start.
> —CECILIA

DOING AGILE OR BEING AGILE?

There is a big difference between doing Agile and being Agile. In the beginning of an Agile transformation, you mostly learn the tools, the new ways of working (WoW), and how the organizational design must change. After some time, the new WoW starts to stick and you can focus more on the culture, organizational values, and the behaviors that need to change.

For Agile to be successful, you need to come to the stage where you are not just using the tools—you have also changed your mindset and work with new principles and a new set of company values that will gradually form your new Agile culture. Not all people have the Agile mindset built into their personality. As discussed in the chapter about Reiss Motivation, people can be more or less Agile. But your personal value structure does not equal your behavior. All people can *behave* in Agile ways, if they are motivated enough.

After some time working with the Agile tools and models, you'll be able to start changing and adopting them by using trial and error. They should fit your organization and your specific needs. Continuous improvement will replace the old tools and you'll know you're on your way to being an Agile organization, not just doing Agile. And when most people start to behave with the Agile principles as their guiding stars, you can let it happen and relax. You are well on your way to succeeding with your transformation.

FULL SPEED AHEAD

> You are here. You cannot create an Agile organization that is self-directed or create a self-organizing team in a year, but you can take your steps to get started. You need to take the small steps that are important for you to develop.
>
> —RIINA

One of the companies I've worked with is ING, a Dutch bank whose management team has realized the value of Agile. They've moved full speed into the future by learning a whole new mindset and using new tools and principles, sometimes not knowing if they will succeed or fail.

They know that it takes time, and that they have to crawl before they can walk. There have been many challenges along the road. But they know that they have embarked on the right track and slowly, bit by bit, they are getting there. When, we look back in ten years' time, I am quite certain that ING will be recognized as one of the large companies that made the difficult transformation from elephant to greyhound, and I wish them the best of luck with their continued Agile adventures.

A lot of large organizations are facing similar challenges. Some of them have started their Agile transformation, some are thinking about it, and some are not even aware that they should. The future belongs to companies that embark on the journey of adapting to the environment and releasing their employees' potential.

Thanks for reading the book! If you want to reach me, send an email to piamia@piamariathoren.com or find me on Linkedin (https://www.linkedin.com/in/piamia/)

IF, THE POEM
BY DR. LEANDRO HERRERO

Dr. Leandro Herrero, one of my favorite organizational architects, writes a blog called "Daily Thoughts." You can find it at leandroherrero.com. The poem below is from one of his blog posts. I think it very nicely summarizes how we should think about organizations.

> *If instead of a company, you had and led a community.*
> *If instead of employees you had internal social activists.*
> *If instead of people in the payroll, colleagues behaved as volunteers.*
> *If instead of a mission you had a cause.*
> *If instead of a culture you had a social movement.*
> *If instead of leaders you had brokers.*
> *If instead of teams and a teamocracy you had peer-to-peer networks with widespread teaming up.*
> *If instead of a budget to spend you had a budget to invest.*

If instead of employee engagement you had employee loving-it-here.

If instead of a business plan to execute you had a business campaign to run.

If instead of annual employee engagement surveys you had a continuous sampling of opinions.

If instead of asking why people left, you asked them why they are still here.

If instead of values on the wall you had non-negotiable behaviors on the ground.

If your organizational structure could self-reconfigure as needed without a noise or hassle.

If the words change management were alien or retired. Or one of them redundant.

If you had a long queue of people wanting to join in.

If you spoke human language as opposed to management dialect.

If work-life balance was an oxymoron, you loved your work and your non work.

If you could walk into a very special place at 9 am everyday and looking forward to it on a Monday morning.

If you could feel that what you personally do has a real visible impact.

Then, "yours is the Earth and everything that's in it,"
And—which is more—you'll be a New Leader, my son!

Agile Glossary

Below you will find a glossary of the most common Agile terms.

Adaptive or adaptable is when project goals and time planning are adapted to how the external circumstances are changing.

Backlog Grooming is the continuous job to keep the product backlog in shape and up to date.

Burndown Chart is a diagram where the remaining work in a sprint is visualized.

Daily Standup or Daily Scrum is a short daily meeting (around fifteen minutes) where the team meets and communicates about tasks and impediments.

Predictive is the opposite of adaptive, for example, when project goals and time planning follow a plan that has only taken into account external circumstances at the time of the project's start.

Product Backlog is a dynamic to-do list containing the project goals and priorities, owned by the product owner, usually prioritized with the most important features at the top.

Product Owner is the role in Scrum that is responsible for the product backlog and who works with the business stakeholders.

Scrum Master is the facilitator for the Scrum team.

Scrum Team consist of the team, the Scrum master, and the product owner.

Self-Organization means that the team decides how work should be accomplished and by whom. It does not mean that the team can decide what work should be done or who can join the team.

Sprint is a "time box" of one to four weeks where the Scrum team is focused on productive work and achieving the goals defined in the updated sprint backlog.

Sprint Backlog is a subset of the product backlog, a to-do list for the sprint. On the first day of the sprint, the product owner meets with the team to explain the priorities and then lets the team decide how much work they can take on in the sprint.

Sprint Retrospective is a meeting that takes place after each sprint where the team thinks about improvements for the next sprint.

Sprint Review is an informal meeting at the end of a sprint where the team presents and demonstrates the finished work in the sprint to management, customers, and the product owner.

Time Box is a unit of time during which something is supposed to be accomplished—for example, a sprint. Deadlines cannot be exceeded; instead, the scope of work needs to change.

DevOps is a software development and delivery process that emphasizes communication and collaboration between product management, software development, and operations professionals.

Principles and Practices

> When it comes to Agile values, transparency is definitely one of them. Transparency and trust. You can't bypass them; you have to have them in a modern organization.
> —CECILIA

PRINCIPLES AND VALUES (TO DO MORE OF)	TOOLS AND PRACTICES (CONCRETE METHODS YOU CAN USE TO SUPPORT AND STRENGTHEN THE PRINCIPLES AND VALUES)	AREA OF HR AND LEADERSHIP (FOR WHICH YOU CAN USE THE TOOLS AND PRACTICES)
Run experiments	Scrum, Kanban	All
Trial and error	Set-based development	All
Face-to-face	Scrum	HR projects
Transparency	OKRs, daily stand-ups	All
Shorter feedback loops	Scrum, sprints, OKRs	Goals and performance, all project-based work
Follow up more often	OKRs, retrospectives	Goals and performance

PRINCIPLES AND VALUES (TO DO MORE OF)	TOOLS AND PRACTICES (CONCRETE METHODS YOU CAN USE TO SUPPORT AND STRENGTHEN THE PRINCIPLES AND VALUES)	AREA OF HR AND LEADERSHIP (FOR WHICH YOU CAN USE THE TOOLS AND PRACTICES)
Judge only yourself	OKRs	Goals and performance
Give more positive feedback	360 dinner, KUDO box and wall	All
Motivate for performance	Reiss Motivation Profile, Moving Motivators	Goals and performance
Steal and tweak	Benchmarking, good practice	All
Agile leadership	Management 3.0	Leadership
Trust	Human View X and Human View Y	Leadership, performance
Flow orientation	Kanban, Trello, lean practices	All, recruitment, transactional processes, HR support processes
Continuous improvement	Retrospective	Goals and performance
Continuous learning	Retrospective	Learning, projects
Collaboration	Reiss Motivation, OKRs	All
Broader roles, cross-functional teams	Cheat sheet, T-shaped people	Job descriptions, job roles

PRINCIPLES AND VALUES (TO DO MORE OF)	TOOLS AND PRACTICES (CONCRETE METHODS YOU CAN USE TO SUPPORT AND STRENGTHEN THE PRINCIPLES AND VALUES)	AREA OF HR AND LEADERSHIP (FOR WHICH YOU CAN USE THE TOOLS AND PRACTICES)
Engagement is the most important of all	Happiness index, Reiss Motivation Profile, squad health check model, delivering happiness, Gallup's twelve questions	Employee engagement
Teamwork	GDQ (Susan Wheelan), Reiss Motivation Profile	HR team
Purpose	OKRs	People strategy
Line-of-sight	OKRs	Goal setting
Build motivated individuals	Ambitions and personal plan, Reiss Motivation Profile, Moving Motivators	Personal development
Salary is a hygiene factor	Salary formula, merit money, six best practices for rewards from Management 3.0	Rewards, salaries
Reduce lead time	WIP-limits	Projects and processes
Delegate/share responsibility and decision making	Delegation Poker, consent from sociocracy	Leadership
No budgets	Beyond budgeting	Goals and performance, rewards

PRINCIPLES AND VALUES (TO DO MORE OF)	TOOLS AND PRACTICES (CONCRETE METHODS YOU CAN USE TO SUPPORT AND STRENGTHEN THE PRINCIPLES AND VALUES)	AREA OF HR AND LEADERSHIP (FOR WHICH YOU CAN USE THE TOOLS AND PRACTICES)
Collective intelligence	Planning poker, OKRs	Time estimation for HR projects
Create customer value	Sprint review	All
Build work around engaged individuals	Engagement grid (employee satisfaction and company contribution)	Employee engagement
Colocation	Daily stand-up, pair work	HR team efficiency

Further Reading

Antman, Peter: *Tear Down the Pyramids Again*
Appelo, Jurgen: *How to Change the World*
Appelo, Jurgen: *Managing for Happiness*
Bogsnes, Bjarte: *Implementing Beyond Budgeting*
Duhigg, Charles: *Smarter, Faster, Better*
Grant, Adam: *The Originals*
Hamel, Gary: *What Matters Now*
Hope, Jeremy, Bunce, Peter, and Roosli, Franz: *The Leader's Dilemma*
Hope, Jeremy, and Fraser, Robin: *Beyond Budgeting*
Kelly, Kevin: *Out of Control*
Kelly, Louis, and Medina, Carmen: *Rebels at Work*
Kruse, Kevin: *Employee Engagement for Everyone*
Laloux, Frederic: *Reinventing Organizations*
Marciano, Paul: *Carrots and Sticks Don't Work*
Morgan, Jacob: *The Future of Work*
McGregor, Douglas: *The Human Side of Enterprise*
Pink, Daniel: *Drive*
Reiss, Steven: *Who Am I? The 16 Basic Desires that Motivate Our Actions and Define Our Personalities*

Reiss, Steven: *The Normal Personality: A New Way of Thinking About People*
Senge, Peter: *The Fifth Dimension*
Thorén Pia-Maria: *Agile People Picturebook*
Thorén Pia-Maria: *Agile People Principles - Your Call to Action for the Future of Work*
Welch, Jack: *Winning*

Appendix

INTERVIEW WITH MATTI KLASSON, PEOPLE DEVELOPMENT, KING AND MANAGEMENT 3.0 FACILITATOR

Have workplaces changed?

They have changed quite significantly. We are standing in front of a paradigm shift where we are moving from hierarchical and traditional structures toward network structures. These changes are reflected in our current society, where social relations and your social life are becoming more important. How you are seen in the public eye and the relationships you have, including your private life, can affect the organization and how you are viewed in the workplace. Hierarchical structures are not that important anymore. It's the social relations at workplaces that are important.

How far have we come?

We're in the middle of it, I'd say. But there are some organizations, tech orgs, in the forefront. It's the place the new labor is moving toward. People are used to working with social relations in a new way. The life of social media is nowadays reflected in workplaces, and it affects how you create new relationships and how important those are.

How difficult is it for large traditional organizations to change?

It's difficult, and it's a true challenge! The fact is they will have to change, to survive. Some organizations are changing radically. For instance, there's a Dutch bank called ING that's adapting to the new paradigm. They got inspired from the Spotify structure with tribes and chapters. ING implemented the Spotify model and people had to (once again) apply for their jobs. All employees may not fit in the new structure, but either way, they chose to change radically to survive. I personally think it could be necessary for the large traditional organizations, because if you don't change, you might not survive in the long run.

So, in this case, it was a top-down initiative?

Yes, it was, and now we have to wait and see what happens. Time will tell if it turns out to be the right decision. It was the same scenario with Zappos. They made a radical change toward a network organization with Holacracy. We still don't know the result; they became quiet after the change. But the change was radical and not all employees agreed with it. I think around 20 percent of the employees quit.

Change itself seems to be hard, regardless. Some organizations were hit harder than others. Do you think a top-down initiative might not be that bad in this case?

What we see is, even if there's a traditional organization with hierarchical structures, people tend to network because relationships are important. The leaders at the top of an organization ask themselves, "Why aren't they doing what we tell them to do?" Their structure doesn't fit with reality. In this case, we get subgroups and suboptimizing, which might not lead to what was desirable in the first place.

There must be both top-down and bottom-up activity. An agreement must take place at the bottom of the organization that the change must occur.

Has leadership changed in order to reflect the new paradigm?

I'd say no. The process is a bit slow, but it must happen. Our leaders need to be trained. In the MBA programs, we find old paradigms being taught. From the beginning of 1900 with Frederick Taylor, everything was viewed as a machine to be optimized. It worked out in the beginning of 1900, but it doesn't work today. We are not acting in a manufacturing industry. We don't view people as resources you can optimize and replace if they're no longer working. But this is what is being taught. The hierarchical structure is, after all, a way of optimizing the workflow. The leadership has to change into a system that thinks with a focus on "the big picture." It's not our job to lead individuals. Instead, we must learn how to create the right conditions and environment for individuals in organizations to thrive in.

Have employees changed? How?

Yes, I think they have changed. They have had less difficulties adapting, because the change is also reflected in their private lives. Employees who build the culture, build the organization. When employees change, the organization changes too. I think employees have had less difficulties than people higher up in the hierarchy.

Why is that? What is at stake?

With responsibility comes risk. And they might not be willing to undertake any risks. In Agile, there are short iterations in place to minimize risk. The longer the iterations get, the higher the risk. The higher someone is in the hierarchy, the more responsibility they have, but there is less willingness to undertake new risks. Therefore, the decisions should be made preferably by the employees themselves, and they can bring their ideas to those higher in the hierarchy.

Has work changed?

It's like Moore's law: it grows faster and it changes. We're moving from a manufacturing industry toward a knowledge and service industry. Just look at the world outside; it's changing. People are willing to move and find other things to do. For instance, it's easy to switch from one phone provider to another, or, if you're over Candy Crush Saga, you can play something else. People are more willing to adapt to new ideas, technology, and processes. One thing we know for sure is that the change will be constant and we have to adapt. When the world becomes quicker, the process of getting new products and services on the market needs to be quicker as well. That's where you start working Agile, to iterate faster and validate against end users as fast as possible.

Changing jobs occurs more frequently and faster than ever. Is that a good or bad thing?

It can be good, in the big picture. There is another dissemination of knowledge that can flow between organizations today compared to the past where people normally stayed with an organization until their retirement. Today, organizations are moving, and people are moving. Everything goes faster; the distance is shorter when everything becomes digital. I have some sort of vision that people will not be employed by organizations in the future. Instead, it looks to me like a network of consultants. You go where you want to be and provide the greatest benefit at the moment. Organizations could have a network, look at their needs, and say, "This is our need. Where's the knowledge?" You could move freely over organizations and hire the talent you need. Like Visa for instance, it's like an association of banks, rather than one organization that provides everything within one card payment. Organizations with a need for this service connect to it. I hope for organizations to act in the same way. Organizations connect and workforce flows freely over the network and over organizational boundaries.

When does transparency become a problem?

Communication goes hand in hand with transparency—how we communicate the information needed will determine if transparency becomes a a problem.

Why Agile HR?

There is not an option in this paradigm shift. HR needs to adapt as the organization changes and requires faster delivery of services and products. How could HR support the new organization if it doesn't adapt itself? So, the question isn't why Agile HR, but when; otherwise, HR will not survive.

Why should the large traditional organizations start with Agile HR?

The organizations must decide when they want to make the change. You cannot take a huge step right away; you must start small. Look into the resources you can find in the organization. Find something local and try it as a small prototype before you scale. I don't think the scenario is *if* companies will question whether this is something for them, but *when* they want to do it.

Could Agile training be misunderstood? What is required to really get the Agile mindset?

It's an inner change that has to occur. (Sarcasm following.) An Agile training could generate a great tool for control, where you visualize a team's workflow and know exactly what they are doing. You have daily stand-ups (reporting) and you can manage the team really hard. It could possibly be the best command and control tool. To be Agile, you need the mindset, the inner change.

Generally, what works less well with HR today?

HR isn't located "inside" of the organization. They try to support from the outside. What they often miss is to be *inlyssnande* (insightful) and adaptive. It's important to have a perfect PM process, "And if that one is in place, we are all set!" But organizational needs look different in real life, and the perfect PM process isn't enough. HR needs to locate themselves amongst managers and employees and listen to their needs. HR must try to understand those and start from there!

In a perfect world, I'd like to see no central HR organization. Sometimes HR takes ownership of processes, which is supposed to result in thriving and productive coworkers who originally belonged to managers and employees. Instead, we're building an external HR organization to take care of that.

If you have trouble with leadership in an organization, check how large the HR organization is. With a large HR organization, you don't expect the manager to be responsible for leadership. In my opinion, the HR work belongs to the managers. That cannot be offloaded on someone else, nor should the ownership be stolen by HR!

How will the traditional role of HR change in an Agile organization?

The traditional role is to create and implement processes and routines, and the Agile way is to be more *inlyssnande* (insightful). Locate as close to the organization as possible, since it's the core in Agile HR. Stay inside of the organization rather than outside.

How can you work with Agile recruitment?

The recruitment process at King is open and the recruitment flow is visualized. At HR we have a recruitment board, a Kanban, where we see all the ongoing processes—open positions and their status. The recruitment team knows what they all are doing, and they are able to support each other. Each recruiter is responsible for a certain area. The recruiters are located inside the organization and are searching for local needs. They ask the managers within each area what needs they have and how they can be supported. Sometimes internal movements are enough, rather than external recruitment. You are able to work more with the talent management process if you visualize, open up, and locate near the organization.

Can Agile improve the recruitment experience?

Absolutely, since the recruitment process isn't transparent or visual only for the recruiters, but also outward. The applicants receive feedback faster, they know exactly where they are in the process, etc. The experience will be better when the expectations are in line. Applicants know exactly what lies ahead, even though our processes are quite long— six to seven interviews. It's really important to have a good experience, even if you don't get hired. You need to feel that you've experienced a great recruitment process. I believe right expectations leads to that.

Is there a difference between Agile leadership and traditional leadership?

We are moving toward organizations where social relationships are more important than hierarchical structures. The big difference is that you work more on the big picture and create the right conditions for employees, rather than build reporting paths/channels that people have to follow. In Agile leadership, information can flow throughout the organization, and the decisions can be made in the right place.

Are there certain values connected to an Agile organization?

You must have an *including* mindset when it comes to decision making and how you work in the organization. Decisions should be made as close to the core worker as possible, and should include those who will be affected. Workers and managers must embrace the including mindset, transparency, and openness regarding everything. Information must flow in the organization for decisions to be made in the right place. People need the right amount of input in order to make a decision.

As an organization, how does HR start becoming Agile?

A good start is to be responsive to the needs of the people within the organization. You can't implement a tool and think that's enough. All organizations are different and therefore a tool won't be enough. That's why you work in Scrum or Kanban, because we don't know what the future will look like. What HR needs to do is listen and understand the needs within the organization, and that happens by being around the people in the organization. In today's organizations, that doesn't happen because they're located offside thinking of how they could support the organization, rather than walking in and asking for the real needs. You can't manage a complex organization externally. You have to look from inside out; it's like the human brain, the most complex thing.

Example: At King, we experienced flaws in the support of our developers a couple of years ago. We wanted to focus on increasing the support the business was giving to developers. In that place, we came up with the idea of development managers, who are still developers, but also coaches. We started small in Stockholm and evaluated it before launching it to other studios. Find the smallest experiment and start from there, which also minimizes the risk.

If you want HR to become Agile, start with small experiments instead of rolling out a brand new performance management process, which implies higher risk from management's point of view. Find a local need in the organization and start from there. It won't hurt the organization.

What tools can be implemented?

It can be hard to just implement Agile HR. But there are tools, Management 3.0 for example, that can be supportive if you want to focus on an including leadership, and understand the needs, for instance. Moving Motivators is a great tool to find an employer's inner drive and how it can be supported in a particular role.

To create the right expectations of who's responsible for what, use Delegation Poker, which we use a lot here at King. All development managers are introduced to Moving Motivators for having healthy dialogues with their developers. Teams are playing Delegation Poker with the stakeholders to set expectations, for instance.

INTERVIEW WITH BONNITTA ROY, CREATOR OF OPO: OPEN PARTICIPATORY ORGANIZATIONS

What is the link between Agile and OPO?

The Agile community really found something in my work that spoke to them. But I think part of the strength is the conversation in my own learning network. The Agile impulse has all this new energy, and some of these new ways are self-evident to them. But they have a little bit of a mythology of why mistakes were made in the past. So, they don't have a lot of insight into that.

What we're trying to do is be completely integrative. Organizations may be faced with a problem and they try to find a solution for it. But in the process, they discover that the possible solution won't work and it escalates the severity and complexity of the problem. When more time is spent and no solution is in sight, frustration sets in. Companies have always grown ad hoc that way. A lot of young companies who start out Agile, as they grow, they find themselves in the same loop. They have the same problem. They move toward a solution and I'll say, "Oh, no, no, no, that's one of those solutions that creates the structures that you actually don't want to do."

I think one of the challenges is to ask, "How do we teach people to identify the indicators, and how can you teach people to know when that kind of loop comes up?" We want them to consider a solution with another mindset.

I'll just give you an example. When I first started doing this work, I was working with a tech who had a lot of offices in Canada and Europe. I had previously worked with a founding partner who grew and came up through the Agile community. In his organization, they teach Agile, certified Scrum, and Management 3.0. But, he admitted that his own company had succumbed to the tyranny of structurelessness. There was not enough structure. The teams had become very siloed themselves and couldn't move. He was working with me to solve that.

When I went into his organizations, I was met with a lot of resistance. We learned a lot through the way we communicated the new approach to them, but one of the things their people said was, "Oh, we don't do that. We have Agile. We make decisions here in a people-centered way or Agile way." But when we looked at their processes, they were functioning more like in an old structural way. It was a throwback to the days when people owed each other favors and nothing happened until you did something and got repaid by having the task completed. It felt like a mafia structure—like I owe you something. It's an old boys' structure.

They understood that in the absence of Agile structure or a people-centered structure or some other governance structure, this old boys' network structure actually crept in. These are the kinds of things we were trying to be the most integrative with.

To me, the future of this work depends on how we learn in terms of our own habits. How do we truly participate in numerous local interactions with each other and still maintain open platforms that allow individuals across many different networks to participate with each other, yet don't function within a single platform to capture all that activity? I think technology is working on the second piece, and people like myself are more interested in working with groups and the human side of it so we can link those two things together.

What is the OPO?

The OPO is a meme. It's just a meme. It's not mine. It's not any specific thing. That's why the Manifesto says these are the kinds of values that we're interested in now. If you work from that value, you can have the kind of structure you might imagine. For me, I was imagining the OPO.

The OPO is a structural thing, but it's really just an attempt to draw out what someone coming from this new paradigm might be thinking about in terms of an organization. It's tricky because the OPO, unlike let's say holocracy, is not a recipe. It's a model of how to get started. It's not a whole package deal. It's a process you can get whether you're a startup and you want to stay Agile, or when you're an Agile company and you want to scale without adapting some of these legacy structures. It's also a process structure that will help large companies who are centralized to decentralize. It's a model or a tool to shift conversations around to the kinds of ways we conventionally think of organizations.

For example, here are some of the techniques: Let's say you're a startup and you're interested in this structure. One of the things we help organizations with is not to build your startup based upon ad hoc roles. This often happens because founders will have cool ideas and work together. You can see they'll naturally take different roles, because you have to make do with what you have. But, they don't stand back and say, "Well, what's a more optimum way we should do this work?" A lot of times, one of the first mistakes made in small startups is that people imagine their company's structure ahead of time without thinking it through. They split it up or they characterize it based upon the personalities at the table. You don't want to work on fixed roles because they are too limiting. You'll always end up having to hire toward roles. Fixed roles create power asymmetry. The very first directive is, don't build this up on roles. So then, how do you build the company?

We build it like a little city. We build it up on a notion of locations. There are two types of locations. The first location is called your core zones, the core operating zone. It's where you're actually producing value. When you work with startups, you say, "Well, what do you actually do? How do you produce value that didn't exist before? What new value are you producing for the client, for the world, and for society?" All organizations have to understand themselves as producing value, so there's a value transaction-out and then there's a value exchange-in.

Now this gets tricky because, in our modern society, it's not easy to answer. For example, Uber is not a taxi company and Airbnb is not a hotel. The first thing people really need to understand is the value they're producing. This is put into play within their core locations. There are three simple prompts: What is happening here? What does good work look like here? And what do we have to do to do good work here? It's a virtual location that's defined by having that conversation. Then, the last prompt is, What values best motivate or allow people to be enthusiastic about doing good work here?

It's kind of like building a house, and if I build it a certain way, I'm going to attract a certain buyer. The better I am about describing the value that could be created here—how people could be enthusiastic about working here and what the requirements are—the more I attract the right talent into that location. This is what we call a starting position. We start as founders defining it as best we can. But once people start to occupy that location, they revisit that and answer those questions so that, over time, the location evolves along with their participation. To get started, you have to begin somewhere, so you imagine what it must be like. But once you get people working in teams and occupying those locations, then they can keep revisiting those questions. They say, "Wait, wait, wait, you know, this is what we're actually doing here now."

Airbnb has been really good at this. At first, they were talking about themselves in a certain way, saying, "Well, this is what we do," and now they're really talking about themselves as enabling people to come together to meet each other globally. The way they understand themselves has evolved over time. It's very important for every location to continually understand why they exist and, more importantly, why they exist in this company.

Once you get really good at that, then people can self-organize within those locations. They can prioritize by understanding why they exist. They already have a strategic alignment with the whole organization. We call that building larger and larger strategic holes, because the locations are defined by why they exist. Contrast that to a very large organization or NGOs or municipalities where somebody might be very good at their job, but all they know is the work comes in here, they do this, and then the work goes out. They have no idea why they exist, and therefore, they can't prioritize anything. The result is that they can't evolve and they can't make decisions that are outside of that role. We completely move out of the constraints of a role and into this notion of location, but then we let the location ask itself those questions. Change is kind of like a house. You can change the way it looks, add a bigger common room and more bedrooms, but then sometimes you want to open up the little room.

That's the first step, to define your core locations. People usually have three. Some people have one or two. If people have like five or six, they probably don't have an understanding of why their company exists. It's not a generalized enough understanding. They've just grown ad hoc and they're kind of splitting it up too much. Because if you have five, six, or seven locations, you get into more divisions, departments, and roles, which means you've lost sight of what you're doing. The first step is to identify your core locations.

As a second step, let's take a look at this example. Steve Jobs and Steve Wozniak are in their garage, doing what they're doing. Natural enthusiasm. Nobody's making them do this.

This is the beginning of them creating core value in this garage. But unless they do a lot of other things, that value would never have been transacted with the world. They would've never become Apple. The second thing a company has to ask itself is, "What are all those other things that need to be done?" When you listen to people or you've worked in many startups like I have—and I've started about five of my own businesses—those questions come in different combinations depending upon your business and the context, but they all come in only four different categories.

To stay lean, the OPO helps us understand that there's only four different types of what we call extra curricular activities— it's what we have to do to create the platform where the core value can be transacted with the world. We call those network zones. They also are locations where we look to see what's happening, what we have to do to do good work here, and what values the people have that will help them be naturally enthusiastic about doing this work. There are four categories in the network zone, and these are the kinds of strategic conversations you have to have in a successful company.

Organizing all these other questions will help you have a very strategic understanding of why you hired those people. With the OPO structure, you can always get back to the bare bones of what you need to do. I think that's what happens to organizations, and then you grow really fast, and you get kind of a bureaucracy or maybe become too complex. Then on a yearly basis or every three years, you can say, "Okay, let's get back to this core structure and re-examine what we need and what we don't need. Let's look at what's grown in an ad hoc manner that's not really working for us." That's the basic structure, and then it's supported by a governance. Once you have the structural integrity understood, the OPO recommends a certain type of governance. We'll get to that in a second, but just remember that in the OPO, every position is a starting position.

The OPO just gives you a template to start from. It doesn't tell you what to do, and it doesn't answer any of those questions. It's a process methodology. So, if you're working as a consultant with OPO, you're just working with these prompts: What is happening here? You're not saying, "This is what you've got to do at the service industry." There are templates you can use while you are starting out. Remember that you're helping people to have conversations from a different paradigm, rather than holocracy, which is much more instructional and follows the rules.

The governance is the same way. It's a minimum structure to get started and it can grow through participation. It doesn't say if you do this structure you will look like this. Or, if you use this governance, you will make decisions like this. It allows you to make decisions, allocate resources, determine how you'll talk together, how you'll vote, and how you decide to evolve as your company evolves, which means it's not a constitutional governance. Constitutional governance sets the parameter of what is possible from the beginning. This is participatory governance. It sets the process so the governance can evolve within the context along with your needs, as you need it.

For example, the first part of your governance is, "We have these locations. This is what's happening here. This is what good work looks like here." You make those statements. Then, when you set up the OPO, you set up a core zone that is identified by the things it does so it can evolve. So, how does it evolve? In the OPO, you start with several things. One is the definition of the zones, and those are called POVs—performance, objectives, and values. You also could start with principles. A principle is like Google saying, "First, do no harm." My company's principles are the six principles of the Open Manifesto. An Agile company might want to start with Agile principles. You have principles and then you have the definition of the zones, which are called POVs. Those would be the start of your governance.

Then, as time goes on and somebody wants to propose a change, you can put a proposal in. Anyone can propose something, but the template the OPO recommends that the proposal come with a story. It should be a real story that illustrates why the principle or the top thing is either inadequate or was ambiguous in the situation. That's the template that the OPO starts with.

Once you get that far, then people say, "But if the proposal and the precedent is there along with the story, then how do we decide to change the principle?" Well, then you'll understand that the governance is going to grow because, from this minimum template, everyone will ask that question. Oh, well, how do you decide? You need a new principle and a new way of making decisions. You state how we make decisions. It's just a starting position. It's not a constitutional thing.

If you're a small company, you'll say, "Well, there's only three of us. This is how we get started. We always agree. We want consensus, 100 percent." So, you just put that there. Even though you know that's not good forever, you don't have to figure out the whole constitutional thing. Why? Because one day a consensus won't work and someone will put in a proposal, tell the story why consensus doesn't work, and then you'll change it. This very minimum process allows your governance to grow like a paramecium and cover the real world events that happen to you in the organization, rather than someone thinking up a constitutional method for solving all problems at all times.

That's kind of the OPO. There are a lot more details, but that's the structure that we offer—the core zones, the network zones where the strategic conversations happen, along with the governance. Teams can move in and out of zones. In small companies, people often wear many hats. In very large companies, there's often a need. It's not ideal to have separate teams doing more strategic work. But when you get a mature company using OPO—which I had the good fortune of meeting three in Stockholm—there's this thing happening where the strategic activities that are arising get operationalized and they're pushed into the core zones so the whole company stays lean over time and there's more distributed intelligence. So, it can get more sophisticated than the way I've just explained, but if you're doing it right, they become more and more integrated over time. That's the OPO.

How do you address the control issue that many managers have?

That's a great question, because simple is not easy, but what simple does is always push the work back to the question of, How can I be better at this? It's one of those questions, How do I learn not to work from control? We kind of turn it around because the need to control—if you actually look at what's happening in your mental model or your emotional body when you feel like taking control—is like you're operating from a state of threat. People don't want to control. They want to get out from the orientation of threat, right?

Then we say in the OPO movement, if you're doing this work, then where does the threat arise? That shifts the conversation from the person who just wants to know where the threat arises from, and then you can see whether it's real or not. In most cases, there's something real in that question, because people's emotional bodies are doing the right thing. They're saying the right thing, but unless you slow down and examine the situation, the problem is not what you originally thought. There's usually something more specific that's like a seed that needs to be examined.

That's interesting work. That's mining the genius of human bodies. When we're organized, a lot of these emotional things are data points about what's actually happening. The idea of control can get really subtle, unless you're really watching carefully. This one startup, for example, consists of eight people. There were four. Now there are eight. Now there are sixteen, and they have an interest in the Agile onboarding process where people volunteer, then they mentor, and then they become the worker class. They become full employees, with profit sharing and everything. But what was happening is they were just growing bigger and bigger and bigger and bigger. This was not actually very effective.

They're a really cool company. I said, "Just think about how you started. It was just four of you, and you tried things, and then you needed a little help and became eight. You already told me that eight was when you really started being efficient and really productive, and now, at sixteen, the work kind of gets divided up and these are some of the problems." I said, "What you've learned already in your context and in your vision, is that between eight and sixteen is your cookie cutter team. What you need to do is hire another eight people. Give them a project so they can learn just like you did to be a team and to solve their own problems. You can't just slowly mentor them as you grow larger and larger."

Maybe they're wondering what it would be like if they made a mistake. But what they will probably say is, "We've learned so much over the last year. We want to help them." But they'll never be a team. You need to reproduce the actual lived experience that made your company cool and alive.

That doesn't mean they shouldn't have a mentor program, but you need to reproduce that cool experience. They'd already had different categories of businesses. I'd say, "So give them that category. Let them do the research. Let them make the contacts. They will be very viable and vigorous just like you were." When I spoke to a woman and pointed out another woman who was a founder of Agile, I told her, "That's the beginning of the control thing." At first, she was a little nervous and then she could see, yes, it comes from a threat.

Part of the OPO is that all the work isn't really coming from this new paradigm. It's just what makes us human, the challenges and the fact that there's always tremendous genius in that, and we can understand our participation from that kind of view.

How do you work with teams?

Working with teams means working with people who are moving toward the notion of defining locations. When people first came together, they would say, "Oh, we're doing this thing and no one's ever done it before, and we can really see that we're doing this." You see, they're basically defining a location. They're getting together and then they sort out their roles. When you're expanding, you have to understand why you need to expand, why more people are needed, and the value you need to deliver. You define it and you attract new teams there.

I met Pia-Maria at King. They had many different locations, and they went to great lengths to make some look like beaches and some look like forests, so they were like walking through a planet and existing in different places. In some of those locations, the values were in putting out one episode of a game every two weeks, but it didn't really change. There was this whole way of doing things but it didn't feel like a startup. It was more like a few ideas, but every two weeks they delivered a new episode, a different color scheme, and a couple new characters.

Another group was producing games that didn't exist before. There were very different environments in there, at different levels. The values in that group were different than the values in the other location. In that location, they felt more like a startup all the time, because they just got done starting up. Whereas in this other location, people who wanted to have that energy and that buzz all the time wouldn't be happy in that location. This is the idea of walking into different locations, different houses. They are different. In my house, you can put your feet up on my coffee table, but in my mom's house, you just know you're not going to do that.

How do you feel that the Agile principles and the OPO thoughts correspond? Is there some way that they don't?

I think there's no contradiction, but I think the Agile principles don't cover everything you need. The Agile principles are more aligned in terms of an operational framework and it doesn't cover the whole paradigm shift or the types of capacities we, as human beings, have to develop. In my OPO Manifesto, I quote the people who wrote the Agile Manifesto saying that they believe there are some deeper *woo-woo* principles underneath what they're saying. Those woo-woo principles are about who we are as people and how we participate together, and they are still unfolding. I don't think there's a contradiction. I just think we keep mining deeper and deeper meaning from that original inspiration.

Can Agile HR, the original Agile principles, and the notion of OPO work together?

Yes, I think they can work together very well. This is how it works. OPO HR is one of those four strategic locations, and there are three others. What Agile has done well is establish a strategic location called access. What do we have? What technologies do we need access to? What knowledge bases? What partners? What customers? What markets? What delivery challenges? That's a strategic activity. HR and OPO are in the location called support, which provides financial and community support. That's HR.

Now, what Agile has done very well in a legacy corporation is siloed the access to strategic activities, which are usually what limits access to the customers. A legacy company only has sales people talking to customers, and then they go and tell the developers what to do. Agile has taken what was previously siloed strategically and they put the customer right in contact with the team. This is part of what is needed when a mature OPO starts. They must have a way to allow all those strategic activities to move deeper into the team. The team is not only cross-functional, but they're inherently strategic.

In the OPO, there's a need for Agile approaches to human resources. It's a process of teaching them how to support themselves and their own growth and development. They're taught not to just have teams, because they have human resources that are siloed in that orientation. You have to develop them, and then you try to push them operationally into these cross-functional teams.

Human resources shifts when you turn to this Agile perspective, but if you silo in these people at human resources, then you will still have made this false dichotomy between strategic activities that happen out here and the teams who are operational. The objective is to continue the learning process right down into the core teams. It's a two-step process.

To succeed, it's ideal when you can "think" with the customer. This hasn't been done before, so I can't give you a really good example. A company will always have some people who are looking for new customers. The teams can't do all that. But when you get a new customer market or customer segment, then you fold that back into the operational teams. The first thing you're doing is innovating what human resources is. Now, you're going to innovate how to let that flow into the core operations. You have this tremendous learning organization.

As that happens, you'll be out looking for even newer things and newer information. You now have local information, but you don't have local capacities inside the core operations. You must keep building this kind of generative capacity.

They're thinking of how they want to embed learning activities that are strategic in nature into our core value teams without overwhelming them. They just need to realize it's not a teaching thing. It's a coaching and facilitation process.

If you have that participatory governance, then every core location will create solutions for their human resources problems in their own context. I think it's a fun job for human resources, because if you think of what it's like to be a human resources person in a legacy organization, it kind of sucks. But this is lively because this location is doing one thing and this location is special. You get to facilitate that, and it's new and fresh and generative all the time, versus just instituting a human resource policy that's not that much fun.

Will HR be superfluous in an Agile organization?

No, I think you will always need them, especially if you allow the organization to change. I don't think you need managers, but human resource people are like sales—they're needed to keep the blood flowing. Teams can't do everything. They can't go find the resources, the exercises, or the fun things. The blood of human resources is always flowing. It goes outside, sees what's new, looks at new ideas, and helps bring back the information. So, you're facilitating that information to flow in, but you're able to scan the larger environment. Core operations don't have a lot of opportunity to go scanning what the larger environment can offer. For the OPO, one of the strategic things that we do is intentionally allow core operations people to go learn something completely new, because they tend to have tasks that demand more specific things than in these other activities.

What would be the reason that an organization can't or won't implement OPO?

I think one of the reasons why we're very lucky is that institutions usually don't change. There's so much inertia in institutions, especially as we have had them now in the modern world. Because it's a feedback-feed-forward loop, not all employees know what to do. If you're a person who's grown up in highly institutionalized, hierarchical organizations, it's very difficult for you to understand how to participate in OPOs. The institution limits the way you can participate, but then, as you mature, you end up not knowing how to do anything differently.

Because technology has given us the ability to be more responsive, effective, leaner-oriented, and faster, there's a huge competitive advantage, and institutions have to change or they'll die. Then someone new will come along and take their place. I think this is pretty evident now and a lot of companies try because they know they have to, but they still don't get it. Try or die.

In the first phase—and Ricardo Semler says it's a coincidence—internet technology gave us the ability for people in organizations to know more, faster, without managers. Prior to the internet, even if managers weren't controlling you, they were the hubs. Somebody had to have a lot of information. It had to be stored somewhere. Storage wasn't a problem; it was still stored on computers, but there was no user interface. So, you had to go ask questions. If you think about it, prior to the internet, the first computers were organizing and storing information, but they couldn't do search and retrieval. Once you could do search and retrieval, it was faster and more efficient for everyone to do their own search and retrieval. For managers who were being used as browsers, their job was done.

This was the first revolution: using a manager as a browser for information and as a communications hub. This completely disrupted organizations. Now what people are doing is building platforms like Slack, and similar platforms are repeating this disruption. I think that's why the old ways are dying and all these new opportunities for careers and organizations are opening up. I think we're really lucky to have lived during that whole curve.

Can all organizations apply these principles or the methodology?

Okay, that's a very good question. This is part of a dialogue that's happening in reinventing organizations. One opinion is that people have to be at a certain level of development to do this. That level of development turns out to be about 11 percent of people who can apply these principles.

I've done a lot of work in developmental psychology, and some of these people who are pioneers in the study are actually my really good friends. In every period during these phases of history, the most important thing to understand about developmental psychology is the move from conventional to post-conventional. If you're in a society where most organizations are legacy organizations, you have to be really smart to be able to see through those structures and consider that something else is possible. The reason why all these young kids say, "Well, it's self-evident," is because they grew up with the internet. The technology is now conventional to them. They don't have to be post-conventional thinkers to act like that because it's become conventional in that society.

For example, a person who comes out of a very patriarchal tribe in the Middle East can work for GE in a legacy corporation. They are actually post-conventional thinkers, because to be born like that and move into a more modern world requires a post-conventional mind.

Over time, these things that are new and have to stretch our imagination become conventional, and then they become limiting because it'll take new post-conventional thinkers to change it. People born into the internet age, and who are born without managers having to retrieve information, already say, "What do I need managers for?" They can see they don't need them. People who came up to the organization as managers were less and less needed, but they couldn't see it because they were conventionally oriented.

So, for me, the OPO governance is cool because it's participatory at different levels. Let's say you have a location like the one at King, where it's a little bit more repetitive. Maybe it's a manufacturing thing. Because that location set its own governance, if you walked in there, they might have a veteran there and some kids. So, they're quite hierarchical. Maybe the veteran can do almost all the work, but they have a summer program and the kids come through. It's a little participatory, but not so much. In different locations, you can have different value schemata being addressed.

Of course, that's challenging. For example, some financial sectors might have a hedge fund branch where the people have to be very aggressive and high risk. When they make very high-risk decisions on intuition, they have a process to help each other. If they fail, they have a culture where they all take that responsibility. This is a completely different value schema than what is required in other contexts.

The OPO, because there's a governance template for the whole organization, gets specified by the people who occupy it. You will see this as an opportunity to include not only other generations but people globally who are at different phases within the organizational dynamics. That's another big advantage of not having a constitutional governance.

About the Author

Pia-Maria Thoren was perhaps the first person in the world to link the terms "Agile" and "HR." Today she is recognized as the pioneer of a fast-growing global movement – Agile People, founded in Sweden in 2013.

A true multi-talent, Pia-Maria describes herself as standing at the intersection of HR, IT, finance, and management. With a background as a consultant and advisor to some of Sweden's largest international companies, she has long been a passionate change agent with a mission: to create organizations where people thrive, feel engaged, deliver customer value – and have fun at the same time.

As Inspiration Director for her company, she continues to be a key influencer in Agile HR, leadership, and motivation. She is a popular keynote speaker, frequently featured in interviews, podcasts, and blogs, where she shares her insights in a personal, informal – and distinctly Scandinavian – style that makes it clear: leadership needs to change.

She is also the author of two other books (Agile People Picturebook and Agile People Principles, Your Call to Action for the Future of Work). Together, the three books form the foundation of Agile People's training programs worldwide.